Jews in Places You Never Thought Of

❖ ❖ ❖

Jews in Places You Never Thought Of

Edited by

Karen Primack

KTAV PUBLISHING HOUSE, INC.
In Association With
KULANU

Copyright ©1998
Kulanu, Inc.

Library of Congress Cataloging-in-Publication Data

Jews in places you never thought of / edited by Karen Primack.
    p.   cm.
Includes bibliographical references.
ISBN 0–88125–608–0
    I. Jewish diaspora. 2. Sephardim—History. 3. Sephardim—Latin America—History. 4. Proselytes and proselyting, Jewish.
I. Primack, Karen.
DS134.J49   1998
909'.04924—dc21   98-12292
                                                                                       CIP

Manufactured in the United States of America
KTAV Publishing House, 900 Jefferson Street, Hoboken NJ, 07030

Table of Contents

Preface xi
    Karen Primack

The Jewish Handshake xv
    Jack Zeller

Meet the Authors xvii

Introduction: Historical Overview 1
1. The Sephardic Diaspora 3
    Joseph Hantman
2. Jewish Roots in Africa 8
    George Lichtblau
3. The Jews of India 14
    Sy Scheinberg

Part I. Descendants of a Lost Tribe:
    The Bnei Menashe (Shinlung) 25
4. Just Who *Are* the Shinlung? 27
    Jack Bresler

5. How I Happened to "Discover" the Bnei Menashe 31
   Eliyahu Avichail
6. Chronology of a Successful Return 38
   Eliyahu Avichail, Bruce Terris, Allenby Sela, Jack Zeller,
   Diane Zeller, Yaacov Levi
7. A New Ritual for Passover: Honoring the Return of a
   Lost Tribe 51
   Jonina Duker

Part II. The Marranos 53
8. That Word "Marrano" 55
   Karen Primack
9. Spain 58
   High Holy Days Among the Spanish Marranos 58
      Gloria Mound
   Judaic Research in the Balearic Islands and São Tome 60
      Gloria Mound
10. Portugal 64
    My Trip to Belmonte: A New Look at Portuguese Marranos 64
       Eytan Berman
    The Marrano Jews of Braganza 74
       Warren Freedman
11. Mexico 77
    Jewish Descendants of Conquistadores? 77
       Joseph Hantman
    Mexico: Land of the Setting Sun and Rising Torah? 79
       Richard A. Kulick
    Frustrations of a Founder 88
       Ignacio Castelan Estrada
    Chanukah in Mexico: A Journey of Renewal 91
       Nancy Helman Shneiderman
12. Brazil 100
    Searching for Brazilian Marranos: A Remnant Returns 100
       Jacques Cukierkorn with Robert H. Lande

We Marranos of Brazil 112
   Julio D'Gabriel
Meeting Four Brazilian Marranos 113
   Ivan Birnbaum, Joaquim Galvao, Eder Barosh,
   Roberto Dias de Oliveira
Portrait of a Leader: Helio Daniel Cordeiro 116
   Karen Primack
A Brazilian Genealogist Speaks 118
   Karen Primack
13. Cape Verde 120
The Jews of Cape Verde 120
   Louise Werlin
An Unusual Society in Cape Verde 123
   M. Mitchell Serels
My Capeverdean Genealogical Account 124
   Donald Wahnon
14. The United States of America 130
Was Columbus Jewish? 130
   Joseph Hantman
Coming Out of the Marrano Closet 136
   Brian P. Haran

Part III. Jewish Roots in Africa 139
15. Fight for the Honor of the Ethiopian Jewish
    Community! 141
   Diane and Jack Zeller
16. Are the Balemba "Jewish"? 144
   Karen and Aron Primack
17. A Lost Tribe in Nigeria? 147
   Warren Freedman

Part IV. Jews in China 149
18. Jews Have Been in China a Long, Long Time 151
   Karen Primack

19. Xu Xin, an Unusual Man 157
    Karen Primack
20. A Delightful Introduction to Chinese Jewry 161
    Jack Zeller

Part V. Communities Seeking Conversion 163
21. Italy 165
    The Case of San Nicandro 165
        Joseph Hantman
22. Uganda 168
    Meet the Abayudaya Jews of Uganda 168
        Aaron Kintu Moses
    Chronology of an Historic Visit 171
        Jacques Cukierkorn, Julia Chamovitz, Matthew S. Meyer,
        David Levine, Karen Primack, Rhoda Posner
    Mikvehs and Cholent in Uganda 202
        J. Hershy Worch
    Let's Send Abayudaya Orphans to School 211
        Karen Primack and Matthew S. Meyer
    Two Fascinating Books About Ugandan Jewry 212
        Irwin Berg
    Living with the Abayudaya and Their Non-Jewish
        Neighbors 223
        Kenneth M. Schultz
23. Peru 245
    Converting Inca Indians 245
        Myron Zuber
24. India 253
    "Discovering" the Telugu Jews of India 253
        Jason Francisco
25. Ghana 263
    Judaism in Ghana 263
        David G. Ahenkorah

The Ghanaian Village That Wants To Be Jewish 264
Daniel Baiden with Robert H. Lande

Part VI. Reflections 271
26. Genealogy on a Grand Scale 273
Jonina Duker
27. Conversion and the Purpose of Jewish Existence 276
Lawrence J. Epstein
28. A Philanthropist Speaks: Zionism for the 1990s 280
Irving Moskowitz
29. Nathan's Prayer 282
Nathan Bliss
30. Celebrating Jewish Diversity 285
Myra D'Gabriel
31. Irony 287
Karen Primack
32. Facilitating Returnees 289
Brian P. Haran
33. Should We Provide a Warm Welcome to Anyone Who Sincerely Wants To (Re)join the Jewish People? 290
Robert H. Lande

Appendix: What *You* Can Do! 297

Glossary 301

Preface

This book is about an unusual subject, presented in an unusual way. It is *not* an encyclopedic directory of information about the little-known communities it describes, and it is not meant to include all such communities in existence. Rather, it comprises personal accounts of interactions with these communities by the authors of the articles. With the exception of a few historical overviews, and views expressed by members of the communities themselves, the pieces were written by people who actually visited these far-off (and often inaccessible) groups—talking, singing, eating, dancing, and praying with them. It is a book about these communities, but it is also a book about personal involvement.

We hope that these articles will encourage the reader to visit or otherwise maintain contact with dispersed Jewish groups (see the appendix for some possibilities). All the communities in this volume practice Judaism in some form, although some may not meet halachic criteria. Some of the groups have Jewish roots; others do not. Most are seeking further education and formal conversion to Judaism—we might view them as "developing" Jewish communities.

The "Reflections" chapter contains a collection of thoughtful essays on some related topics, most having to do with why the individual writers feel that contact with developing Jewish communities is vital today, both to increase our numbers and to enrich our religious practice by enhancing our own appreciation of Judaism.

The reader will notice that a great deal of space in this work is devoted to a small, newly "discovered" community (the Abayudaya Jews of Uganda), while another larger, better-known, long-standing community (the Jews of Ethiopia) receives relatively scant attention. The volume of the material is not meant to indicate the importance or size of a group, but is rather a reflection of the extent of the writers' opportunities and contacts.

As the reader may be aware, large segments of world Jewry have been lost through the course of history as a result of war, exile, and forced conversions. The greater part of the Jewish people was "lost" in the eighth century B.C.E., when the ten northern Israelite tribes were conquered by Assyria and the captives were forcibly resettled. Today their descendants can be found in India, Burma, Afghanistan, Pakistan, and China.

Another large group of Jews was "lost" during the period of forced conversions to Christianity in Spain and Portugal in the fifteenth and sixteenth centuries. Many of them, the so-called Marranos, continued to practice Judaism in secret. Some of their descendants can be found today in Brazil, Mexico, and the southwestern United States, as well as Spain and Portugal.

In addition, there are communities made up of people who have no Jewish ancestry but desire to embrace Judaism. One example is the group of Inca Indians in Trujillo, Peru, whose leader, a Catholic named Villanueva, decided in 1966 to become Jewish after pondering the Bible. Much of his community followed him, and after study with a rabbi in the late 1980s, three hundred of them were converted by a *beth din* from Israel and made aliyah. Another example are the Abayudaya, a group of native Ugandans who have been practicing Judaism since 1919, when their leader, a local governor named Semei Kakungulu, studied and meditated on the "Old Testament" and adopted the observance of all Moses' commandments, including circumcision. Over the next seven decades, the Abayudaya were visited by American, European, and Israeli Jewish travelers who instructed them in postbiblical Judaism.

Several organizations, listed in the appendix, are doing excellent work in assisting these lost and developing Jewish communities and making world Jewry aware of them. Figuring prominently in this book is one of these entities, Kulanu ("All of Us"), a nonprofit organization of Jews of varied backgrounds and practices dedicated to finding lost and dispersed remnants of the Jewish people and assisting those who wish to rejoin the Jewish community. (An earlier version of many of the chapters in this book appeared initially in Kulanu's quarterly newsletter.) Kulanu has undertaken a variety of activities worldwide on behalf of these dispersed groups, including research, contacts, visits, education, donation of religious books and articles, facilitation of conversion when requested, and help with relocation to Israel if desired. Kulanu was inspired by an Israeli organization, Amishav ("My People Return"), founded in 1975 by Rabbi Eliyahu Avichail.

K. P.
December, 1997

The Jewish Handshake
Jack Zeller

There is something remarkable about how one Jew greets another who is otherwise a stranger. Jews feel an immediate kinship with other Jews—a feeling that non-Jewish friends often describe with amazement and envy.

The universality of the enthusiastic greeting of one Jew to another is what we tried to capture in the planning of this book.

Jews are often to be found in unlikely places. The prophets foretold that the Diaspora would be worldwide. And our siddur repeatedly refers to the four corners of the earth.

One purpose of this work is to preserve and enhance the enthusiasm of one Jew meeting another, even if it occurs in the most unlikely place, and the other Jew is of a darker skin color or different appearance, or practices a Judaism that is non-rabbinic in origin, or is a newly arrived Jew by choice.

Our goal is to ask all Jews to consider the spiritually elevating practice of befriending other Jews as a treasured birthright that must be experienced—not simply learned in books, heard in sermons, or described by our bubbes and zeydes. This practice of *doing* is deliberate, delightful, and full of surprise and meaning. This practice is self-identifying and critical to our identity.

Kulanu sometimes receives inquiries from people who may or may not belong to synagogues or other Jewish organizations, asking how they can visit the Shinlung Jewish community in India, the Abayudaya in Uganda, the Marranos in Brazil or Santa Fe, as if this were a most Jewishly intuitive and reasonable request. And it is! But we want to make it easier.

Jews travel. We have traveled far and wide, often against our will, to find a more likely place to survive. Now, even those of us who have been fortunate enough to travel often will find that the pleasure of travel is richly enhanced by meeting the local Jewish population. We encourage you to travel for this pleasure. We suggest contacting one of the many communities we describe in this book. The accommodations are not elegant, but then again our ancestors, who gave us the opportunity to do this, were not thinking about luxury. Their reward was the warm greeting, learning about the quality of local Jewish life, and discussing how Divine Providence intended them to behave.

Since the Jewish communities described in this book have suffered from chronic and almost complete isolation, your visit with them will have a profound and electrifying effect. You may be asked the most difficult questions by people who sincerely believe that Western Jews must know it all. And when you ask your own questions and find the reply is a more penetrating question, you know that we are all part of *K'lal Yisrael*. You may start your journey thinking you are helping another, only to find that you are also a major beneficiary.

For what can be more moving than to grapple with our nature and destiny?

Much of Jewish living has occurred in the Diaspora. We've been here far longer than in Eretz Yisrael. And we will probably be here for a long time to come. Never before in Jewish history has it been easier to meet remote and virtually ignored or newly developing Jewish communities. We can do it by phone, fax, e-mail, and best of all, an in-person handshake. Many of us have done some or all of these. You shouldn't miss out!

Meet the Authors

Eliyahu Avichail. A leading Orthodox rabbi in Israel whose interest in the Ten Lost Tribes resulted in the founding of Amishav in 1975 and frequent visits to lost and dispersed Jewish communities around the globe.

Daniel Baiden. A Ghana-born Jew who moved to the United States in 1979 and revisited his native land in 1996 to check out reports of a Ghanaian group interested in embracing Judaism.

Eder Barosh. A Marrano raised in Brazil without knowledge of Judaism who was influenced by the Jewish community in Natal to become an active participant in the Associacao Religiosa Israelita Marrana.

Irwin Berg. A New York attorney and Jewish history buff who has visited Marranos in Portugal and Brazil and the Abayudaya in Uganda.

Eytan Berman. An engineer of Dutch and Spanish descent currently working in Israel.

Ivan Birnbaum. A Brazilian Marrano whose interest in Judaism increased when he was in the Brazilian Navy and met other Jews; moved to Natal with his family and helped found the Associacao Religiosa Israelita Marrana.

Nathan Bliss. A teenager in a Spanish-immersion program who keeps busy with tennis, desktop publishing, computer illustration, his temple youth group, and studying cello.

Jack Bresler. A rabbi and teacher of Jewish Studies who became interested in the Far East as an Army intelligence officer in Vietnam; he and his Taiwanese-Jewish wife are active in Kulanu.

Julia Chamovitz. An American who, while a college undergraduate in 1992, studied in Kenya, came to know a few Abayudaya Jews of Uganda, and subsequently traveled to their villages for an unforgettable Shabbat.

Jacques Cukierkorn. Brazilian-born Reform rabbi who has studied and visited crypto-Jewish communities in Brazil as well as the Abayudaya in Uganda; a founder and rabbinical advisor of Kulanu.

Julio D'Gabriel. A resident of Canada who went to northeastern Brazil and organized and encouraged descendants of Marranos to return to Judaism; founded and presided over the Associacao Religiosa Israelita Marrana.

Myra D'Gabriel. A Scottish-born Ashkenazic Jew of Russian and Sikh heritage who was an activist with the Associacao Religiosa Israelita Marrana in Natal, Brazil.

Roberto Dias de Oliveira. A Brazilian Marrano raised with the awareness that he was a Jew; began studying Hebrew in 1981 and has become a Jewish leader in Natal.

Jonina Duker. A board member and lecturer for the Jewish Genealogy Society of Greater Washington who is also particularly interested in writing and collecting Jewish lifecycle and holiday rituals.

Lawrence J. Epstein. An English professor who writes extensively on conversion; recently authored *Conversion to Judaism: A Guidebook* (Jacob Aronson, 1994).

Ignacio Castelan Estrada. A Mexican Marrano, raised outwardly as a Catholic, who learned Judaism from his grandparents, began studying and practicing it with his wife and children in the intimacy of their home, and eventually founded the Puebla synagogue.

Jason Francisco. A photographer and writer, currently at work on a book on everyday life and labor in the Indian countryside.

Warren Freedman. An attorney, former judge, and author of legal treatises whose avocation is writing and teaching about the Ten Lost Tribes of Israel.

Joachim Galvão. A Brazilian raised with knowledge of his Marrano heritage who "returned" to the public practice of Judaism.

Joseph Hantman. A retired U.S. government employee (forty-two years of military and civilian service involving much overseas travel) who has done considerable research and lectured widely on Jewish communities around the world, specializing in the history of the Jews of Spain.

Brian P. Haran. An Irish-American Sephardic Jew who speaks *nine* languages. and uses them all in his position with a major airline at Dulles Airport; he has lived and worked in eleven countries.

Richard A. Kulick. A long-time Hispanic community activist and student of Jewish mysticism who works to investigate and preserve the converso heritage.

Robert H. Lande. A law professor who was a co-founder and treasurer of the Washington Association for Ethiopian Jews as well as a co-founder and treasurer of Kulanu.

Yaacov Levi. An American-born immigrant to Israel who has settled near and befriended Bnei Menashe immigrants.

David Levine. A Peace Corps volunteer near Mbale, Uganda, through July 1993, who spent time with and became an admirer of the Abayudaya.

George Lichtblau. A retired Foreign Service officer in Israel and Africa whose long African experience made him aware of the interest of West Africans in their Jewish roots and led him to study French sources on the subject; he received a Rockefeller grant to travel throughout Africa and write a book, *Politics of African Trade Unionism*.

Matthew S. Meyer. A Teach-for-America teacher in Washington who, when a student at Brown University studying for a year in Kenya, "discovered" the Abayudaya Jews of Uganda; he has visited them on nine separate occasions.

Aaron Kintu Moses. Secretary of the Abayudaya Congregation in Mbale, Uganda.

Irving Moskowitz. A Miami Beach dentist, builder, supporter of yeshivas and of Amishav, and philanthropist.

Gloria Mound. A scholar who has researched, written, and lectured on the Jewish history of the Balearic Islands; founder and executive director of the Institute for Marrano (Anusim) Studies in Israel.

Rhoda Posner. A case worker at Jewish Family Services in Baltimore who participated in Kulanu's mission to the Abayudaya in Uganda in 1995.

Aron Primack. A physician and anthropologist who has lived in Africa and traveled extensively, having visited Jewish communities in Latin America, Africa, Asia, and Europe; he participated in Kulanu's mission to Uganda in 1995.

Karen Primack. Retired attorney who is interested in Judaic and environmental causes; edits Kulanu's newsletter and produced a commercial recording of Abayudaya music for Kulanu.

Sy Scheinberg. Professor of history and chair of the department of history at California State University, Fullerton.

Kenneth M. Schultz. A graduate of the University of Rochester, where he participated in the Senior Scholar Program through his research and writings about the Abayudaya; currently a law/social work student at Washington University in St. Louis.

Allenby Sela. A Bnei Menashe from Mizoram who studied in a yeshiva in Bombay.

M. Mitchell Serels. Director of Sephardic Community Programs at Yeshiva University; visited the Cape Verde Islands, researching gravesites and lecturing on Jewish history.

Nancy Helman Shneiderman. A psychotherapist and musician who gives lectures, performances, and workshops on Jewish lifecycle events.

Bruce Terris. A Washington attorney who travels frequently to his home in Israel; an active member and treasurer of Amishav.

Donald Wahnon. A retired engineer currently living in Massachusetts, who has traced his family roots. His family came from Morocco, through Gibraltar, Cape Verde, and Brazil, to the United States.

Louise Werlin. A country development officer with the Agency for International Development's Office of Sahel and West African Affairs.

J. Hershy Worch. An Orthodox rabbi currently residing in Illinois who has visited the Abayudaya Jews of Uganda.

Diane Zeller. An African historian with expertise in Uganda and an activist for many Jewish causes, including Ethiopian Jewry, Hillel, Kulanu, and her synagogue.

Jack Zeller. A physician-activist who is the co-founder and president of Kulanu, and a past president of the American Association for Ethiopian Jewry.

Myron Zuber. A Lubavitch rabbi and retired scientist who prepared Inca Indians in Peru for formal conversion to Judaism.

Introduction
Historical Overview

1

The Sephardic Diaspora
Joseph Hantman

So many of the renascent and potentially renascent Jewish communities we read about are of Sephardic origin that it is appropriate to present a brief overview of the origins and history of the Jews of Spain and Portugal.

From their earliest history, Jews and Jewish communities existed along the shores of the Mediterranean. In Spain they appeared first as trading outposts and later as well-settled communities in agriculture, trade, and crafts. Their religious identity was maintained by ongoing communication with Jewish institutions in Jerusalem and Babylon. Both the Greek historian Strabo (born in 63 B.C.E.) and the Roman statesman Pliny (62–113 C.E.) cited the existence of Jewish communities in Spain. It is believed that the name Sefarad, as it appears in the biblical book of Obadiah, refers to Spain.

In pre-Christian Spain Jews flourished and, in fact, gained converts from among the local population. In early Christian times relations between Jews and pre-trinitarian Christians were relatively peaceful. However, with the arrival of Visigothic tribes in Spain and their ultimate conversion to Roman-dominated Christianity, the status of the Jews declined rapidly. Under a series of Visigothic kings, Jewish children were forcibly taken from their parents, and by the year 580 C.E. Judaism was outlawed.

Although overt Judaism disappeared from the scene, we know that crypto-Judaism, which was to be strongly identified with Sephardic Jews, continued to exist.

This became evident in the year 711, when Arab armies under Tarik, carrying the banner of Islam, crossed from North Africa into Jib al Tarik (Gibraltar) and invaded Spain. Large numbers of Spanish Jews, whose identity as Jews had hardly been apparent until then, joined the victorious Arab armies. In the immediate wake of the invasion there was a large-scale movement of population from North Africa to Spain—among them many Jews. (Jews had been in North Africa for hundreds of years, going back at least to the Second Temple period. With the fall of the Temple in 70 C.E. many more fled to the existing Jewish communities in North Africa, and their number was further increased after the defeat of the Bar Kochba revolt and the harsh reprisals by Rome in 135 C.E.) These newcomers, entering Spain from 711 C.E. on, became the foundation upon which Sephardi Jewry was built.

In the years that followed, the Arabs continued to pursue the Christian forces northward, leaving small garrisons in the cities which, together with the Jews, administered the land.

This was the beginning of a relationship controlled by Islam, but under which Jews (and in fact many Christians) continued to flourish. It led to what has been called the Golden Age of Spanish Jewry, producing such great figures as Chasdai Ibn Shaprut, diplomat, linguist, and statesman for the caliph; Yehudah Halevi, great poet; Ibn Gabirol, scientist and mathematician; Ibn Nagrila, military leader of Islamic armies; Ibn Ezra, renowned talmudic scholar; and many others. They all served in the Arab courts but remained learned and faithful to the Jewish religion and the Jewish people.

The greatest product of Sephardic Judaism was, of course, Maimonides (Moshe ben Maimon, 1135–1204). Born in Cordova, he had to flee with his family to North Africa (1148) and then to Egypt under pressure from fanatical Islamic groups.

5 / The Sephardic Diaspora

After their defeat, Christian Spaniards began a slow but relentless battle to reconquer Spain. The "Reconquista" proceeded province by province, culminating in 1492 with the fall of Granada and the unification of Spain under Ferdinand and Isabella.

In the early years of the reconquest Christians sought, and frequently gained, the support of Jews, whom they needed as administrators and financial advisors. Jews were rewarded with large estates and soon found themselves in high positions in most of Christian Spain. In the 1300s this led to much resentment by the Church, the nobility, and a rising class of Christian merchants. Laws were passed restricting Jewish activity. Riots and mob violence against the Jews broke out, culminating in 1391 in mass forced conversions. Other Jews, succumbing to Christian pressure, voluntarily went to the baptismal font. Many of those who accepted Catholicism were freed of anti-Jewish restrictions and soon resumed their old positions of prominence—this time as "New Christians" rather than Jews. The Jews of Spain soon fell into three categories: (1) Conversos—individuals who had accepted Christianity and just wanted to continue their lives; they were not trusted and frequently were hounded by the Church and later by the Inquisition. (2) Marranos—converts who remained loyal to Judaism but had to practice it in secret; they were hounded by the Inquisition and if caught were subject to severe penalties, including death. (3) Jews who did not convert; their freedom, economic opportunity, and social status were severely limited. There were, of course, some exceptions, some professing Jews, such as Abravanel and Senhor, who remained Jewish and later joined the expulsion, despite pleas by the monarch to convert and remain in Spain.

In 1492 King Ferdinand and Queen Isabella issued a decree expelling all Jews from Spain, citing as one of the reasons the continuing influence of practicing Jews upon former Jews who had converted. Thus ended some of the most glorious years in Jewish history.

It is estimated that close to 300,000 Jews left Spain—many to Portugal, where a few years later they were forced to convert on pain of death. Many other Spanish Jews fled to Holland, Italy, and, most of all, to the lands of the Ottoman Empire—Turkey, Egypt, Palestine, North Africa, the Balkans. Many lost their lives en route to pirates, corrupt ship captains, etc. Those exiles who survived often found a refuge in existing Jewish communities. Within a generation or two the Sephardic culture, educational level, and language (Ladino, Judeo-Spanish) had come to dominate most of the local populations. These, then, were the Sephardic communities which existed for hundreds of years, and after the creation of Israel made aliyah in great numbers; today they constitute more than half the population of the Jewish state.

In Spain, after 1492, and Portugal after 1497, only conversos and crypto-Jews (Marranos) remained. Hounded by the Inquisition, many, using their Christian identity, joined the expeditions that explored and colonized the New World, hoping to find freedom there. Some were with Cortez's conquistadores in Mexico, where the Inquisition pursued them. After public burnings (*autos-da-fé*) in Mexico City, the survivors merged into the Christian community and lost their identity or went north with military expeditions. Over the generations even their crypto-Judaism disappeared, and all that is left are family traditions and practices which some now identify as vestiges of their Jewish roots. These are the well-publicized "Marranos" of the southwestern United States, a few of whom have returned to Judaism. Some small communities in Mexico which claim descent from Cortez's Marranos are now also reentering the Jewish fold.

In Brazil, Portuguese Jews found freedom under the Dutch in Recife, but when that city fell to the Portuguese in 1654, the Jews were forced to leave. Most went to Holland and a few settled in New Amsterdam, but many others were lost into the local population. The descendants of those who remained and developed

Brazil's sugar-refining industry, as well as of some Jews who came later, are those seeking Jewish identity today.

It was Sephardic Jews escaping from Mexico who established the Jewish communities in Barbados, St. Thomas, Curaçao, Surinam, and other Caribbean islands. Many typically Sephardic synagogues remain on the islands, but the congregations today are for the most part Ashkenazic.

In Majorca, today host to many cruise ships, an entire segment of the population, known as Chuetas, is of Jewish origin. The Chuetas have been practicing Catholics since the forced conversions in 1391, but their identity as Jews has kept them apart from the main population, and family names, neighborhoods, occupations, and practices still reflect their origins. Some of them have shown an interest in Judaism, and a few have visited Israel.

On the nearby smaller islands of Ibiza and Formentera, Jewish practices and observances were never completely obliterated and continue to this day. On the islands of São Tome e Principe, off the coast of Africa, descendants of Portuguese Jews are also seeking out their roots. These last groups have been researched by Gloria Mound, executive director of Casa Shalom, the Institute for Marrano (Anusim) Studies in Israel. In other far-flung outposts of former Portuguese colonies, vestiges of early conversos and/or Marrano families are being sought out by their descendants.

There is no doubt that more will be heard on this subject.

2

Jewish Roots in Africa
George E. Lichtblau

Claims of an historic presence of Jewish communities in certain regions of Africa, notably West and Southern Africa, seem esoteric when first mentioned. This presence, in fact, goes back not just centuries, but even to biblical times.

Of course in two areas such a communal presence on the African continent remains a firmly acknowledged part of Jewish history and experience–North Africa and Egypt/Ethiopia. A Jewish presence in Egypt and the former Kingdom of Cush are described in the Book of Exodus. Yet even after their departure from Egypt and their settlement in the land of Israel, the Jewish tribes retained certain nomadic characteristics which are reflected throughout their history.

For example, in the tenth and ninth centuries B.C.E. Kings David and Solomon sought to expand Jewish influence and trade throughout the Mediterranean, including North Africa, Egypt, the Arab Peninsula, and the Horn of Africa, as well as Persia. Often such trade-promotion and colonization drives were arranged in cooperation with the Canaanites and the neighboring Kingdom of Tyre. These kingdoms often lent their military backing to colonizing efforts that led to the establishment of numerous settlements by Jewish artisans and traders throughout these regions.

But the subsequent scattering of a Jewish presence and influence reaching deep into the African continent is less widely acknowledged.

Pressed by sweeping regional conflicts, Jews settled as traders and warriors in Yemen, the Horn of Africa, Egypt, the Kingdom of Cush and Nubia, North African Punic settlements (Carthage and Velubilis), and areas now covered by Mauritania. More emigrants followed the early Jewish settlers to Northern Africa following the Assyrian conquest of Israel in the eighth century B.C.E., and again two hundred years later, when Jerusalem was conquered by the Babylonians, leading to the destruction of the First Temple.

This catastrophic event not only drove many Jews into exile in Babylonia, but also led to the establishment of exile communities around the Mediterranean, including in North Africa. Then, with Israel coming under Greek, Persian, and later Roman rule and dependence, renewed waves of Jewish traders and artisans began to set up communities in Egypt, Cyrenaica, Nubia, and the Punic Empire, notably in Carthage, whence they began to scatter into various newly emerging communities south of the Atlas Mountains. Several Jewish nomadic groups also started to move across the Sahara from Nubia and the ancient Kingdom of Cush.

The Jewish presence in Africa began to expand significantly in the second and third centuries of the Christian era, extending not only into the Sahara Desert, but also reaching down along the West African coast, and possibly also to some Bantu tribes of Southern Africa (where some forty thousand members of the Lemba tribe still claim Jewish roots). The names of old Jewish communities south of the Atlas Mountains, many of which existed well into Renaissance times, have been found in documents in synagogue archives in Cairo.

In addition, Jewish, Arab, and Christian accounts cite the existence of Jewish rulers of certain tribal groups and clans identifying themselves as Jewish, scattered throughout Mauritania, Senegal, the western Sudan, Nigeria, and Ghana. Among notable Arab historians referring to their existence are Ibn Khaldun, who lived in the thirteenth century, a respected authority on Berber history; the famous geographer al-Idrisi, born in Ceuta, Spain, in the twelfth century, who wrote about Jewish Negroes in the western Sudan; and the sixteenth-century historian and traveler Leon Africanus, a Muslim from Spain who was raised by a Jewish woman working in his family's household, who is said to have taught him Hebrew and emigrated with the family to Morocco in 1492. Leon Africanus later converted to Catholicism but remained interested in Jewish communities he encountered throughout his travels in West Africa.

Some evidence can also be derived from surviving tribal traditions of some African ethnic groups, including links to biblical ancestors, names of localities, and ceremonies with affinities to Jewish ritual practices. Moreover, the writings of several modern West African historians and two personal anecdotes indicate that memories of an influential Jewish historical past in West Africa continue to survive.

I still remember from my assignments in the 1960s as a Foreign Service officer an encounter with Mr. Bubu Hama, then president of the National Assembly in Niger and a prolific writer on African history. He told me that the Tuaregs had a Jewish queen in early medieval times, and that some Jewish Tuareg clans had preserved their adherence to that faith, in defiance of both Islamic and Christian missionary pressure, until the eighteenth century. In several of his books Hama even cites some genealogies of Jewish rulers of the Tuareg and Hausa kingdoms.

A related story about surviving memories of Jewish roots in West Africa was told to me around 1976 by Shimon Peres, the former Israeli prime minister. He had just returned from a meeting of the Socialist International, during which he had met with President Leopold Senghor of Senegal. In the course of their discussion about the possibility of normalizing Senegalese-Israeli relations, Senghor told Peres that he too had Jewish ancestors. When

Feres recounted the incident, we both smiled somewhat incredulously. Yet, indeed, there are a number of historical records of small Jewish kingdoms and tribal groups known as Beni Israel that were part of the Wolof and Mandinge communities. These existed in Senegal from the early Middle Ages up to the eighteenth century, when they were forced to convert to Islam. Some of these claimed to be descendants of the tribe of Dan, the traditional tribe of Jewish gold and metal artisans, who are also said to have built the Golden Calf.

A Jewish presence is said to have been introduced into Senegal, Mauritania, and numerous other West African countries south of the Sahara in part through the migration of Jewish Berber groups and later through exiles from Spain who first settled in North Africa and then crossed the Atlas Mountains. Other even earlier arrivals are said to have come from Cyrenaica (now part of Libya, Egypt, the Sudan, and Ethiopia), having crossed the Sahara to West Africa and eventually also moved farther south.

In addition to the groups in Senegal that claim to be descendants of the tribe of Dan, the Ethiopian Jews also trace their ancestry to Dan. Some of these transmigrants established communities in such still renowned places as Gao, Timbuktu (where UNESCO still maintains notable archives containing records of the old Jewish community), Bamako, Agadez, Kano, and Ibadan. A notable number of Berber and African nomad tribal groups joined up with the Jewish communal groups trying to resist aggressive Arab Islamic efforts or as a bulwark against Christian proselytizing, sometimes going so far as to convert to Judaism. Notable among these were some Tuareg, Peul, and Ibadiya groups.

Another source at the root of this Jewish presence and influence was the spreading gold trade emanating from Persia, with Jews becoming involved as important intermediary traders. These traders came to rely on contacts with scattered Jewish communities they encountered in their West African travels in search for gold, a trade prohibited to Muslims as usurious under Islamic law. Thus, for instance, various historical accounts claim that Jewish travelers from Persia organized exchanges of Chinese silk for gold in the Kingdom of Ghana; the Ashanti needed the silk for weaving Kente cloth. To this day it is said that the Ashanti words for numbers relate to those in Parsi, the language of Persia. Under the impact of this Jewish influence, a number of ruling families in Ghana converted to Judaism, and for nearly two hundred years the Kingdom of Ghana, which extended at that time far north into western Sudan, was ruled by Jewish kings.

Because of their skills, ability, and multilingual knowledge, Jews became important intermediaries in regional trade relations and as artisans, grouping together as craft guilds. They are said to have formed the roots of a powerful craft tradition among the still-renowned Senegalese goldsmiths, jewelers, and other metal artisans. The name of an old Senegalese province, Juddala, is said to attest to the notable impact Jews made in this part of the world.

The Jewish presence is also confirmed by numerous surviving accounts of Portuguese and other European visitors in the fourteenth and fifteenth centuries, as well as by North African and Arab historical records. Gradually most of these communities disappeared. Since they existed largely in isolation, there was a good deal of intermarriage, which for a while reinforced their influence and expansion. As a result they were increasingly viewed as a threat by Muslim rulers, and most of the Jewish communities and nomad groups south of the Atlas Mountains were either forced to convert to Islam or massacred; the remainder fled to North Africa, Egypt, or the Sudan, and a few also fled to Cameroon and Southern Africa.

Reviewing the various Jewish and non-Jewish sources on the origins of these Jewish communities involves complicated and at times seemingly contradictory stories about tribal and religious wars and resultant alliances and transformations. These originated with the Roman and Byzantine persecutions of Jews and the promotion of Christianity beginning under the emperors Diocletian and Constantine. There was also a wave of Jewish proselytizing and conversions of nations and tribal groups to Judaism. For instance, the people of Yemen converted to Judaism in the fifth century under King Du-Nuas, as did a major Berber tribal group under Queen Kahina in the seventh century. These were followed by forced conversions of Jewish communities to Christianity and later to Islam, but with some Jewish consciousness and traditions surviving.

The conflicting references to biblical sources by Jewish, Muslim, Berber, and Christian sources survive not only to legitimize their respective spiritual claims but also as indicators of their transitions through a common past.

There has been an historical Jewish ambivalence about legitimizing mass conversions to Judaism and much looking askance at those who do not "look Jewish." In part such attitudes are reinforced by the fact that certain Jewish communities, for historical reasons or due to prolonged isolation, evolved ritual and ceremonial standards linked to older sources and traditions, thus becoming somewhat differentiated from those authorized by the dominant rabbinical authorities. These differences sometimes involved such questions as the acceptance of the Talmud. At times this put into question the authority of even so prominent a Jewish sage as Moses Maimonides.

Even before Maimonides these issues led to the now virtually forgotten split by the Karaites, who rejected the Talmud as divine law as well as the hierarchical authority of the rabbinate. Yet, despite their current obscurity, the Karaites played a significant historical role in the expansion of Judaism and also as advocates of a greater religious role for women. Karaite influence extended to Judeo-Berber communities and West African tribal communities such as the Malinke, Peul, Foulani, Mossi, Fanti, Songhay, Yoruba, and Hausa.

3

The Jews of India
Sy Scheinberg

This article was written before the existence of the Telugu Jews of India became known in America. A separate article on the Telugu, by Jason Francisco, appears in this book.

It is difficult to find an inhabited area of the world where Jews did not locate sometime in their varied and hectic history. One of the more exotic countries which the Jews called home was India.

Legend and tradition date the arrival of the Jews in India back to the destruction of the Second Temple of Jerusalem in 70 C.E., though some claim origins dating back to the reign of Solomon in the tenth century B.C.E. Unfortunately, there is no documentary evidence to support either of these claims, although references to India are found in a number of biblical texts and in the Talmud. The first concrete documentary evidence available that relates to Jews in India is a pair of copper plates with inscriptions that clearly identify their recipients as Jews. These plates were issued by the Hindu ruler of Malabar, Rajah Bhaskira Ravivarman, to Joseph Rabban, granting the local Jews, of whom he was the leader, property rights to a Jewish settlement near Cranganore about the year 1020 C.E.

COCHINIS

The Jewish community of Cranganore remained and expanded slightly over the next three centuries, after which its members gradually moved to Cochin, which came to supersede Cranganore in importance. Here too they had the good fortune to live under beneficent rulers, despite persistent persecution by the Portuguese between 1502 and 1663. A Cochin rajah in 1565 gave the Jews a large strip of land adjoining his palace, and it remains a significant site of the Jewish community in South India. According to historian David G. Mandelbaum, the famous Paradesi Synagogue was permitted to be constructed within yards of the rajah's private temple, "so that the adoration of Siva is heard in the synagogue and prayers to the God of Israel echo through the palace compound."

During the period of the Dutch presence in Malabar (1663–1795), the Jews of Cochin enjoyed complete freedom to practice their religion and prospered. As news of their existence in this remote land reached Europe, the local population was augmented by visitors and immigrants, causing some disruption in the social structure of the community, which probably never totaled more than twenty-five hundred members. During the 1780s Cochin was the busiest and most prosperous of the Dutch holdings, but by 1789 it was clear that the British were coming. The Jews of Cochin viewed a possible takeover by the British with a great deal of trepidation.

This situation prompted Jewish merchants to negotiate with the Travancore rajah, hoping that he would buy Cochin in order to keep it out of the hands of the British. The defeat of the Dutch and of Tipu Sultan established the British firmly in South India. Cochin was placed under direct British management in 1809, but despite continued religious tolerance, the status of the community declined. Over the next century many members migrated north to Bombay, lending numerical strength to the Bene Israel community in that city (see below), and after 1948 even more migrated to Israel. The result is that only a small handful remain today.

Before Jews were permanently established in the major cities of the country, they arrived as peripatetic merchants in Mughul India during the sixteenth century, with some of them settling in Delhi, Lahore, Fathepur Sikri, and Kashmir. They played a more significant role in the economic life of the country during the period of British rule, operating mainly out of Surat and Madras. Their main interest appears to have been the prospect of a lucrative trade in diamonds and pearls, and in that pursuit they contributed to the expansion of British trade.

BENE ISRAEL

The Bene Israel (Children of Israel) of Bombay today comprise the largest Jewish community in India. Its actual origins have not yet been established, though a number of theories and legends are repeated by members of the community.

A number of them in the second century were allegedly shipwrecked off the Konkan coast, about 20 miles south of Bombay, near the village of Navagaon. The survivors are said to have been seven men and seven women. Unfortunately, there is virtually no documentation of their activity over the succeeding centuries.

In time this group is supposed to have expanded and found employment as oil-pressers, whence they were known as Shanwar Telis, or "Saturday Oilmen," indicating their occupation and the religious requirement of resting on the Sabbath. Isolated on the Konkan, they were unaware that other Jews had settled elsewhere in the country. It was not until the mid-eighteenth century that a number of them appeared in Bombay. The apparent reason for their visit to the metropolis was to seek jobs and/or enlist in the native regiments of the British East India Company.

It was not long afterwards that the Bene Israelis were discovered for the first time by Jews from Cochin. Although they had lost touch with the Hebrew language, adopting Marathi as their native tongue, and had forgotten many of the prayers and rituals, they had preserved the fundamentals of Jewish tradition and practice, such as circumcision, the dietary laws, the Sabbath, and some festivals. Contact with the Cochini Jews led to a revival of Judaism among the Bene Israelis and in 1796 the first synagogue in Bombay, Sha'ar he-Rahamin ("Gate of Mercy"), was built.

In Bombay the earliest official designation of the Bene Israel was "Native Jew Caste," or simply "Jew Caste."

The last decade of the eighteenth century saw some expansion of the community as a whole. Additional synagogues were established and schools were built. Bene Israel did not enter any of the traditional Jewish occupations, such as high finance and international trade. The principal source of employment for the Bene Israel had been oil pressing, which they gave up shortly before moving to Bombay. They could no longer be identified with any particular vocation, thus losing one of their forms of identity. Most were poor and came to be employed in low-paid occupations.

Some entered the crafts, but the majority found employment as clerks in government offices and private businesses. They were thus often identified as members of the clerk caste. This became so common that when a member of the community was once told that many Jews elsewhere owned their own businesses, he remarked, "How very strange! How unlike Jews to go into business."

BAGHDADIS

Lending impetus to the growth of the community in Bombay, and providing additional religious inspiration, was a second wave of Jews arriving toward the end of the eighteenth century. It consisted of Arabic-speaking groups coming first from Iraq and then from Persia and Afghanistan; they are generally referred to as Baghdadis or Iraqis. Although most settled in and around Bombay, some continued on to Calcutta. These groups came in search of new economic opportunities. The Ezras and Eliases built jute and tobacco empires in Calcutta, while the Sassoons built a commercial empire in Bombay based on the opium trade and later on textiles. The family of David S. Sassoon became famous not only for its wealth but also for its philanthropic support of museums, libraries, hospitals, and synagogues. It employed thousands of people and thus earned for itself the sobriquet "Rothschilds of the East." Up through the 1980s the family's wealth supported more than two dozen institutions and hundreds of less fortunate Jews who received allotments of food and money from the continuing Sassoon trusts. The Sassoons thus became a major factor in the cultural and social fabric of Calcutta, Bombay, and Poona.

Although the Baghdadi Jews initially supported and worked with the Bene Israel, especially by instilling in them a greater sense of orthodoxy, by 1836 the sharp contrasts between the two groups began to take its toll. Differences in observance, language, appearance, and vocation caused the Baghdadis to withdraw from their early association with the Bene Israel; by the end of the nineteenth century the separation was nearly complete.

The Baghdadis built their own schools and synagogues. They went so far as to erect a wall to divide the Bombay cemetery in half, separating the graves of the two groups. This estrangement, though softened over the years, has continued to the present day.

Although several cities, including New Delhi, acquired small congregations, the only other city with a Jewish community of any numerical significance is Calcutta. It was a single Syrian Jew, Shalom ben Aaron ben Abadiah Ha-Cohen (1762–1836), and his descendants who laid the foundations of the community in that city in 1798. Much smaller in size than the community in Bombay, Calcutta Jewry never numbered never more than about five thousand.

It was, nevertheless, a very active, thriving group, eventually supporting a wide variety of institutions, including three synagogues, three schools, a clinic, a hospital, and a large cemetery. The economic basis of the successful families in the city were cotton, jute, and tobacco processing, though opium in the early years contributed enormously to their initial wealth. There were many successful Jewish merchants in Calcutta, but the principal names, once again, are Sassoon, Ezra, and Elias.

One of the outstanding features of the community is its dedication to social welfare. Through continuing trusts, it supports schools, provides housing and food for students, and supplies money and food to the indigent and unemployable.

When Israel and India gained their independence within a year of each other, the inclination to emigrate to Israel received impetus from the economic decline the Jewish community was experiencing throughout the country. Today the number of Jews in Calcutta has been reduced to less than one hundred, and throughout India the total is no more than five thousand.

In addition to these more or less traditional groups in India, there has recently come to light the existence of two, and possibly more, groups on the subcontinent that at least lay claim to being Jewish and to being descended from one of the Ten Lost Tribes. One such group is located in Kashmir, and another in northeastern India.

KASHMIRIS

After several years of trying, a Kashmiri village of self-proclaimed Jews apparently was successful in emigrating to Israel under the Law of Return. The details surrounding their success constitute one of the more bizarre tales relating to the Jews of India. Members of this Kashmiri community appealed first to the Israeli consulate in Bombay for recognition as bona fide Jews, so that they would be eligible to apply for entry to Israel under the Law of Return. Unable to grant such recognition due to very sketchy, unsatisfactory evidence, the consul-general turned them down. They then appealed directly to officials in Israel. A rabbi arrived, spoke with members of the group, and, apparently satisfied that they were bona fide Jews, approved their acceptance by the Israeli government. According to the consul-general, the only proof submitted was a room purportedly used as a prayer hall. The bizarre irony, according to the consul-general, is that these people were apparently Muslims who had fled Pakistan and settled in India. Furthermore, adding insult to injury, not long after their arrival in Israel, they disappeared!

SHINLUNG

The peoples that settled in northeastern India are more numerous, more active, and have a longer history, at least as described by the elders of the community. They are concentrated in the states of Manipur and Mizoram, and they tell a fascinating tale describing their origins.

Their basic claim is that they are descended from the tribe of Manasseh (Menashe in Hebrew). About four hundred years after the defeat of the Kingdom of Israel by Assyria in 722 B.C.E. and the dispersion of the Ten Tribes, many were pushed eastward before the onslaught of Alexander the Great. From Afghanistan they fled into Tibet and then on into central and southern China, settling eventually in Kaifeng (east of Loyang, in Honan province on the Yellow River) in 231 C.E.

The new arrivals and their descendants lived in relative peace until the Mongol period (1280–1368). At that point the existence of the Jewish colony was threatened by absorption into local Chinese communities and conversion to Christianity.

A large number are said to have fled China, with one segment making their way into Indo-China, where they took refuge in what they called "Cave Valley." It is difficult to determine exactly where this was, but the claim is made that they survived there for at least two generations. They had carried their sacred scrolls (the Torah) with them and continued to practice their religion. They appear to have lived a somewhat primitive existence, with little protection against the weather and never enough food. They were called Khul or Chinlung ("Cave Dwellers") by the local inhabitants. Then, say the Manipuris, the Chinese authorities discovered their existence in the caves of Indo-China and sent an army to drive them out.

All of the group's religious materials and sacred scrolls were either destroyed by the Chinese or buried by the group's priests in order to avoid their destruction. Due to Chinese pressure the colony of Jews migrated north through Thailand into Burma, where they followed the Irawaddy River toward Mandalay. Not far from that city they were able to settle in a village called Aupatuang. However, they were not there long before they were dragooned as forced laborers to build a palace for the Burmese king.

In time, due to famine and other vicissitudes, they moved to the town of Kalemyo north along the Chindwin River, where they remained a few years. From there they traveled west into the Chin Hills and then to the Khampat Valley east of Manipur. In Burma they were called "Luse" by the Kachins, which is interpreted to mean "of the Ten Tribes."

In 1830 some members of the community migrated to Mizoram and Manipur in India. They apparently were not well received, and it was a while before they felt comfortable in their new surroundings. By the middle of the nineteenth century, however, they claim they were overwhelmed by Christianity with the arrival of Baptist missionaries in the area.

The individual specifically identified for his missionary work in the area was William Pettigrew (1869–1943). Rev. Pettigrew was stationed in Manipur and, between 1891 and 1934, established missions in Churachandpur, north among the Nagas, and at Kangpokpi.

The first five years of his tenure in Bengal and Manipur were under the authority of the Aborigines Mission, sponsored by Robert Arthington of Leeds, England. American missionaries began arriving after 1910 and added to the difficulty the remaining Jews faced in maintaining their identity.

Apparently it was not until the mid-1950s that several groups in Manipur and Mizoram somehow realized that they were of Jewish descent. It is difficult to determine with any precision when this discovery occurred and how soon afterwards they returned to the teachings of Moses. According to their own records, as they began to reclaim their Judaism they faced some mistreatment by the native tribes, a situation that did not, however, last very long.

Especially curious is the fact that the Jewish communities in Manipur and Mizoram continued to survive without any knowledge of other Jewish groups elsewhere on the subcontinent. It was not until 1971, when they learned that an Indian government architect temporarily working in Manipur was Jewish, that members of the community came forward and identified themselves as Jews. They were astounded to learn that there were other Jews in India. Upon discovering, further, that there were schools catering to Jews in Bombay, the president of the United Tribal Jews of North East India, Vaniah L. Benjamin, proceeded to that city, where he met with the directors of the Jewish boys' and girls' ORT schools.

The directors were very suspicious of Benjamin's motives and questioned the validity of his origins and his claims to being Jewish. They therefore refused to admit any Shinlung students. Benjamin persisted, and in 1975 the boys' and girls' institutions finally accepted Shinlung students. Ten youngsters were admitted as boarders and received their entire training, education, room and board free of charge.

The ORT school for boys teaches machine-shop skills, while that for girls offers sewing, cooking, secretarial skills, and hair dressing. One entire class of Shinlung students completed the three-year course of study and, with one exception, returned to Manipur and Mizoram, and a group of new students arrived to begin the program.

The present Shinlung community is distributed among thirteen villages, the principal one being Aizawl, the capital of Mizoram. The young people cannot remember the practices of their grand-

23 / The Jews of India

parents, but along with the adults they all apparently attempt to celebrate the important holidays throughout the year, including Israeli Independence Day. Attendance at Sabbath services is expected of all members of the community. There is a prayer hall, Beth Shalom, in Churachandpur used for this purpose, and in Aizawl it is a room in the home of one of the members. A small transliterated prayer pamphlet was published and serves as the basic reference for worship.

The exposure to the Jews of India, as well as to outside visitors, prompted community leaders to seek recognition from Israel. In correspondence with Israel they noted that they had been practicing Jews since 1959.

To date their existence can be documented from about 1970. The 1971 Indian census identifies a small handful of Jews in Meghalaya and Mizoram: eleven in all. Photographs of the community, dated 1970, however, show a number of members in front of the prayer hall, while others picture individuals celebrating Jewish holidays. This would suggest that they are living as Jews and probably had been for some time before. A few artifacts are reported to have been found that are quite old, but they have not been scientifically dated. These include a small wooden board with a Hebrew inscription and a framed board with a Star of David on one side and a configuration of intertwined *nagas* (cobras) on the other.

Ever since 1982 the Shinlung have been in touch with Amishav in Israel and, since 1994, Kulanu in the United States, two organizations that are interested in assisting them to get to Israel. Since Israel will not recognize the Shinlung as bona fide Jews, these organizations have solicited funds to subsidize Shinlung members to travel to Israel. Their efforts have been delightfully successful up to a point. As of the spring of 1996, almost two hundred Shinlung have entered Israel, where they have studied for about a year, learned Hebrew, and been converted according to rabbinic law. They are then accepted as Jews by the chief rabbi's office and become eligible for Israeli citizenship. Those who have made the trip have done exceptionally well.

In addition to the claims of the community itself, there appears to be a general belief among certain Christian groups in northeastern India that all Manipuris were descended from the Ten Tribes. An interesting footnote to the entire situation is the observation of Rev. Frederick S. Downs, a Baptist missionary who worked in the area for about twenty years and is now teaching at the United Theological College in Bangalore. "It was not," he wrote, "a matter of Christians converting these 'Israelites,' but of the 'Israelites' converting the Christians!"

Much more work needs to be done on this subject before we can really know exactly who these people were, where they came from, and the circumstances of their Judaism. That they are presently practicing Jews is an accepted fact.

* * *

In 1970 Benjamin J. Israel wrote a fitting tribute to the Bene Israel and to India. It can be applied very appropriately to all of India's Jewish communities: "[The demise of the Bene Israel] will be a loss to India, if not World Jewry. However insignificant a part the Bene Israel played in the general life of India, by their very existence in sizable numbers on the West Coast, they have constituted a Jewish presence in India which in its small way has enriched its multi-faceted culture. More important, they have provided living evidence that, in at least one country in the world, Jews can exist in pride and honour and without any need for self-consciousness or protective withdrawal into a self-created ghetto."

Part I

*Descendants of a Lost Tribe:
The Bnei Menashe (Shinlung)*

4

Just Who Are the Shinlung?
Rabbi Jack Bresler

Background

The Shinlung are a group of tribes of approximately two million people who reside in several northeastern Indian states, including Manipur, Mizoram, Assam, and Nagaland. They also reside in the Chin mountains of Burma and the Chittagong tracts of Bangladesh. *Shinlung* is the Chinkuki word for "cave," but some say it means "closed valley." The Shinlung have also been called Mizos, from the state of Mizoram, but *mizos* also happens to mean "spread out" in Hebrew.

As was noted in the introductory overview on Jews in India, members of the Shinlung tribe believe they are descended from the tribe of Menashe (Manasseh), and many wish to come back to their true Jewish roots and migrate to Israel. About five to ten thousand of them are actively involved in practicing Judaism, trying to follow the Torah and perform the mitzvot. But these members of the Shinlung say they find it difficult to live as observant Jews in their local setting.

The Shinlung were "discovered" about a hundred years ago by Christian missionaries, who became excited when they realized that these people were probably Jews, since they had customs very similar to the Jews, and felt they would be able to convert them to

Christianity. With the help of British troops, the missionaries were able to rob the Shinlung of their religious treasures and destroy their religious hierarchy, thus preventing the Shinlung leaders and people from performing their own Jewish religious customs and practices.

One problem the Shinlung face is that their neighbors deride them for acting like Muslims (for instance, by wearing kippot) in an area where Muslims are hated. It was recently reported that in Burma huge numbers of Muslim villages were destroyed and their populations killed, forced into manual labor, or deported to Bangladesh. It has also been reported that members of the Shinlung tribe are sometimes murdered by other inhabitants of the area. Another problem the Shinlung have faced is not being accepted as "real Jews" and not being given priority over non-Jews in studying at training facilities such as the ORT in India.

CUSTOMS

The Shinlung call their deity Y'wa, although some use the term Pathien. They have feast days corresponding to the Jewish holidays and an elaborate system of animal sacrifices resembling the Jewish sacrificial system. They practiced levirate marriage (wherein a man marries his deceased brother's widow), buried their dead simply (no cremations), and maintained the patriarchal system of inheritance. On the eighth day a newborn boy was sanctified. They also slaughtered an animal and drained its blood before eating it, and wore blue-and-white tzitzit.

At the heart of the Shinlungs' identification with Judaism is the belief that all two million of them are descended from the tribe of Menashe, the son of Joseph. They sing the following traditional song:

We observed the Sipkui festival,
crossing over the Red Sea running dry before us,

29 / Just Who Are the Shinlung?

and the walking enemies of mine,
the riding foes of mine,
were swallowed by the sea in the thousands.
We were led by fire at night
and by cloud in the day.
Thou art Manmasi [Menashe], begot forefathers
coming from beyond the river.
Following the rivers and streams,
Passing through the mountains and hills,
Brought us thou into the land of strangers.

According to the Shinlung, the tribe of Menashe settled in Persia and was eventually driven eastward to Afghanistan and then to China. Around 600 C.E. (some say during the time of the Mongol invasion) religious persecution forced them to flee from China and settle in Vietnam, where they lived as cave dwellers (*shinlung*). During that time the Shinlung lived continually in a state of fear and hunger, and found it impossible to rest on Shabbat.

They were eventually driven from Vietnam by a Chinese king (at that time China controlled Vietnam, and the Vietnamese were fighting for independence). They lost their Sefer Torahs and were forced to follow their traditions by memory. They wandered around Thailand and then through Burma for hundreds of years. Their priesthood was preserved until the middle of the nineteenth century, when Christian missionaries, supported by foreign troops, were able to end their traditions. In 1854, the American Baptist Mission was established in Manipur. By 1890 Presbyterian missionaries were also active in the region. By 1990, 90 percent of the tribal people in Mizoram had been converted to Christianity.

Thirty years ago a local prophet named Tanruma of Manipur began preaching to the Shinlung, saying that they would be destroyed if they did not go back to their old Jewish faith. He told them that they were all destined to return to Israel. The return to Judaism started in Churachandpur in southwestern Manipur and has since spread throughout the area. Small synagogues have been established around towns in the Imphal area. Those who have returned to Judaism but have had exposure to Christianity may still have some belief in Jesus, while others with less exposure will not have this belief. The Shinlung who at present want to go on aliyah do not have this belief and are eager to study Judaism.

5

How I Happened to "Discover" the Bnei Menashe
Rabbi Eliyahu Avichail

In 1960, when I was a rabbi and teacher of Talmud in the Nahalim yeshiva high school near Petach Tikvah, I invited a guest speaker on the topic of the Ten Lost Tribes. The speaker was Rabbi Avraham Zonenshein from Tel Aviv, the head of an association by the name of Or Hadash Betzion ("New Light in Zion"), founded by him in 1958. Rav Zonenshein (today over eighty years old), a Hasid and Holocaust survivor, full of imagination and enthusiasm, devoted himself completely to this subject.

To a certain degree, he founded a new direction in investigating the subject because even with his creativity, he tried, more than his predecessors, to base his conclusions on fact.

His words and book interested me and revealed to me a "new world" that did not compare to the normal literature on the Ten Tribes, which was mainly based on imagination rather than fact. For example, it had been written that the Ten Tribes lived a full Jewish life with Kings, Kohanim, and Levite priests beyond the Sambatyon River. "Facts" were told through unfounded rumors which were accepted even by the great religious leaders of Israel. Due to my limited experience in research, I too turned to literature of this type when I began to be interested in this topic—without being helped by it much.

I learned early that I would have to interest myself in peoples of the present, and not so much in books or stories from the past. I returned to collecting information from testimonies and books on peoples with signs of Jewish roots. After fifteen years I started to round out my theory on the Ten Lost Tribes, which I presented (in Hebrew) in the fourth edition of my book *The Tribes of Israel*.

On Jerusalem Day 1975, I was invited to lecture about the Ten Tribes at Yeshivat Mercaz Ha-Rav in Jerusalem. I was very excited to lecture in front of my peers and teachers, especially Rav Zvi Yehuda Kook. The next day I was asked by the Rav, through a friend, why I didn't act on this issue. My answer was that a single person couldn't do it alone and an organization was needed. Rav Kook took up the challenge and, by providing a recommendation, helped in the founding of the organization when I approached the Chief Rabbi. Thus Amishav ("My People Return") came into being.

In 1979 I received a letter sent by a group calling itself "Jews of North East India," asking for assistance. So started my connection with the Shinlung.

It was not clear that the writers represented only a small community within a large ethnic group of over a million people. The members of this community had split from the whole group, which had embraced Christianity, and had begun living Jewish lives.

The Shinlung reside on the two sides of the India-Myanmar (Burma) border. They live in the Indian states of Manipur and Mizoram and in the Tidim region of the Chin Mountains in Myanmar. Those who live as Jews call themselves the Menashe Tribe or Children of Menashe (Bnei Menashe).

After a correspondence of sixteen years with this group, meetings with members of Menashe in Israel and India, and letters and writings of other knowledgeable individuals, the following picture arises:

When Christian missionaries arrived in Burma at the beginning of the eighteenth century, they were surprised to find people who were aware of biblical stories, and who believed in one God whom they called Yahve, even though there had been no previously known Jewish or Christian influences in the area. The various peoples in the area had a common tradition of a parchment or book which they had lost and which one day would be brought back to them by a white man. They also had a tradition of an escape from China in the distant past.

In addition to the Shinlung, the above story is also shared by the Karens (a group numbering three to four million) in East Myanmar (Burma), and perhaps also the Shans (five to six million). These people also had a tradition of sacrifices, levirate marriage, etc. The Shinlung were sometimes known as Lu-Si, Chinese for "Ten Tribes." In addition, the concept of Bnei Menashe appears in many of their ancient prayers and songs.

It seems that the origin of these tribes was in the Chinese state of Sichuan, where the Chiang ethnic group resides. Like the Shinlung, the Chiang converted to Christianity some eighty years ago. The Chiang also have a tradition of sacrificial offerings in purity, levirate marriage, etc. During the sacrificial offering they mounted twelve flags beside the altar representing their national forefathers (Tribes of Israel?). In times of trouble they called upon a God named Yahve. It is interesting to note that the Chiang numbered some eight million several hundred years ago but today number only about a quarter of a million.

Several hundred years ago the Chinese, who were enemies of the Chiang, conquered the Chiang, killing many and placing the rest under a severe servitude. After an extended period the Chiang escaped to southern China and from there to Burma. Some of them reached Burma through Thailand.

Some fifty years ago, one of their spiritual leaders, who was considered a prophet, announced that the time had arrived for them to return to the Land of Israel ("land of our forefathers"). They started to prepare their aliyah, which was halted by pressure from local authorities. With the establishment of the State of Israel, the

Shinlung approached Jewish leaders around the world asking for assistance to return to their homeland, but none responded.

About twenty-five years ago, aware that a return to Israel must be preceded by a return to Judaism, groups within the Shinlung started leading Jewish lives. They circumcised themselves, built synagogues, and fulfilled the commandments to the best of their ability. They sent their children to study at the ORT school in Bombay (about 600 miles from home). So started the development of a Jewish religious community among the Shinlung which today numbers some five thousand people in the whole region.

In 1980 we asked the group to send two representatives to study Judaism in Israel. They arrived at the end of 1980—Gideon Rei and Shimon Gin. They studied Hebrew at Kibbutz Be'erot Yitzchak and continued their religious studies at Machon Meir and the Kever Yosef Yeshiva. When they returned to India, Gideon became the spiritual leader of the Bnei Menashe, and Shimon became the spiritual leader of the Churachandpur community, as well as its teacher of Hebrew.

In 1981 Rivka Benjamin came to Israel from Manipur to study and pass the conversion course at Kibbutz Shluchot. After her conversion she married an Israeli, and they live today in Elon Moreh.

During my visit to India in 1982, I attempted to reach the Menashe without success. In 1984 a "congress" with the Menashe was planned to take place in Silchar, Assam State, but although we had received a state permit to enter the state, we were not allowed to reach our destination. Only seven leaders of the group arrived in Calcutta. We studied Judaism and Bible together for three days, and discussed the future.

In 1985, during an important journey to India, Japan, Mexico, and the United States that dealt with research, conversion, and fund-raising, Rabbi David Shelousch, Chief Rabbi of Netanya, joined us in order to convert thirty young members of the Bnei Menashe in Bombay or Calcutta. There were many problems and the conversion did not take place. In 1988, however, twenty-four of the Bnei Menashe were converted by a beth din (rabbinic tribunal) presided over by Rabbi Yacov Neuman, who was a presiding judge of the beth din in South Africa. The conversion took place in Bombay. After lengthy negotiations with the Ministry of the Interior, the group immigrated to Israel a year later.

In 1991 we miraculously succeeded in entering Manipur and Mizoram. We were greeted with great honor and pomp; the government of Mizoram sent two ministers to welcome us—they had to travel for seven hours in order to do so—and provided us with a chauffeured vehicle as well as lodgings in a government-run inn. On entering the territory of Mizoram we were escorted continuously by a government-supplied bus adorned with a banner reading *Am Yisrael Chai* ("Long live the people of Israel") and filled with wonderful young people of the Bnei Menashe who kept singing Israeli songs.

The receptions in the cities were marvelous, and signs such as "Take Us to Israel" were unforgettable. In Aizawl, the capital of Mizoram, we had important and emotional meetings, one with fifteen hundred citizens of Mizoram in the largest hall in the territory! Here, too, the government assisted with a choir and dance troupe. The program was more than three hours long, and yet, even though it was a regular working day, the people didn't want to leave.

Over the past few years individuals and groups of Bnei Menashe have arrived in Israel to study at kibbutz ulpanim and have continued their Jewish studies in Jerusalem. In 1993 a change took place in the character of the Bnei Menashe immigration. This occurred when interested Israelis began urging us to bring more Bnei Menashe to Israel. These requests came mainly from farmers in the Gush Katif region, where employing Arab workers had become dangerous. Dr. Irving Moskowitz and his son-in-law Yigal Hirsh, both of Florida, were willing to cover the cost of this immigration.

We approached the Chief Rabbis of Israel, who had just been

inducted into office, to obtain their opinion on this issue, but we received no reply. I then wrote to the Lubavitcher Rebbe, of blessed memory, asking his opinion regarding the immigration of youths from India to Gush Katif. His reply (within three days) was to bring them and convert them in the Holy Land, starting with single individuals.

A group of forty arrived in August 1993 on a work-study program. Two of them were stabbed by Arabs while working in greenhouses in Gush Katif—Stanley Sharon (a day after his circumcision) and Orly Menashe. (Stanley has since been married, on the exact spot where he was stabbed, and Orly is now married to an Israeli and lives in Kiryat Arba.) After a period of eight months in Israel and conversion, the group moved to Jerusalem to continue their Jewish and Hebrew studies at the Ein Hazvi Yeshiva.

With the completion of their absorption, the Interior Ministry agreed that an additional twenty families and a group of young singles could immigrate to Israel. In April 1994 a delegation from Amishav went to India to select and prepare those who were qualified for conversion and immigration to Israel according to the following criteria: number of years connected to the Jewish community, knowledge of halacha (Jewish law) and Bible, age, fluency in English, and social aptitude.

In Manipur and Mizoram some forty-two singles and sixteen families were chosen, totaling 110 individuals. The first part of this group arrived in Israel in August 1994, exactly a year after the arrival of the original one. It included fifty-seven persons—thirty young singles and seven families. The expenses for this immigration were also covered by Dr. Moskowitz of Florida.

The singles went to Jerusalem to study Judaism and Hebrew, while the families, not being able to be absorbed by religious kibbutzim, settled in Kiryat Arba, where they were accepted with open arms.

Due to delays caused by the Interior Ministry, the remainder of the original group of 110 arrived only after another year. Thank God this group was absorbed well.

In the summer of 1995 it was arranged that the beth din of Sydney, Australia, would convert Bnei Menashe in India with the financial support of Amishav, which would be responsible for preparing them for conversion—conditional upon approval of the Chief Rabbinate of Israel.

In February 1996 the Sephardic Chief Rabbi of Israel, Rabbi Bakshi-Doron, agreed to the conversion in India of the parents of the young singles living in Israel, in groups of forty every half year.

The first *shaliach* (emissary) to Manipur began working to prepare these converts in March 1996. He had joined our delegation, which had traveled to Myanmar (Burma) and then to Imphal, the capital of Manipur. During this visit we concluded several practical matters, such as plans for the construction of a community center and synagogue in Imphal and the establishment of a center near the city to include a seminary and kibbutz for Jewish and Hebrew studies for the Bnei Menashe.

To facilitate future immigration, this seminary/kibbutz project was designed by communities in Mizoram and Manipur with the help of the first generation of immigrants who have successfully completed absorption in Israel. Construction is scheduled to start in late 1996 in Manipur. The seminary will train fifty teachers for adults and children, and after a three-year course, the teachers will go to synagogues and schools throughout Manipur and Mizoram. The faculty of the seminary will consist of both Bnei Menashe and Israelis. The seminary will have several classrooms, a dining room, and a synagogue. The kibbutz will be used to expand and deepen the Jewish education of families for six months prior to making aliyah. About twenty families will work at the kibbutz at any one time, supporting themselves with kibbutz industries. Huts will be built at the kibbutz to accommodate the families.

6

Chronology of a Successful Return

Although no one knew it at the time, the arrival of the first forty-one Bnei Menashe in Israel in August 1993 marked the beginning of one of the most successful homecomings in Jewish history. While it is only a ripple of immigration, the quality of the absorption and the historical significance of the return of a Lost Tribe make the story a stirring one. Added to its importance is the fact that the initial settlers succeeded without assistance from the Israeli government (Amishav is a privately funded organization), and against a backdrop of malicious scare tactics.

As this book goes to press, exactly three years have elapsed since that first arrival. About two hundred Menashe have emigrated to Israel and formally converted to Judaism. Join us as we review the exciting chronology, as recorded in the pages of Kulanu's newsletter.

Autumn 1993
Forty-one Shinlung Have Come Home!
Rabbi Eliyahu Avichail

Warmest greetings to my dear friends in the United States! Our organization, Amishav, has undertaken the difficult yet tremendous task of helping to bring the dispersed Jews of the world back to the Jewish religion and to Israel. Our role is to be a bridge to dispersed Jews around the world. We open a door for their future return.

Jews have returned to Israel from many nations and are currently returning from Russia, Syria, Yemen, and other nations. Almost all of the returnees, however, have been from the two tribes of Judah and Benjamin. But there now appears to be the beginning of a stirring among the dispersed of the Ten Lost Tribes of Israel, as it is written: "And He will gather the dispersed of Israel and assemble the scattered of Judah" (Isaiah 11:12).

The exile of the Ten Tribes of Israel is different from the exile of the tribes of Judah, in two ways. First, the Ten Tribes of Israel live generally as non-Jews, with only some indications of their Jewishness, and will largely return as converts. As the Palestinian Talmud says: "They [the Ten Tribes of Israel] will be converts to Judaism in the future" (Sanhedrin 10:6). Second, with exceptions (such as the Ethiopian Jews), they will largely come from the east: "From the east I will bring your offspring, and from the west I will assemble you" (Isaiah 43:5).

Although our task is tremendous, our means are meager. We have managed to work in cooperation with others on some of our projects, such as our project to facilitate the return of the descendants of Marranos in Belmonte, Portugal. But for many other projects we have to act largely by ourselves—such as our project to bring to Israel and back to Judaism some members of the tribe of Menashe who are from India. (According to tradition, the tribe of Menashe will be the first of the Ten Lost Tribes to return from the east.)

The forty-one young Shinlung men and women from the tribe of Menashe arrived from northern India (Mizoram and Manipur). The group of thirty-nine who came on August 2, together with two who arrived earlier, were greeted at Ben-Gurion Airport with flowers and new kippot by members of the board of Amishav and representatives of the Gan-Or settlement, which absorbed the group. We rented a special bus from Jerusalem that took the group and the greeting party to the Gush Katif area.

The ride, the dancing, and the reception they received in Gan-Or was a very moving experience. The occasion was taped on a home video camera, and I will show the tape during my next visit to America. In Gan-Or they were housed in new homes where they are working and studying Hebrew and Judaism. The work that they are doing, in hothouses, is difficult, but all of the people we have brought are young, strong, and willing to work hard while living Jewishly and learning about Judaism. The arrangements for their absorption necessitated a special financial effort which we still need to continue.

Following their arrival, some twenty articles appeared in the local press as well as several appearances by myself on television and radio. Most of the articles were favorable, but there were those who did not grasp the fact that new converts need a warm, comfortable, and religious atmosphere where there is ample employment. All these conditions are found in the Gush Katif area. The cost of their transportation to Israel, $20,500, was covered by our dear friend and member Dr. Irving Moskowitz and his son-in-law, Yigal Hirsh. We are hoping that other friends of Amishav will help cover the cost of the ulpan for these new immigrants until their formal conversion to Judaism. After they have converted, the Israel Absorption Ministry will pay their expenses.

We hope to bring another group of forty individuals from the Menashe tribe to Israel. Of course, we would like very much to find someone who would be willing to cover part or all of the expense involved.

We here in Israel cannot do our work alone. We turn to you, members of the Jewish community in the United States, to give us support. We ask you to contribute to the redemption of the Jewish people by helping Amishav undertake projects like the one that is bringing the Shinlung to Israel and to Judaism. We have to provide for their material and spiritual needs, for the sake of all of us. May God help us toward the complete redemption of Israel.

Autumn 1993
My Visit with the Shinlung Immigrants
Bruce Terris

Early in August 1993, a group of about forty young members of the Shinlung tribe arrived in Israel. They came from northeastern India near the Burma border. None had been outside their country before.

I had the good fortune to visit them on August 11, just a week after their arrival in Israel. I went with Rabbi Avichail, who had helped them come to Israel, and a television newsman, who was filming for a program to be shown nationwide in India. They had come to a moshav where they are earning their way by working in the morning in hothouses where tomatoes, melons and other produce are grown. Then they spend their afternoons learning Hebrew. They are filled with enthusiasm for Israel and Judaism.

The television reporter tried hard to see if the young people had any dissatisfaction with Israel. Their only criticism was that it was a little hot and humid in Gaza. But as their enthusiastic singing of Hebrew songs demonstrated, they were thrilled to be Home.

All this may sound as if they have been missionized for Judaism the way other people have been proselytized by other religions. But this is absolutely untrue. They come from a tribe which has an ancient tradition that they are descendants of the lost tribe of Menashe. In the nineteenth century, as a result of missionary activity, they became Christians. However, about thirty years ago a small group began, entirely on its own, to return to Judaism. This group has grown until there are now approximately five thousand or more practicing Jews among the Shinlung in India, and perhaps more in Burma, out of a total Shinlung population of approximately two million.

Rabbi Avichail discovered these Jewish Indians about fifteen years ago. He has worked with them until now and has readied them to rejoin the Jewish people. It is truly an inspiration to see their spirit and dedication. They have been very well received on the moshav because of their spirit, enthusiasm, and energy. The moshav has told us to bring as many additional Menashe as we are able.

Winter 1993–94
The Forty-one Bnei Menashe Are Settling In
Rabbi Eliyahu Avichail

The forty-one Tribe of Menashe immigrants from India have been moved to Midreshet Hadarom. This has turned out to be a very positive location, and I am pleased with this arrangement. The Bnei Menashe work in agriculture in the mornings and spend their afternoons in intensive study, rediscovering their Jewish roots. Obviously, their work does not begin to cover the cost of teaching and sustaining them. The rent on their rooms comes to $20,000 a year; clothing and footwear will cost $200 per person; equipment for classrooms costs $4,000; and so on!

These people, who for hundreds of years were denied their roots, have come home to their homeland. We would love to bring visitors here to meet our newly discovered brethren and to see what is being done for them, and what they are doing for themselves. They are not sitting around, waiting for a handout. They work. If you are planning a trip to Israel, please contact me, and I will arrange for you to meet these impressive immigrants.

We are confident that you in the Diaspora will want to be active partners in the absorption of Bnei Menashe.

Spring 1994
We Mizo Jews Are Increasing in India
Allenby Sela

As the people of the world now know, descendants of one of the Lost Tribes of Israel, the Shinlung of Menashe tribe, are found in northeastern India, and some of them are being brought back to Israel by the director of Amishav, Rav E. Avichail and his friends. With the help of HaShem, we Shinlung are very interested in Judaism and want to get our own original tradition back, and practice the Jewish life, to live as real, pure Jews—even though we are in the Mizoram Diaspora.

Even though we were influenced and converted by Christian missionaries one hundred years ago, we really never forgot our own identity within our deepest hearts.

After living as Christians for fifty years, some of our elders abandoned the Christian community and started living as Jews, even though they did not know anything about Judaism. Years later, we Mizo people realized that we are descendants of Menashe, but there was no way to go back to Israel or follow the halacha because of our poor knowledge.

When we were discovered fifteen years ago by Rav E. Avichail, we Mizo people were so excited about getting our original tradition back, we were unable to apply ourselves to anything else. After Rav Avichail brought some of our young members to Israel, many of the Shinlung wavered from faith in Christianity. People were more and more unsatisfied in Christianity and abandoned Christian doctrines. More people wanted to follow Judaism, but no Jews influenced us except Rav Avichail.

News about the group of thirty-nine who arrived in Israel on August 2, 1993, reverberated all over the world. The Mizo Christians are very interested and watch us. We Judaism followers are becoming greater in number. Even the great leaders of Mizo Christians are also interested in Judaism, but Christian missionaries from foreign places encourage them not to follow Judaism, and they sent a big fund for their community, as they always did before. Nevertheless, we Mizo Jews are increasing even though we don't have any assistance and help from our Jewish brothers around the world with higher living standards. We are poor, but we don't hesitate to express our feeling, our belief, and faith in HaShem.

Summer 1994
The Shinlung Are Growing!
Rabbi Eliyahu Avichail

A second group from the Tribe of Menashe of northeastern India has arrived in Israel, twenty families comprising more than one hundred individuals. They will be given lessons in Judaism and Hebrew, and will be aided in their adjustment to their new home, a settlement north of Be'ersheva. Families will be working but will also need financial assistance to supplement their learning schedule of twenty hours a week. They will also need medical insurance, furniture, blankets, etc., at a cost of $2,500 per family for the first year.

By the end of their first year in Israel all will have finished their conversions to become completely Jewish, accepted by all as Jewish and entitled to rights as new immigrants. All the members of this group have been carefully selected for their desire to resume their "lost" Jewish heritage and rejoin the Jewish people in the Jewish land. Now, with the approval of the Chief Rabbis and key government leaders, all are extremely enthusiastic for the program's success.

The project has been assisted by a few very generous individuals—Dr. Irving Moskowitz of Miami Beach, Simon Wapnick of New York, and A. Sabah of Netanya.

Autumn 1994
A Scare Tactic
Jack Zeller

Recently, Rabbi Eliyahu Avichail has been rudely charged by a few members of the established Jewish community in Israel of planning to bring millions of African and Asiatic Jews to Israel. This charge, totally untrue, was an ugly scare tactic—used by those who want to change the Law of Return—which has no applicability to the Shinlung (Tribe of Menashe) immigrants from India to Israel, who entered as non-Jews.

Whatever merit there may be to changing the Law of Return, it is not served by lies and racial innuendoes. But the worst aspect of the criticism is that it distracts Rabbi Avichail from his efforts on behalf of fifty-three Shinlung in India who are ready and waiting to make aliyah. These individuals and families have been so carefully and individually screened that upon arrival in Israel it is assured that they will be motivated to work and study and qualify for conversion at the end of a year.

The Shinlung (also referred to as the Chikimi) do not get any support from the Jewish Agency and do not sit idly in absorption centers, the victims of government maladministration. They work and study and make the most of what they have, which is breathing the spirit of Jewish life and aspirations.

And, contrary to the scare-tactics message, these are not impoverished people seeking economic asylum; to the contrary, they are middle-class, educated immigrants from Mizoram who are making well-informed choices, including a diminution of their living standard and often a change of professions.

It requires remarkably little to absorb the Shinlung. But that small amount ($3,000 per person) is still more than Rabbi Avichail currently has to bring over the remainder of the group that is waiting in Mizoram. These and other needs are mentioned elsewhere in this newsletter. We urge you to show your support for the Shinlung at a time when they are shamefully maligned. And, at the same time, you will send a message to those who use deceit to humiliate themselves, the Shinlung, and the Jewish people in Israel and the Diaspora.

Summer 1995
A Truly Successful Absorption
Jack and Diane Zeller

We were standing in a cabbage field enclosed by a large plastic roof and walls and asked to admire the crop that was almost ready for harvest.

"Our crop is a good one," said Sharon Benjamin. The "our" tells the real story about how the Shinlung are being absorbed in Israel. They feel at home with their Israeli colleagues, who have given them training, work, friendship, a Jewish environment, education, and attention to their family needs. The Shinlung spoke in Hebrew to their Israeli counterparts and in English to us. Their Hebrew is smooth and comfortable, much the way they feel in their aliyah.

How can it be? we asked Rabbi Eliyahu Avichail, founder of Amishav, an Israeli organization that assists potential immigrants with Jewish roots.

He said it is simple: "The first day of arrival in Israel is to celebrate, and the next day begins work." Rabbi Avichail in former years was a kibbutznik, and he very much admires the "will do, can do" method of absorption. And while performing physical work from sunrise to sunset, they follow an observant Jewish life which includes observing mitzvot, intense study, and daily prayer.

It was Thursday evening just before 9 p.m., and Rabbi Avichail's small dining room and adjoining living room were already overflowing with people who had come for his lecture. The rabbi spoke in Hebrew, and occasionally in English to help us along.

There were pleasant introductions of us as representatives of Kulanu from the United States. It was very important to the Shinlung students that Kulanu recognized their contribution to the Jewish people and Israel. They were especially excited that night to read an article about themselves in a Kulanu newsletter. The stack of newsletters we had brought disappeared in seconds.

Among the Shinlung, we felt comfortable and awkward at the same time. Comfortable because we were in such admiration of the intelligence, skill, good cheer, and sterling character of those we met, and awkward because deep in our hearts we felt they were more Jewish in their deeds and decisions than we had ever been. We urged them to keep good diaries so that Jewish historians will have an easy time when writing about their contribution to Jewish civilization.

Readers may recall that some prominent officials of the Israeli government think that you can't really be Jewish if you look Asiatic. Although the Shinlung come to Israel as visitors and do not ask for absorption rights under the Law of Return or to be recognized as Jews without prior conversion, the Foreign Ministry, Ministry of Absorption, and Ministry of Interior are not friendly. This does not disturb the Shinlung. They are in Israel and are warmly received by everyone they meet. Employers who hire them ask if there are more where they came from. There are; and we, in our very small way, have the honor of adding to the chorus of those who say *Baruch haba* ("Welcome").

Autumn 1995
In Praise of My Menashe Neighbors
Yaacov Levi

Shalom. I am writing in reference to the Bnei Menashe that have recently been discussed in your newsletter.

First, my own personal endorsement—I have been an *oleh* (immigrant) here in Kiryat Arba for two years. I made aliyah from upstate New York with a background in law enforcement and as a lifelong farmer.

I have studied with the Bnei Menashe in ulpan, worked with them on a job, davened with them in *beit knesset* (synagogue), and lived with them in the community; and on all counts, and many more, they are good people and an asset wherever they are. Well worth whatever support that they can be provided.

They have just organized an association among themselves for mutual assistance and local leadership. Their goal, and mine as a friend of many of them, is to enable other members of the community in Manipur, India, to make aliyah.

There is much that can and needs to be done to help bring the Bnei Menashe home. Rabbi Avichail in Jerusalem, through Amishav, is a good start.

Be well and be blessed.

Autumn 1995
An Appeal for the Shinlung
Rabbi Eliyahu Avichail

As you may know from previous newsletters, the Shinlung Jewish community (the Bnei Menashe) of northeastern India—who are of Chinese extraction—never come to Israel under the Law of Return. The reason is this: The community is very proud and does not want to be accused of abusing a law that is already criticized as being too generous. This is quite painful, since the Shinlung feel awkward whenever they do something which diminishes their historical claim to Jewish origins.

Therefore, the day after Shinlung arrive in Israel they begin working to support themselves, at the same time that they begin absorption and formal training for conversion by the Chief Rabbinate. It is a remarkable feat when you consider how much money the Jewish Agency (through your federations) spends for absorption centers to the same end.

The one expense that the Shinlung need help with is transportation costs to Israel. There are now thirty Shinlung who are ready to leave for Israel, and there is a shortfall in transportation expenses. While the impediment to their arrival once lay with unsympathetic ministries, the current impediment is something *we* can easily overcome.

I am asking those who believe in the legitimacy of the Bnei Menashe or Judaism-by-choice (take your pick) to act now to help keep the Chinese Diaspora aliyah alive.

Winter 1995–96
Menashe Rites of Passage
Rabbi Eliyahu Avichail

Baruch HaShem, the Shinlung (Bnei Menashe) families that arrived here in Israel last April have successfully undergone the process of *giur* (conversion), and all had Jewish marriage ceremonies.

J. K. Gangte, a Menashe leader, arrived last July with his wife. They immediately went through *giur*, and also had their marriage ceremony performed along with the young couples in Gush Katif—one of them was their son! Six children of theirs are now living in Israel, three of them married with children; Yehuda, one of the four sons, is currently in the military.

In November we had two joint weddings of young people in Gush Katif. One of the young men, Yoel Misao, who recently completed his military training, married Idith. The other couple is Stanley and Rina Sharon; Stanley is the boy who was seriously wounded by an Arab terrorist's knife eighteen months ago in Gush Katif.

The first complete family of official new Menashe immigrants, Yehuda Vaiphei with his wife and two children, arrived in September.

Four families, comprising sixteen souls, arrived from Manipur in December, and we hope to bring the remainder of the group waiting to make aliyah (fourteen people) in February or March 1996.

The Haukip family, from the new group, have been blessed with a new baby girl, and also Mr. Sharon Benjamin and his wife, Suzanne, have been blessed with their second newborn daughter.

Three young Menashe families in Gush Katif will soon have their own greenhouses, currently under construction.

We hope to function with the authorization of the Chief Rabbinate and the Ministry of Interior to bring, as soon as possible, the parents of each young immigrant, as well as their remaining children.

7

A New Ritual for Passover Honoring the Return of a Lost Tribe
by Jonina Duker

The following is suggested as a Pesach Seder reading just before the recitation of Dayenu.

From the time of the Assyrian Exile in 722 B.C.E. until the present, segments of the Jewish people have been forcibly separated from us through persecution and expulsion.

One such segment previously lost to the Jewish community is a people now known by at least three names: Bnei Menashe (since they trace their ancestry to the tribe of Manasseh), Shinlung (after the caves in which they once found refuge), and Chikimi (after the Chin, Kuki, and Mizo ethnic groups from which they spring). The Bnei Menashe believe that their ancestors were exiled in 722 B.C.E. and wandered across many lands. They live now in a mountainous region on the India-Burma border. Knowledge of various ritual observances was handed down orally for twenty-six centuries. Since 1993, approximately two hundred Bnei Menashe have immigrated to Israel, worked to support themselves, and studied for conversion (back) to Judaism under the auspices of the Chief Rabbinate. We recite a poem that, according to tradition, accompanied the Bnei Menashe throughout their migrations.

Copyright © 1995 Jonina Duker

Red Sea Song

We must keep the Passover festival
Because we crossed the Red Sea on the dry land.
At night we crossed with a fire
And by day with a cloud.
Enemies pursued us with chariots
And the sea swallowed them up
And used them as food for the fish;
And when we were thirsty
We received water from the rock.[1]

We pause during our Seder to reaffirm our unity with the Bnei Menashe and with *K'lal Yisrael*, all the Jewish people:

We and They

As we have wandered, so have they.
As we have suffered for our beliefs, so have they.
As we have retained our faith, so have they.
As we have clung to our precious identity, so have they.
As we long to lead Jewish lives, so do they.
As we believe in the Promised Land, so do they.
As we pray "You are One", so do they.

May those among the Bnei Menashe, and anyone else who desires to return to or turn to Judaism, celebrate Passover Seders next year in peace and tranquillity.

L'SHANA TOVA TIKATEVU

---

[1] From E. Avichail, *The Tribes of Israel* (1990).

Part II
The Marranos

8

That Word "Marrano"

Karen Primack

Perhaps it goes without saying that we would never intentionally call people by a name that is offensive to them. The real question is, If we use the word "Marrano," have we unintentionally used an offensive term? Is this term, moreover, the best one to describe the people at issue?

Some, such as Schulamith Halevy, an Israeli scholar, prefer the word *anus* (plural *anusim*), Hebrew for "forced one," but *anus* could refer to other converts throughout history, including those forced under Islam, as well as to people forced in other circumstances (the word's root also means "compel" in the sense of rape). Also, the word is not well known outside of Israel. And Rabbi Peter Tarlow, who speaks to and sometimes converts such individuals, finds the use of *anus* misleading, since not all Jewish converts to Christianity around the time of the Inquisition were forced to do so; some, on the fringes of Judaism, accepted Christianity willingly (although he is quick to add that these individuals did not escape the wrath of the Inquisitor or the *limpieza de sangre* requirements that kept New Christians with "impure" Jewish blood from participating in various occupations and institutions in Spain).

Tarlow and others prefer the term *converso*, but this usage is ambiguous, since the translation is simply "convert," which could refer to fifteenth-century Spanish Jews who became good Catholics (i.e., *not* secret practitioners of Judaism) or even to any modern convert from one religion to another.

Others prefer "crypto-Jew" (literally, "secret Jew"). This, again, is nonspecific. For example, the *Encyclopaedia Judaica* refers to crypto-Jews under the Visigoths in seventh-century Spain, under the Almohads in twelfth-century North Africa and Spain, and under the Muslims in nineteenth-century Persia; it also lists the Neofiti in southern Italy from the thirteenth century and the Doenmehs in Turkey and Salonika from the seventeenth century.

The term "Marrano" is employed by knowledgeable authors in this book, including Rabbi Jacques Cukierkorn, who is of Brazilian origin and who studied Marrano communities in northeastern Brazil for his master's thesis, and Joseph Hantman, who teaches numerous courses on dispersed Jewish communities. Also, the reader will note in these pages articles written by members of Brazil's Associacão Religiosa Israelita Marrana (ARIM). Its members obviously do not find the word offensive since they apply it to themselves. In addition, Brian P. Haran, who wrote an article herein on "coming out of the Marrano closet," is one, and uses the term. Gloria Mound, a distinguished scholar on the Jewish history of Spain's Balearic Islands, founded an Israeli organization, the Institute for Marrano (Anusim) Studies.

In addition the word is used by Helio Cordeiro, a distinguished Brazilian Jewish editor and self-described Marrano who founded the Society for the Study of Marranismo in Brazil, and published a book called *Os Marranos e a Diaspora Sefardita* ("The Marranos and the Sephardic Diaspora").

According to Rabbi Cukierkorn, the forced conversions were more a Portuguese than a Spanish phenomenon, and the source of the word "Marrano" is the Old Portuguese verb *marrar*, meaning "to force." In Old Portuguese, *marrano* means "forced one." If one looks up the definition of *anus* (Hebrew for "forced one") in a Hebrew-Portuguese dictionary, one will find *marrano*.

57 / That Word "Marrano"

Coming at the issue from a different angle, Joseph Hantman points out that whatever the origin of the word, historians, including the eminent Cecil Roth, commonly use it. And if the word is indeed a pejorative (Cecil Roth claims that *marrano* is a medieval Spanish term meaning "swine"), it has become a term of honor over the years to refer to those forced converts who retained their Jewish identity and secretly continued to practice Judaism, at least to some degree. Hantman also notes that the Persian Jews in Mashad who were forced to convert to Islam in 1835 but continued to practice Judaism in secret referred to themselves as "Persian Marranos," and that is how historians refer to them too.

There being no truly satisfactory solution, we opt for the term "Marrano" because it is well known and clearly conveys what we mean in these pages—Spanish and Portuguese converts to Christianity around the time of the Inquisition beginning in the fifteenth century, many of whom converted against their will, and many of whom continued to practice Judaism in secret, often at great personal risk.

We mean no disrespect to those who may be offended by use of the term. There is no perfectly suitable name, only a convenient one. We recognize that the word may have been used as a pejorative at one time, but perhaps that can usefully remind us of the disgrace with which these people were once viewed, which will remind us of the desperate conditions of the past and the need for understanding and sensitive outreach today.

Someday, very soon, may the descendants of the survivors of the Inquisitions and forced conversions raise their voices, reassemble, and find their true voice and name.

9

Spain

High Holy Days Among the Spanish Marranos
Gloria Mound

Five centuries ago, the Spanish Marranos indeed regarded the Days of Awe with a sense of awe, but uppermost was *fear*—of being discovered by the Inquisition.

Therefore, the fact that Rosh Hashanah is but ten days apart from Yom Kippur made most secret communities weigh which of the two festivals was paramount. The fear was to take time off from work twice in such close succession, regardless of what excuse one wished to make, or even if one was self-employed. To be seen as desisting from work first for two consecutive days, and then for another day but ten days later, was, for the majority, just too risky.

And so in the passage of a very few years after the expulsion of the Jews from Spain, and particularly in the Balearic Islands, only Yom Kippur was observed. The Marranos, or Chuetas, as they were called on the island of Majorca, called Yom Kippur "El Dia Puro." Fasting was something that they found easy to do without detection. Gathering for prayers was far more difficult. Yet somehow they managed it throughout the centuries. The fact that the Jewish calendar is lunar was a tremendous help to isolated groups.

One of the most thrilling reports of Marranos praying together in secret was reported in the 1930s, when Ezriel Carlebach, editor of the *Jewish Daily Forward* in New York, found himself in the capital of the Balearic Islands, Palma de Majorca, on Kol Nidre night. The biggest problem for the American was to convince the Chuetas that he was indeed a Jew and wished to pray with them. After so many centuries the Chuetas knew almost no Hebrew, but the one common word between them and Carlebach was *Adonai*. Later, when this had convinced them, Carlebach saw how the prayers, even in Spanish, still had the form and order of the service that so many Jews around the world know.

In my visits and studies to the more tolerant smaller Balearic Islands, especially Ibiza and Formentera, the third and more jovial festival of Sukkot, with its pastoral, agricultural emphasis, seems to have been far easier to observe.

To this day, one village has a fiesta, which is set by the moon's cycle and usually seems to fall on the intermediate days of Sukkot. There is a procession around the village, with a proportion of the men dressed in creamy white shawls fringed at the corners. In their arms they carry an exact replica of the lulav, but the etrog is missing. Another nearby place has a sixteenth-century folksong about how the Jews, Moors, and Christians celebrated fiestas together at a time when, officially, no practicing Jew was allowed to live in Spain!

Here in Israel we are free to observe our festivals, but if our forefathers in times of danger had not somehow remembered and tried to practice Judaism, would there still be Jews and a State of Israel? I admit I stand in awe of their tenacity and faith, and I try to remember them in my own prayers.

Judaic Research in the Balearic Islands and São Tome
Gloria Mound

As an individual researcher in the 1970s, then very part-time, I started to study the Jewish history of the islands of Ibiza and Formentera, in the Balearics, near southern Spain. I was fortunate enough in this exceptionally insular society to be introduced to a number of persons who were willing to admit that these two small islands not only had a Jewish history, but that a community had continued there until modern times. When the Jews of the controlling island of Majorca had only two choices in the fifteenth century, to either flee or convert, a community of Jews continued there, protected by the islanders.

In the course of the next twenty years, I discovered two secret synagogues in use until the Spanish Civil War in 1936, a Megilla Esther from the fourteenth century (at present being restored by the Spanish government), and numerous families who (when I finally gained their confidence) told me many things about the traditions and customs of this community.

I lived with my family in London, but by 1985 our children were already married and living in Israel, and my husband and I knew we would eventually make aliyah. However, we decided to spend some time living in these islands to learn more about their Jewish history. Our stay lengthened from one year to three, during which we held open house on Shabbat, opened a cheder for children that expanded to accommodate their parents and grandparents, and held an annual seder, packing in as many as our tiny flat would hold.

Later our research extended to Majorca and Minorca, where I discovered two synagogues and a cemetery, as well as other Jewish artifacts and documents.

Upon arrival in Israel, on a minimal budget, my husband and I decided to collate all the Marrano/Anusim material we held, as well as our unique book collection, so as to be a data base for those interested in the subject. I started to receive invitations to lecture in the United Kingdom and America and to publish my findings. In 1988 I was given the honor, on account of my discoveries, to be made an Honorary Research Fellow of the prestigious University of Glasgow, Scotland, an honor that has been renewed each year since. I have also lectured at Oxford and Cambridge, as well as several American universities.

From these visits I have had the opportunity to investigate other secret Jewish communities and their history in places like Mexico, New Mexico, the Caribbean, and São Tome y Principe, and to be consulted by other researchers as well as individuals searching out their Jewish roots.

The Jewish history of São Tome y Principe, two small islands off the west coast of Africa, close to Guinea, includes a tragic era. In 1493, one year after the Jews were expelled from Spain, a large percentage of them had taken refuge in Portugal, where the edicts of banishment did not begin until 1496. King Manuel of Portugal, seeking funds to finance his program of considerable colonial expansion, exacted huge head taxes on the Jews, with very little time to pay, and fines if not paid by a certain date.

The king wanted to colonize the islands of São Tome y Principe (to "whiten the race," as he put it), but the Portuguese did not relish settling in the fever- and crocodile-infested islands. When it was seen that there was very little likelihood that the majority of the Jews would pay the demanded tax, the king deported their young children, aged two to ten, to São Tome y Principe. In the port of Lisbon, no fewer than two thousand children were torn from their parents and herded onto boats as slaves (Samuel Usque reports this in his book, *Tribulations of Israel*). Within a year, only six hundred of the children remained alive. Usque recorded that when the parents of the children saw that the deportation was inevitable, they impressed on the children to keep to the Laws of Moses; some even married them off amongst each other.

The entreaties of the parents apparently were not in vain, for reports soon began reaching the Office of the Inquisition in Lisbon that in São Tome there were incidents of obvious Jewish observance. The local church was greatly incensed. The bishop appointed in 1616, Pedro da Cunha Lobo, became obsessed with the problem. According to an historical source, on Simhat Torah 1621, he was awakened by a procession, rushed out to confront them, and was so heartily abused by the demonstrators that in disgust he gave up and took the next ship back to Portugal.

There was a small influx of Jewish cocoa and sugar traders to the islands in the nineteenth and twentieth centuries, two of whom are buried in the São Tome cemetery.

Today, these islands of approximately one hundred thousand inhabitants are independent of Portugal. Two years ago Israel's first ambassador, Dr. Mose Liba, was warmly received. He found that the descendants of the child slaves were still a very distinctive segment of the population (recognizable by their whiter skins), proud of their historical past and desirous of contact with other Jews. Some Jewish customs seem to have continued, although by now mixed with the values and culture of the heavily Creole society.

In order to commemorate the children who were torn from their parents in the fifteenth century, an international conference was held to coincide with the islands' twentieth Independence Day, on July 12, 1995. Participants attended from Israel, the United States, France, Holland, Portugal, Spain, and South America. Two on-site research projects were begun which are yielding some most interesting results. Many youngsters there are now looking closely at their roots! It is hoped that sponsorship will come forward for further research and studies in the area. Inquisition archives in São Tome, closed for hundreds of years, have now been opened to researchers and are eagerly being studied at the Institute for Marrano (Anusim) Studies in Gan Yavneh, Israel. It is hoped that interested persons will come forward to enable this valuable opportunity to be used by giving support. Slide lectures on the subject were given in the United States in 1996, and more are planned.

10

Portugal

My Trip to Belmonte
A New Look at the Portuguese Marranos
Eytan Berman

Vibrant is the only way to describe Belmonte's Jewish community, an important native Jewish community of Portugal. From the smallest boy to the oldest man, when they prayed they shouted in the small one-room shul. They didn't miss a word. They tried to catch up with all they had missed over five hundred years. I couldn't stay on the wrong page in the siddur for more than two seconds without being corrected. They watched me furtively for signs of approval. It could be confirmed that, yes, I was one of them. I could pray with them, and the wide smiles on their faces affirmed this.

When they took off their tallitot they suddenly looked like Portuguese villagers, dressed in dark jackets and pants of 1940s vintage. I have never seen anything like it. These are the last small-town Jews in the world.

I had been in Belmonte for a couple of days and had met many of the people. This is a fascinating piece of Jewish history, and a miracle. There are about 250 Jews in Belmonte, and the Jewish movement is strong. There had been an Orthodox rabbi and his wife from Israel in the town for one year. The Jews refrain from work on Shabbat, eat kosher, and attend services daily in the small shul. One Shabbat there were fifty people (thirty-five men and fifteen women) in attendance; approximately seventy-five Marranos have been converted to Orthodox Judaism, and many more are preparing to be converted. Some Marranos who practice Judaism with devotion do not qualify for conversion under the rabbi's interpretations because of a non-Jewish maternal ancestor. Others are not interested in religion, are intermarried, or still practice crypto-Judaism in private with the old customs (more about this later).

Their crypto-Judaism is a blend of Catholic and Jewish practices with adherents rarely knowing which practices come from which religion. Over the years, Jewish prayers and customs were passed down from mother to daughter orally, written works being too great a risk. Their crypto-Judaism evolved out of twenty generations of this iterative process.

Some of Belmonte's Jews look like American Jews. Others look like Portuguese peasants, their clothes and culture unmistakably Old World European. The old women dress in black and have dark skin browned from the sun. The men dress in dirty dark jackets and wool pants.

The community of Belmonte is apparently the only surviving Marrano community in Portugal. It started five hundred years ago when six or seven poor families arrived from Spain's Seville and Cordoba. They couldn't leave Portugal during the expulsion because of poverty. For hundreds of years the families married among themselves. Now they are all related. Some can't see at night because of vision problems due to small-group interfamily marriages. Most are obese or very thin.

Why did I go? A responsibility to witness a miracle and . . . curiosity. What would these Jews be like, separated from mainstream Judaism for five hundred years, perhaps the only community of Jews in mainland Europe unscathed by the Holocaust? This was a peek into the past, opening a history book to the year 1500. Could I answer their questions on Judaism? Are they better left undisturbed?

My Yiddishkeit weak, and with no planned agenda, I took the thirty-six-hour train ride from Amsterdam to Oporto, Portugal. I was delirious from the train ride. It took a strong Portuguese coffee to get me adjusted to solid ground again. I walked aimlessly up the narrow, busy street to a corner where I could eat my sandwich.

Rejuvenated with food and caffeine, I began my learning curve for Portugal. A new country always presents challenges—new language and money system, where to sleep, eat, and be safe—the basics that most of us take for granted. I changed some money and found a reasonably priced *pensão* (bed and breakfast inn). It was wonderful to be freed of my baggage. I wanted to explore immediately. There was much to do in Oporto. I couldn't waste time as it was already December 21 and I wanted to be in Belmonte by Christmas to observe any unusual Marrano practices relating to this most important Christian holiday.

Oporto was the home of Artur Carlos de Barros Basto, a highly decorated, influential officer in the Portuguese Army during World War I. His family, like other Marrano families, practiced Judaism in secret, but his Jewish feelings had prompted him to expose his religion to the public. He was, in a sense, the first Marrano to "come out of the closet." He had worshipped publicly in synagogue with the Jews of Lisbon, and the existence of Marranos in Portugal had become known. Although he had been humiliated in the Catholic press and lost his military rank, Barros Basto was a charismatic leader who traveled to Marrano villages and encouraged many others to follow his path. He had attracted international headlines and funding from the Jewish community in England and the wealthy Kadoorie family in Shanghai. When a bitterly anti-Semitic socialist government came to power in the 1930s, the Marranos were driven back to their secret ways; Barros Basto died a broken, poverty-stricken man whose vision had never fully come to fruition.

What to do first in Oporto? Many of the books mention Amilcar Paulo as the most prominent Marrano after Barros Basto. Paulo, once a young student in the synagogue yeshiva Barros Basto had built in Oporto, had discovered Basto's papers years after the leader's death and devoted his life to recording Marrano history. I looked him up in the phone book and was surprised to find him listed. I called and a woman answered. She turned out to be his wife, Lourdo Paulo. To my great disappointment I learned that he had died ten years earlier, in his mid-fifties. His wife was willing to meet me that evening to discuss his work. Through bus, walking, and finally taxi, I arrived at her apartment on Rua de Covelho.

When Ms. Paulo opened the door I knew it was worth the effort. The house was full of historical treasures. Her English was broken, so I used my broken Portuguese mixed with some English. We managed to understand each other. She told me about her husband, his work, his trips to Israel, and the existence of other communities of Jews in northern Portugal. She showed me his library, the world's cradle of information on Portuguese Marranos. Among the volumes of neatly stacked books stood a lamp that the Marranos had used as their Sabbath candles. Ms. Paulo described the synagogue, the small-group interfamily marriage problems, and the emigration of Jews to find work in other countries. She cooked Portugal's native codfish, *bacalhau*, for dinner, and it was delicious.

After the meeting with Ms. Paulo, there was only one other important thing to do in Oporto, and that was to visit the Kadoorie Synagogue. Named after the famous Kadoorie family of Shanghai, who funded it in the early 1920s, the extravagant synagogue is so large that its pews can hold hundreds. The potential number of Marranos returning to Judaism was fifteen thousand. A yeshiva for Marrano children was established. Unfortunately the revival was short-lived. The synagogue only filled up on its inauguration and was later used by Jewish refugees who had fled Germany in the early 1930s.

By the time I arrived at the synagogue only ghosts remained. The most troubling aspect of the synagogue was the silence. Synagogues are not built to become museums. Oporto does not have enough active Jews to maintain a minyan, and there isn't a rabbi for hundreds of miles. The synagogue is cared for by a non-Jewish woman, and a dog protects the fenced-in property. The synagogue is in a nice neighborhood but is still disproportionately beautiful. A synagogue this large, surrounded by palm trees, belongs in Beverly Hills!

As the woman escorted me through, I was awed by the concept of a structure so Jewish in the middle of a population so Christian. Unlike the rest of Europe, the Portuguese Jews were not known as Jews. The Marranos had acted as Catholics, so when they reverted to Judaism in the early 'teens and built a synagogue, it was sensational. The Portuguese knew little about Judaism, and some still believe the synagogue is a church.

I was sad to leave the synagogue. The Kadoories still pay for its maintenance, and the woman probably takes good care of it, but for the last fifty years it has remained a shell, a reminder of the missed potential of the Marranos of northern Portugal. How long would it be before another Jew came to visit?

Arrival in Belmonte

I took a bus to Belmonte. Two or three passengers smiled wide, toothless grins at me. It was a sunny day, and the hills were decorated with olive trees and huge boulders. It reminded me of Israel. As we approached I saw the mountain and someone pointed out the town perched on top. Belmonte means "beautiful mountain."

Slightly intimidated by this new Old World, I got off the bus and threw my bags on the ground. Later I learned that everyone in town knows each other, and I must have stood out like a zoo exhibit. I walked up the street, exhausted and not knowing where to find a *pensão* or the Jews.

I saw an old man with a hat and old slacks; he didn't have many teeth. I don't believe he understood me very well, but he responded to the word *Judeo*, and I nodded excitedly. He pointed at me saying "*Judeo*" and I nodded. He quickly led me around the corner to a fabric store. A telephone call was made, and within a couple of minutes the bearded young rabbi of the community drove up in his new Honda. I wasn't sure what language to speak. We settled on a combination of Hebrew and Portuguese.

We were both excited and hungry for information about each other's world. At his apartment I met his beautiful wife. She lit the Shabbat candles and we enjoyed a wonderful meal as we discussed the Jews of Belmonte. It became clear to me that the rabbi and his wife had not been sent to Belmonte to uphold the status quo. Their mission is to lead and teach the Marranos in Orthodox Judaism.

They are both young Israelis, he of Moroccan birth and she a Sabra. He leads the congregation, teaches the adults how to live as Orthodox Jews, converts Marranos to Judaism, and oversees the kosher slaughtering. She teaches the children Hebrew and Judaism. A new synagogue and mikveh are in the planning stages. They told me that all the Jews are in the clothing business, some rich and some poor. They spend long hours in outdoor markets.

We discussed the question of "What is a Jew," and this led to some lively debate. I was told there are only seventy or so Jews, but I knew that 10 percent of the town's two thousand people were Marranos, whom I considered to be fully Jewish. My definition of a Jew was different from the rabbi's. He required the strict definition of a Jew to be applied: a clean Jewish mother-line, circumcision, and the study and practice of Judaism. I wasn't as rigorous and stressed the feeling of Jewishness.

After Shabbat dinner we went to services. I was simply dressed and arrived in synagogue with the rabbi. We waited for the minyan. People came in slowly, touching the mezuzah as they entered the synagogue. Each man carefully shook my hand. The women entered an adjoining room. All the men greeted the rabbi with "*Shabbat shalom, Rabino.*" The teenagers enjoyed seeing a young Jew from the "outside." The older men sensed an attachment and looked into my eyes, as if to consummate a connection from the past. They didn't say much, but the look was apparent: "It's good to be back."

They spoke to me a little but didn't completely open up until the rabbi left; then their curiosity was unleashed. One man asked if I was *Judeo*. I nodded. Then if I was Sephardic. They wanted to know what Judaism is like in the United States and what I thought of them. They wondered if they were good enough to be Jews and about my reason for visiting. The air permeated of Judaism and we savored it in every breath.

The next morning I went to Shabbat services. Among the sixty people were about three or four male teenagers and four or five toddlers. The services started. The congregants followed the rabbi's lead with hands raised to the Torah. All were involved in the service. They were equals during the service, rich and poor. They kissed the Torah the same way the rabbi did, with all four corners of the tallit. Belmonte was ripe for Orthodoxy.

I was impressed. These people learn quickly because they are like sponges—thirsty for knowledge. There are advantages and disadvantages with an Orthodox rabbi, as there would be with a Conservative or Reform rabbi. To me, one of the greatest disadvantages of this particular rabbi's interpretation is that some Marranos were not accepted for conversion. They don't have proof of Jewish maternal ancestry or don't live in a Jewish community, such as Belmonte, with access to a synagogue and kosher meat.

After Shabbat services, I was fortunate to meet a woman from the neighboring town of Covilha. Helene was introduced to me as a Marrano, but unlike the Belmonte Jews, she has lost the insular look and feel. She dresses fashionably, free from the restrictions of poverty and physical labor. Her worldly manner and education make her as comfortable with non-Jews as with Jews.

She was kind and offered to show me around Belmonte. Involved in several Jewish organizations, she has an intimate knowledge of the Belmonte Jews' problems and needs. Ironically, she is not recognized by the rabbi as Jewish because she lives in the neighboring town of Covilha, 12 miles away, a town without a Jewish community, kosher food, or synagogue.

Helene gave me an insider's tour of Belmonte. From the shul we walked up a winding path along the edge of the mountain that separated the sloping meadows from the walls of the fortress above us. The gravel path soon took us past old houses cradled together with a grand view of the valley below. This was the old Jewish Quarter.

At one time, the Jews of Belmonte lived only in this part of town. The houses are old, built from stone and mortar. They are simple squares with orange-shingled roofs. Each of the houses is distinguished from the other homes in Belmonte by the prominent display of a cross scratched into its outside wall. The Marranos who lived in these houses were terrified of being found out as Jews. They overcompensated by an outward display of Catholicism. Inside the houses was a different story.

A Secret Compartment

We continued through the Jewish Quarter, knocking on the doors of Jews, but no one seemed to be home. At three in the afternoon on Shabbat most of the older Jews who still live in the old quarter visit their children and grandchildren. We continued up the path to one of the modern Jewish houses and knocked. A middle-aged Jewish woman answered the door and immediately invited us in. Inside we met her mother-in-law, an old woman dressed in black.

I was fascinated by the old lady, a link to the past. Her face was heavy with years, and her skin leathery and browned from the sun. Helene's child was carrying a puppy, and the old woman broke into a toothless smile every time she touched the puppy. This was no ordinary Jewish woman. She held many secrets but wasn't about to unburden them on me, a stranger. I had seen her before on the street and in the synagogue. She kept to herself, and her presence was ethereal. She was a history book locked shut. In her nineties, she is well versed in the oral tradition passed to her from her mother and grandmother. I could not understand a word she spoke, and she not a word I spoke. Helene tried to ask her some questions, but she would not answer.

We departed with the key to one of the old Jewish houses, but encountered the woman of the house on the street. The house had two doors, one used for merchandise storage and the other as an entrance. The house was cold, with uneven concrete floors, and sparsely furnished. We were led to the living room, where the woman of the house proudly showed us the secret compartment in the wall, housing an old lamp made from fused, roughly cut pieces of tin. It was such a simple design, but I have never seen anything like it. It had been used regularly by her, her mother, and her grandmother to welcome in the Shabbat. Once the lamp was lit, the secret storage space was closed so that unexpected visitors would not see the telltale light. The prayer the women would recite when lighting the oil lamp was, "Blessed be my God, my Lord, my Adoshem, who ordains us and commands us with His blessed and most holy commandments to kindle this holy wick." I am told that if you find an older woman in the streets of northern Portugal's small towns, chances are high that she will recognize one of these lamps.

We then went to the kitchen, where there were large buckets of black olives. The only natural light in the house was through the back door, as there were no windows. I don't know if this had to do with their being Marranos or for protection from the cold temperatures of northern Portugal's winters.

The back yard revealed a breathtaking view of a valley with rolling hills, the olive trees, weeping willows, and land cut into tracts for farms. Chickens and dogs ran freely, and goatskins dried in the cool mountain air. There was no electricity or plumbing. The man who lived in the house assisted the rabbi in the butchering of goats and chickens to provide the Jewish community with kosher meat. Unfortunately, I couldn't take pictures of the interior of the house as it was Shabbat.

Helene told me that one of the old houses in the Jewish Quarter had recently been sold. I was concerned that a slice of history would disappear if all the houses fell out of Jewish ownership, dissolving the legacy of the Marranos' secret home worship. Most younger Jews who have some money build modern houses outside the Jewish Quarter. Helene showed me a plot of land in the Jewish Quarter where the Jewish community has bought a piece of land and will construct a synagogue and mikveh. Funds have been secured for half of the $100,000 cost of the project.

Helene and I continued on our walk up past the fortress. On the street she would point out Jewish people. The children are somewhat shy to outsiders. They like Belmonte, its small-town life being the only life they know. Lisbon is regarded as fast-paced and impersonal. Unfortunately, the children are not educated because they are pulled out of school young to help in their parents' businesses.

The Jews in Belmonte are all involved in the clothing business, from linen to socks to suits. There are five clothing shops and boutiques in town. Other Jews travel to surrounding towns' markets to sell their wares. There is one factory in town owned by Obelio, a Marrano convert to Orthodox Judaism, who is one of the thousand wealthiest people in Portugal.

Belmonte's Marranos used to have their own marriage and funeral rites. Each couple was married twice, first at home and then, to make it legal, in church. Non-Jewish friends were only welcome at the second ceremony. Parents would make matches. "Marriage is the best deal you can make," parents would tell their children. There were no dissolved marriages; members were expelled from the community if they intermarried. Recently Moises Nunes and his female cousin, both single and of marriageable age, went to Israel in search of spouses on the advice of doctors. Belmonte needs a new gene pool to fight physical and psychological diseases due to in-marriage. They returned from Israel with the news that they were engaged to each other!

Funerals used to take place in church and were followed by the Jewish seven days of mourning at home. On the eighth day and again on the thirtieth day, and every three months thereafter until a year of mourning had passed, the relatives fasted. There was no Jewish cemetery. Marranos left the world as Christians buried under crosses in Belmonte's Christian cemetery. Now there is a Jewish cemetery, and most of the Jews are married and buried according to Orthodox Jewish law. For example, a Marrano recently died and his family wanted to bury him in the Jewish cemetery. The rabbi, following certain customs, wouldn't allow it unless the dead man underwent a circumcision.

Belmonte is a sociological and religious gold mine, a pure gene pool of Spanish Jews completely insulated from the rest of world Jewry for over twenty generations. How have these people survived for so long? Their secret Judaism, the only Judaism they knew, kept them together as a people and apart from all others. They have been insulated from Jewish movements, celebrations, and disasters for over five hundred years. They are transplants out of the fifteenth century in the Petri dish of modernity.

The Marrano Jews of Braganza
Warren Freedman

In the northeastern corner of Portugal, at the Spanish border, is the city of Braganza, where many of Portugal's estimated one million Marrano Jews (one-tenth of Portugal's population) reside. (In central Portugal, also near the Spanish border, is another Marrano center, Belmonte.)

Braganza is the site where only a few years ago I had the pleasure of meeting with Ephraim Eldar, Israel's ambassador to Portugal, who was similarly visiting with the Marranos. I was then a visiting journalist accompanied by an official Portuguese guide from New York for the purpose of studying the Marrano presence in Portugal.

It was noteworthy that the State of Israel was then "interested" in recognition of the Marrano Jew, although subsequent events brought forth little success. In point of fact, I had offered one-way plane tickets from Lisbon to Tel Aviv to a Marrano family named Rodriques, only to have Israel's Minister of Immigration and Absorption turn down the request for acceptance under the Law of Return.

During my visit to Braganza I was aware of the fact that Jews first settled in Portugal long before 1492, when the Jewish population was strikingly increased by the arrival of thousands of refugee Spanish Jews who had crossed the border to escape the Inquisition. But in 1547, under Pope Paul III, the Portuguese Inquisition brought death to thirty thousand Jews, although it spared thousands of others who accepted conversion but continued secretly to practice the Jewish religion in their homes.

Thereafter, except for transients during World War II, Portugal never had more than a thousand Jewish citizens. These secret Jews, or Marranos, maintained their religion these many years only to come forth in numbers in 1948 with the birth of the modern State of Israel.

The Marranos are distinguishable from other Portuguese by (1) possession of Hebrew writings, Hebrew prayer books, religious objects, art, and miscellany; (2) circumcision on the eighth day; (3) Friday night ceremony for lighting candles; (4) separation of meat and milk foods; (5) observance of Jewish holidays, to wit: (a) ten days after the new moon in September, a day of fasting is observed and everyone dresses in white clothing; (b) eight days after the new moon in February, a fast is observed, probably Purim and the Fast of Queen Esther; (c) on the fourteenth day of the new moon in March, Passover is observed; for two days no bread is eaten, but on the third day unleavened bread is eaten, and a whole lamb is roasted; (d) on the Sabbath cooking of food is not permitted; and (e) meat and poultry are soaked and salted; (6) after a funeral the mourners sit on special low benches in their homes for seven days and burn a special oil lamp; and (7) the wedding ceremony includes a blessing in the name of the God of Abraham, Isaac, and Jacob.

11

Mexico

Jewish Descendants of Conquistadores?
Joseph Hantman

Fourteen ninety-two marks the year of expulsion from Spain and the beginning of the Sephardic Diaspora. However, for one hundred years before and for many hundreds of years after that date, Jews who had been forced into Catholicism continued to lead secret Jewish lives. They were the Marranos who were hounded, sought out, and frequently put to death by the Inquisition.

Many Marranos fled to Holland, Turkey, and other countries where they resumed their identity as Jews. Others, ostensibly as Catholics, joined Spanish explorers and colonizers in various colonies around the world. Some ultimately found refuge in Dutch and British colonies in the Caribbean, where they resumed their Jewish identity; their synagogues and burial grounds remain today in such places as Barbados, Curaçao, and the Virgin Islands.

One group accompanied the Spanish Conquistadores who conquered Mexico in 1521. Here the desire by the Spanish conquerors for riches, gold, land, and expansion was so great that the leaders had little zeal for or interest in hunting down or exposing those among them who in secret practiced some Jewish rituals and observances. Thus, the secret Jews flourished and rose to positions of relative power in the administration and economy of New Spain. They lived as Catholics in public but as Jews in private, and maintained a network with other secret Jews. Their secret was passed from parents to children, and the double life became their way.

Unfortunately, the dreaded Inquisition soon came to Mexico, with the predictable horrendous consequences. Those who practiced Judaism were tracked down, arrested, and tried, and many were put to death by burning at the stake in central Mexico City. Hernando Alonso, one of the soldiers who arrived with Cortez, had the distinction of being the first Jew burned at the stake on the North American continent. This tragic repetition of Spanish history is well documented in the records of the Inquisition. Names, dates, and places are published and are available for study.

As a result of frightening pressure from the Inquisition, many Marranos gave up their secret Judaism, but others moved north to the frontiers of Spanish colonial life to areas which are now California, New Mexico, Texas, and Arizona. Here much of the secret Jewish life continued through the eighteenth and nineteenth centuries, apparently with diminishing strength, until it was thought to have disappeared in the twentieth century.

Now, however, thanks to the work of such historical researchers as Dr. Stanley Hordes at the University of New Mexico, a new and fascinating picture has emerged of descendants of those secret Jews living today as Catholics or Protestants but keeping alive family traditions which are unmistakably clear indications of Jewish origins.

Some families to this day light candles on Friday night, circumcise newborn sons, eat thin flat bread at Pesach, use biblical names, and have family traditions of not eating pork. For the most part they considered such activities family traditions and did not necessarily ascribe them to Jewish identity until, in recent years, such facts have been made clear to them. Some have expressed interest in learning more about modern Judaism with a view toward reentering the Jewish mainstream. Others are comfortable in their present religious affiliation but are intrigued by their history.

Mexico:
Land of the Setting Sun and Rising Torah?
Richard A. Kulick

I have served as Kulanu's shaliach, or regional representative, to Mexico since July 1993, visiting on an annual or semi-annual basis to monitor the progress of a number of small converso havurot, particularly in Mexico City and Puebla. I have also provided technical assistance to the Liberal Jewish Forum of Mexico. The tableau that I entered is one of a small, affluent, and recently established immigrant community which confronts a much poorer Catholic and increasingly Protestant population. Within this environment, tiny "pockets" of individuals encouraging the practice of Judaism have surfaced periodically since the time of the conquest of Mexico under Hernan Cortes.

Mexican Jewry has been an important player in the context of Latin American Jewry as a whole, as well as in Zionist politics. Latin America, in general, is a region of sparse Jewish settlement, reaching a high of approximately 700,000 Jews in 1960, and declining to about 460,000 today. The reasons for this demographic decline are varied, but include the movement of some 75,000 Latin Jews to Israel, 25,000 to Spain, and 25,000–50,000 to the United States, with the balance of the loss due to the typical processes of assimilation, intermarriage, and a low birth rate.

The remaining Jewish population is organized around four axes of ideological commitment: Zionism, secular Jewish culture, resurgent Orthodoxy, and "American imports," such as Conservative Judaism. Unlike in the United States, the Reform movement is hardly present in the region, while the Conservative movement has enjoyed significant growth, probably commanding the loyalty of about 20 percent of the region's Jews. Zionism is likely the most influential movement, given the noted pattern of resettlement, though its influence is declining among the young in favor of increasing "haredization," or the rising influence of Neo-Orthodoxy and Hasidism. Indeed, throughout Europe, Latin America, Australia, and New Zealand, the small Jewish communities have seen a tremendous increase in enrollment in Jewish schools and Orthodox commitment.

This trend has had a major impact on Kulanu's work. In the 1930s and the 1970s, regional Vaad Harabonim, or rabbinical councils, affirmed strict stands against both intermarriage and conversion, reasoning that whatever gains were made through conversionary efforts would be outweighed by the attrition resulting from loss of communal cohesion. Over time, much of this reasoning has proved correct, especially if one compares the rates of activism between Mexican and U.S. Jewry. However, it makes tremendously complex the work of any group such as Kulanu, committed as we are to outreach to those now distant from their Jewish heritage.

Adin Steinsaltz states in his book *Teshuvah* that it takes three generations to make a Jew. The Talmud traditionally required discouraging would-be converts to Judaism by warning them of the suffering they would face on becoming Jewish. It therefore becomes obvious that Orthodoxy's attitude to converts has never been one of evangelical enthusiasm. Indeed, traditional Judaism takes the view that to be a Jew is difficult and challenging, and to convert should require one to pass many tests of commitment to Jewish faith and ritual demands. This means that, especially in communities where Orthodox Jewry is the majority, conversion and welcoming those long lost to the Jewish people will be a careful and select process, requiring any shaliach to work "one by one by one." This has been my experience with Mexican Jewry and the small, struggling Marrano havurot that Kulanu helps.

Mexico's total Jewish population is currently about fifty thousand, of whom 4–5 percent are conversos, 70 percent Ashkenazi, and 25 percent Sephardi. Ninety percent live in Mexico City, with much smaller communities in Monterrey (100 miles south of

Brownsville, Texas), Guadalajara, Puebla, Veracruz, Jalapa, Venta Prieta/Pachuca (near Mexico City) and Tijuana, adjoining San Diego. The communities in Veracruz/Jalapa, Puebla, Venta Prieta/Pachuca, and two study groups in Mexico City are composed of indigenous Mexican Catholics and Protestants and those of Marrano ancestry interested in converting to Judaism, and constitute about three hundred families, or between seven hundred and nine hundred conversos, in total.

It should be noted that this has led, over time, to a division between the "established" Jewish community, which is largely affluent and Orthodox or Conservative, and the small, struggling converso groups, which are becoming more religious. Since the phenomenon began in the 1930s with the founding of converso synagogues in Mexico City and Venta Prieta, the established community has treated such groups with a mixture of curiosity, distance, condescension, and, occasionally, welcome. Both groups also assert very different histories. The conversos allege that they are the true heirs of Mexican Judaism, having ancestry in the country since the first Spanish settlement in the region in 1519.

The "established" community and many scholars of Judaic studies have always dismissed such claims as unproven, but neither are they disprovable. The most respected historian of the conversos in Mexico, Benjamin Laureano Luna, has told me that the conversos knew of each other and remained in-married as a community from the time of the Conquest through the present. However, documentary proof of such claims is rare. In any case, given their tiny numbers, Jews have never been more than a token presence in Mexico, though, as in the United States, their influence, at least in business and industry, has been significantly greater than their numbers would suggest.

The history of the established Jewish community began with the arrival of a group of Sephardic Jews from Syria in 1912, starting a wave of immigration which brought some twenty-five thousand Jews to the country by 1949, including the majority of the

Ashkenazic community, who began arriving after 1920. By the late 1930s, some anti-Semitism began developing in the country, largely sustained by merchants of German and French ancestry, who agitated against Jewish and Chinese immigration, even provoking a riot against Jewish merchants in the Merced central market in 1937. However, anti-Semitic acts and unpopular sentiment have been virtually unheard-of since then, and the Jewish community, especially in Mexico City, has developed a vibrant and fairly affluent, if somewhat self-enclosed, community life. The great majority of Mexican Jews make their living in the business community, the technical professions (i.e., engineering) or the trades.

Currently in Mexico City one can find ten functioning synagogues: four Orthodox Askenazi, four Orthodox Sephardi, and two Conservative. There are nearly 150 Jewish communal groups currently active in Mexico City, and Jewish communal life is strongly oriented under Zionist auspices and activities. The community supports the large Jewish Sports Center, located on approximately five acres of parkland near the main Bull Arena on the western edge of the city, and has a membership of six thousand families, or almost eighteen thousand people. Synagogue life is somewhat more enthusiastic than in the United States, with at least two Conservative shuls having full sanctuaries every Shabbat, and one, known as Bet El, so filled each week that it is building a community center to rival the Jewish Sports Center in size.

The same problems of assimilation and intermarriage that plague other Diaspora Jewish communities are present here, but have so far had a much less corrosive effect on Jewish life in Mexico than in the United States. For example, nearly 70 percent of Jewish children in Mexico City attend the nine Jewish day schools currently in operation. However, the low level of assimilation may have much to do with the community being more recently established than in the United States as well as being 80 percent Orthodox. Mexican Jews have been accused by many of their Gentile neighbors of being elitist, due to the very strict stand many of the synagogues take against interdating and intermarriage with non-Jews.

An example of the select process of admission to Mexican Jewry, related by Rabbi Samuel Lehrer, is the case of the "Diaz" family (not their real name). Diaz worked for a Jewish family in Mexico City that had a cloth factory. The owners of the plant would give any damaged cloth to him, which he then sold at a profit on his days off. He soon made enough money to open a clothing store, which has been expanded into a small department store. In time, he was able to open three more stores, and many of his eight children have started businesses of their own. The Diaz family initially began their conversion to Judaism through the Venta Prieta synagogue, then moved to the Beth Israel Community Center in Mexico City, where they worked with Rabbi Lehrer. The Nidche Israel Ashkenazi Orthodox community began making overtures to them, and they now make their spiritual home there.

The Sephardi communities are particularly adamant in their opposition to any form of conversion being allowed in Mexico. A friend of mine who married an American diplomat was told she would have to go to the United States or Israel to undergo conversion. This was a major factor in the couple's decision to leave Mexico and move to the United States. Once there, she converted under Orthodox auspices.

In opposition to this strong stance, the Liberal Jewish Forum has been convened by Dr. Bill Landau, a psychiatrist of German ancestry, for the purpose of advancing education about human rights and the open acceptance of converts in Mexico City's Jewish community. The Forum was initially attracted to the ideas of Dr. Mordecai Kaplan and the Reconstructionist movement, but many wanted a more determinedly secular outlook, and contacts developed with the Society for Humanistic Judaism in Birmingham, Michigan. The Society's founder, Rabbi Sherwin T. Wine, has since held several seminars in Mexico City, and currently the group has an active membership of thirty.

The Jewish community in Mexico does not include a progressive or liberal nexus, as exists in the United States influenced by the Reform movement. Rather, the "Jewish street" in Mexico is very Orthodox or Orthodox-influenced, and thus, even though at least four of the sixteen synagogues in the country are Conservative, all of them, with the exception of the Liberal Jewish Forum and its allied organizations, follow an Orthodox policy of conversion and intermarriage. That is, they are totally against intermarriage and, therefore, discourage conversion. Only one rabbi in Mexico currently accepts converts: Rabbi Samuel Lehrer, Israeli-born and ordained by Rabbi Abraham Isaac Kook in Jerusalem in 1935.

Rabbi Lehrer is spiritual head of the Beth Israel Community Center, a Conservative, bilingual (English/Spanish) synagogue in a wealthy neighborhood of western Mexico City. Since his arrival in 1968, Dr. Lehrer has converted about two thousand Mexicans to Judaism, including members of the rural indigenous communities mentioned above, with the exception of one of the two study groups in Mexico City and the Venta Prieta community (the second study group is currently studying to convert under Rabbi Lehrer). Approximately 20 percent of the total number have made aliyah to Israel.

Dr. Lehrer currently serves as rabbi for the largest of the indigenous communities, in Venta Prieta, which was originally an evangelical Protestant church until the mid-1930s, when the minister, Balthazar Laraine Ramirez, became involved in a protracted dispute with the leaders of the Church of God Israelite (the sect's name) in Mexico City, and converted to Judaism, taking his church with him. The Church of God Israelite is a loosely organized, but fairly large, Mexican Protestant denomination with three or four hundred member churches throughout the country. While they believe in Jesus to some degree, they consider themselves Jews, using Hebrew liberally in their church symbols and liturgy, and, according to Rabbi Lehrer, having a strong Zionist commitment.

The same phenomenon is apparently behind the consistent, if small-scale interest noted by Rabbi Lehrer, in various parts of Mexico, in studying and/or converting to Judaism. While some in the Orthodox and other Jewish communities view this as an attempt by such groups to improve their socioeconomic status by identifying with a wealthy group such as the Jewish community, a religious interest cannot be denied. The recent wave of Protestant evangelical activity throughout Latin America has brought a large-scale reappraisal of previous anti-Semitic folk attitudes in many parts of the region, as have Israeli military successes.

The Venta Prieta synagogue is located 55 miles northwest of Mexico City and currently has a membership of one hundred families, with its own building, cheder, mikveh, ark, and Torah scrolls. It has been extensively written about (too much for some members) and is very firmly Jewish and Zionist—but not accepted by the mainstream Orthodox in Mexico City, who continue to shun them.

The communities in Veracruz and Jalapa are somewhat smaller and already have a relationship with Kulanu. Rabbi Lehrer originally converted these groups (about fifty families) under Conservative auspices between 1978 and 1983. As some of their leaders wished to make aliyah, they contacted members of the Orthodox community, who referred them to Rabbi Eliyahu Avichail in Jerusalem, who came to Veracruz and Jalapa in 1991 and performed a second conversion. Subsequently, about 70 percent of the one hundred-plus members of the Veracruz synagogue made aliyah to Israel. The communities of Veracruz and Jalapa are continuing to hold weekly services (in members' homes in Jalapa) and maintain the Veracruz synagogue building with the members they have attracted.

The community in Puebla is the newest and probably the most integrated into mainstream Mexican Jewry. Located 90 miles east of Mexico City, and with a population of 1.2 million, Puebla is one of Mexico's traditional "Silver Cities," with a city center endowed with beautiful Spanish colonial architecture. Long the capital of Mexico's textile industry, it has recently begun to diversify its economic base while weathering hard economic times.

Jewish life in Puebla did exist at one point, from approximately 1550 to 1700, with the presence of several wealthy Marrano families who maintained Jewish ritual in secret. However, after this period, they forgot such rituals and became exclusively Catholic. Other families in the town maintained their memories of Jewish heritage but did not practice the religion in any organized fashion. Puebla's Jewish community is now trying to recover the use of some of the properties of the old Marrano families for communal use but has had little success, since all of these homes are in use as either museums, banks, or educational centers.

Contemporary Jewish life in Puebla has a relatively short history, beginning in the late 1970s when Ignacio Castelan Estrada, then the president of the Church of God Israelite in Mexico, began to feel a sense of "metaphysical disquiet" as a result of an increasing consciousness of his Marrano heritage and the effect this understanding was having on his interpretation of the Bible. Raised from birth with a strong consciousness of Marrano ancestry and its attendant "secret Shabbatot" and other vaguely Jewish home rituals, he had always been more strongly attracted to the Hebrew Bible than the Christian Bible. He believed that Jesus had come to fulfill and energize Jewish commitment to ritual practice, not to supplant Judaism with a new religion.

Over time, this conviction grew, as did his belief in the overall validity of the Hebrew Bible, and what he regarded as the dubious claims of the Christian tradition. In 1978, after a number of years as a church leader, he decided to pull away and begin a small havurah in Puebla. Throughout the 1980s, he studied Jewish texts on his own, watched the birth and growth of his children, and slowly built a small proto-Jewish community.

By 1990–91, the group had grown to ten families, almost all of whom had known Castelan. It was then that a small, white-washed synagogue was built by the community on the eastern outskirts of Puebla, much in the style of evangelical Protestant churches throughout the region. Except in this instance it was a shul, not a church. Since 1990, Castelan has been in regular touch with the Central Israelite Committee of Mexico, the representative Jewish body in Mexico, and in 1995 he became its representative in Puebla. In addition, the ten "native" or "born" Jewish families of Puebla have now joined the ten converso families to worship on a regular basis in their small synagogue.

Castelan receives spiritual guidance from the "established" Orthodox Ashkenazi synagogue in Mexico City, Nidche Israel, and is an "otherwise" typical Mexican Jew. The "otherwise" is that he cannot find a rabbi who will convert him and his family or their community. However, regardless of their current status, they mark the first glimmering of Jewish life in Puebla in three hundred years.

The future of these small, fledgling communities may not at this point appear bright. With a total membership of three hundred families and living in isolated areas, they lack the critical mass to establish the kind of autonomous, self-generating Jewish life found in larger communities. However, the same could be said of the small mainstream communities in Guadalajara and Monterrey, which have, at most, a thousand Jewish families and two synagogues between them. Another problem to be faced is the communal consensus of the Mexican Jewish leadership and laity regarding the inadvisability of encouraging conversion.

It has, however, been shown that small, isolated Jewish communities can survive for centuries without much outside contact, as did the Jewish community in Kaifeng, China, from the eighth to the eighteenth century. While the possibility of obtaining conversion in Mexico would seem limited at this time, there has been interest expressed in Israel in facilitating conversion to Judaism in such communities, to encourage aliyah.

The Jewish people were called "an ever-dying people" by the late philosopher Simon Rawidowicz. In every generation since

Sinai, the Jewish people have dealt with the same threats and temptations leading to communal extinction: intermarriage, assimilation, Amalek-style threats of genocide, anti-Jewish violence, and diminished commitment. Yet there always remains a *Sherut Yisrael*, a faithful remnant who eventually reconstitute a flourishing, or at least viable, Jewish communal presence. So it is with all of the communities with which *Kulanu* works. While they struggle to maintain some sense of forward momentum, they still adhere, as does all of *K'lal Yisrael*, to the vision of the prophet Ezekiel, of the dead bones of Israel taking flesh and breath to prove that Israel is indeed eternal.

The Frustrations of a Founder
Ignacio Castelan Estrada

Translated from the Spanish by Richard A. Kulick

I was born in 1943 in Mexico City, as the eldest son of Eligio Castelan Calderon and Juana Estrada Mendez. In those years they identified as Catholics, and a few months after my birth we moved to the provinces to live with my paternal grandparents, Ignacio Castelana Herrera and Juana Calderon Carcamo. There we lived until I was eighteen years old, and I learned some of the Jewish dietary laws, not to eat pork, observing the Sabbath on Saturdays, and some of the other festivals of the Torah. One day my father informed me that he had gone to Mexico City to talk with a rabbi, to arrange for my conversion, but I heard nothing more after that, as he told me that the requirements for conversion could not be fulfilled at that time.

When I arrived in Puebla to study engineering, I encountered a group called the Church of God Israelite, in which my grandparents were also believers, and was told that they followed the Jewish people in many aspects. However, after some time in association with this movement, I began to understand that they actually had very little to do with the Jewish people, and so I decided to leave the organization (at this point, I met my wife Mary, who then was a professing Catholic). In the privacy of our home, with our children Ada, Abner, Jemima, and Hartus, we have always practiced Jewish rituals: receiving Shabbat and lighting candles, guided by some Jewish books I purchased in Mexico City, such as the *Shulchan Arukh*.

We began visiting other persons of our ancestry who knew of our desire to serve the Eternal, and also understood the meaning of the Shema, and we began meeting in one another's homes to celebrate Shabbat. Sometime after this, as we became better integrated as a group, we acquired some land, where we have constructed a modest synagogue. However, at that point I felt some degree of disquiet with the amount of support I was receiving from my community, and did not feel that I was developing sufficient Jewish background with the books of Torah I had, so I established contact with the offices of Keren Kayemeth (the Jewish National Fund) in Mexico City.

Meanwhile, our small community was growing, with ceremonies for births, marriages, deaths, and illnesses all falling on my shoulders to conduct, which I accomplished as best I could in my ignorance. Finally, I managed to make contact with the director of Keren Kayemeth, then Isaac Saad, and I spoke of my community's situation. He attempted to put me in touch with Rabbi Abraham Bartfeld of the Nidche Israel Ashkenazi synagogue, but I never managed to make contact with anyone other than his secretary, who provided me with some books the rabbi had written.

When I again met with Mr. Saad, he recommended that I meet with Rabbi Abraham Palti of the Monte Sinai synagogue, who received me with my son Abner. We spoke of our community's need for spiritual guidance, and while he said he thought the situation of our group was interesting, nothing more happened than a second meeting. I later returned to Keren Kayemeth to make a donation to support Israel during the Gulf War.

I attempted to meet with Mr. Saad one more time, but could not make contact, but I did meet Manuel Levinsky, president of Keren Kayemeth in Mexico, who set a date to visit with us in Puebla. He also put me in touch with Rabbi Samuel Lehrer of the Beth Israel Community Center, who met with me that afternoon. Rabbi Lehrer asked me many questions, and also set a date to visit with me in Puebla.

Mr. Levinsky and his family then visited our community for Shabbat on May 29, 1993, and an article about this was published in Mexico City's weekly Jewish newspaper, Kesher. Many blessings on Mr. Levinsky and his family!

However, the greatest moment in my life as a Jew joined with the house of Israel was being able to receive Rabbi Lehrer in my humble home. May God bless him and keep him in good health! This meeting took place on Sunday, January 30, 1994, or 18 Shevet 5754, here in Puebla. Rick Kulick from Kulanu was also present.

We hope to construct a new synagogue building for our congregation, Beth Shmuel, in the near future. We have a total of twelve families in our community, including thirty-six adults and twenty-three children. At this point we don't have enough financial resources to have a budget per se, but we do have a funding committee, chaired by my daughter Ada, which equitably distributes any resources which we may come across.

Chanukah in Mexico: A Journey of Renewal
Nancy Helman Shneiderman

THE PRELUDE

Late one night, while I was wending my way through a dense paperwork thicket, my home-office jungle yielded a true treasure—a neglected frequent-flyer coupon. Alarmed by its imminent expiration, I quickly telephoned the airline. The agent vigorously explored qualified international destinations, finding Hawaii and Mexico still available. A perfumed recollection of Hawaii's outrageous pleasures on a trip there some years earlier remained etched indelibly into my life-gallery of all-time favorites. Why, then, did I choose Mexico? Kulanu.

This decision had been sourced by a fascinating article in a recent Kulanu newsletter. Mexico, it had informed me, was the home of several indigenous crypto-Jewish communities. Those in Puebla and Veracruz, part crypto, part converso, had recently been featured. To say I felt a strong affinity with the descendants of Inquisition survivors in the New World was an understatement. Despite half a millennium of oppression, repression, coercion, and assimilation almost to the point of extinction, the current generation of crypto-Jews were recombinating their Hebraic identities successfully. Even with the Holocaust to serve as their most recent historical disincentive, neither could they, nor would they, be denied their Jewish heritage any longer. I sensed that we had something in common.

As a woman, I too had known marginalization in Judaism. Lighting the chanukiah in Puebla at the winter solstice would be a joyful affirmation of the Life Source during the darkest time of the year. We could, together, celebrate the power of hope, the miracle of survival, theirs and mine, and the renewal of Jews who, like

---

Copyright © 1996 Nancy Helman Shneiderman

myself, might have turned away, but didn't. Instead, our quest for wholeness required full tribal recognition, in our own contexts, *kulanu* ("all of us").

I knew that these communities were not entirely accepted by mainstream Mexican Jews and were looked upon with considerable suspicion by some in Israel. I admired their tenacity. By reconnecting the unraveled fringes of our people's cloth of continuity, we Jews have repaired ourselves time and again. Recovering and rediscovering forgotten ancestors, the crypto-Jewish story-strands were being reattached daily, like tzitzit, into the total Jewish garment. I knew it took dedicated leaders with courage, vision, patience, and, most of all, faith. This is holy work. I hoped that our visit and songs might offer comfort, affirmation, connection, and new threads of meaning to these groups' challenging retrieval process. Aware that our encounter would further define my own role and responsibilities as a contemporary Jewish woman, songwriter, and liturgist, I prayed for a Chanukah blessing in Mexico.

The memory buds of Hebraic heritage, tribal custom, and religious practice had, in large part, lain dormant in Mexico for many centuries. Selectively maintained by the subtle balance between what could be said and done and what could not, parents, teachers, and the communal norms of each succeeding generation had carried the seeds of tradition from town to town, shaping the crypto-Jews' consciousness. Withstanding each cultural, political, and industrial shift in historic Mexico, these potent seeds of tradition, though inert, contained a robust Jewish possibility. From time to time they would be revitalized by certain events or unanticipated confluences. Occasionally this potential flowered fully within one exceptional, charismatic individual. My quick review of the Kulanu article suggested that the founder of Puebla's Beth Shmuel, Ignacio Castelan Estrada, was such a person.

The Contact

Speaking little Spanish myself, I invited Allan Griff, a friend fluent in the language and my Jewish singing partner, to help with travel plans and to accompany me on this journey. We placed phone calls to both Puebla and Veracruz. Soon we realized that both communities bore the same name: Beth Shmuel. This was, of course, no coincidence. Over the years, a now elderly Conservative rabbi, Samuel Lehrer, spiritual leader of Beth Israel Community Center in Mexico City—a large congregation comprised mostly of Ashkenazim, but with considerable Sephardic and Marrano representation as well—had made numerous visits to both Puebla and Veracruz. To honor Rabbi Lehrer's blessings, and to show appreciation for his officiating at various life-cycle rituals (marriages, bris, and conversions), these two congregations had been given his name.

We had hoped to meet Rabbi Lehrer in person but were disappointed. He told us on the telephone that he would be out of town during our entire holiday stay, as would most of his beach-bound congregants.

Our luck improved with Ignacio Castelan of Puebla and Saul Ruiseco of Veracruz. Both were not only able but happy to celebrate our visit with special Chanukah feasts and candle-lighting. Both warmly extended home hospitality. We accepted, offering to sing for our supper and bring gifts for the children. My vision had taken root. We would indeed spend Chanukah with our Mexican extended family, *kulanu*.

The Visit to Veracruz

Saul Ruiseco, from Veracruz, is extraordinarily proud of his Spanish ancestry. Displayed prominently over his bedroom mirror, an eighth-century crested coat of arms hangs, complete with the Ruiseco family name. Under the watchful eye of his ancestors,

Saul sleeps, perhaps joining with those who went before in dreamtime. The total effect of this is quite dramatic. Saul is a slender, terse, yet pleasant man, probably in his late thirties. He is light-skinned, tracing his origins back to Spain and Portugal. Saul, his mother, and his elderly grandmother graciously greeted us, even though our arrival was inconveniently late.

Though our party wasn't scheduled until the day following, Saul's mother shyly requested a private concert in her kitchen over tea. I couldn't have been happier to agree. She listened to my *niggunim* (wordless melodies) and her reserve dissolved. A deep, intimate, common well of feeling opened between us, lifting our veils. From her shining eyes tears of joy flowed and were reflected in mine. The words of Shneur Zalman of Lyady, a Hasidic rebbe, echoed as we sang. "The songs of the souls, at the time they are swaying in the high regions, drink from the well of the Almighty." Sentimental smiles of tribal recognition as Jewish women passed between us. One human being to the other, one Jew, one woman, one Source. One. *Kulanu.*

The next evening we walked to the beachfront synagogue of this southern coastal town. The sea air blew wind in warm, sibilant gusts around the corners, brazenly ballooning the ladies' skirts. *Ruach!* The chazan, embracing a well-dressed Torah, wailed familiar Sephardic melodies in a sanctuary of the same ambiance. When the dark wooden ark once again protected its precious contents, we all retired upstairs to the social hall. Our feast consisted of tamales, cake, pasta, and the ever present rice and beans. Our rendition of a Flory Jagoda song in Ladino, "Oco Kandelikas," lent itself well to our multigenerational sing-along. Then, with the expert assistance of Saul and the smallest community children, the little windows of a large Chanukah "Advent" card were opened. Counting out the eight days of Chanukah, the Maccabee story was retold. Finally, when our bonding through story and song was done, all the lights were dimmed. We lit the chanukiah, and silence filled the darkness. The magic of the glowing tapers spread in a shining, expanding circle. As I sang a song from my commercial tape, "The Solstice Chanukiah" (*Like a Tree: Songs and Life-cycle Celebrations for All People*), we were joined together, *kulanu*, in the mystery of our separate, linked histories:

And the echoed voices harmonize an ancient melody,
Our Ancestors in Unity stand with us as we light,
Sing with us as we light
Dance with us as we light
Pray with us as we light the Chanukiah,
Dark winged Shechina, Etz Chayim, Tree of Life, Amen!
Pray now,
Hope,
Hold our Souls!

THE VISIT TO PUEBLA

For personal reasons, we had to ask Ignacio Castelan Estrada and his lovely wife, Mary, to accept us a day early and extra, to which they graciously agreed. After a late start, the enthusiasm with which we had begun the two-hour journey from Mexico City to Puebla faded. Long shadows grew quickly, bringing the deep solstice darkness up right behind. Arriving in Puebla, a city the size of Washington, D.C., we started to ascend ultra-steep hills, a cobblestoned territory with no crest in sight. Night fell. Higher and higher we climbed into what appeared to be an increasingly unsavory neighborhood. The unavoidably numerous speed bumps of unimaginable height seemed to leap out of the pavement without warning like ominous pinball ghosts. The odds of our rental vehicle's underbelly being marooned atop a particularly large bump seemed high. Decreasing our speed seemed to have little effect on the constant banging and scraping. Gradually, our uneasiness transformed into fear.

Suddenly, a pleasant Hispanic voice called out in melodic singsong, "Senor Allan! Senora Nancy!" Like the proverbial circus car, a tiny VW Beetle, piled to overflowing with grinning people in party clothes, beeped wildly. It pulled up next to us, and a stunning beauty in a cocktail dress hung out of the window up to her waist and waved her hands at us frantically. "I'm Ada, Ignacio's daughter! I knew you must be lost. I told the others we should go out to find you. And now, here you are!" she chirped. "Follow us!" she gestured gaily, turning the Volkswagen on a dime and gunning it down the steep incline into the night.

We soon arrived on a relatively flat dead-end street. One lovely home, with appealing aesthetic touches, stood apart from all the others. Lovely tiles appointed the verandah. Flowers dripped from a decorative wrought-iron fence which closed with a splendid menorah gate. Behind it stood Mary, her black hair and berry-brown face flashing a wide, warm welcome smile. Her husband, Ignacio, strode out to greet us in full Maccabean command. Happy, if a bit hurried, he shooed us indoors, where, to our amazement, sat the entire community. Dressed to the nines, they applauded enthusiastically. A great hand-cut gold banner with the words WELCOME NANCY AND ALLAN was strung across an elegant buffet. As we got our bearings, we saw the small sea of joyous, hopeful Chanukah celebrants reaching out to greet us with their eyes, hands, and hearts. We saw also the great importance of our visit to this community, and their yearning for more connection to the Jewish world at large, *kulanu*.

The evening was spent sharing stories in Spanish and English. We identified ourselves much as they do in the Bible, sharing ancestral names and places whenever possible. Several of the families were recent converts. Ignacio later told us about others who were interested in conversion. He had been clearly discouraged by Rabbi Lehrer from pursuing these inquiries. His desire to go to Israel with his family and the rest of the community was a delicate matter. Though he, his wife, and their four children would probably be accepted for making aliyah, leaving the others behind was not a real option. Their Jewish lives and worship were genuine. To be cut off and left behind in Puebla because they had been born without some Jewish lineage would be unbearable. The smallest children knew all the Hebrew words to all the songs and prayers by memory. If they were old enough to read at all, they read Hebrew. I knew that few Jews in the United States could make such a claim. In fact, the entire community read the text flawlessly.

Our Thursday night service-party was just an introduction, ending with jovial singing and dancing around the table. During the next two intense days, we worshipped with this group at home and in their small, simple cinderblock synagogue. Seldom had I experienced such spirit, such intense joy, in a group. Particularly poignant was the reverence for their one tiny Torah, one of those eight-inch miniatures sold in Jerusalem. I prayed that the community might receive a Torah large enough to hold and to hug.

Though there was an aisle dividing the men and women, the feeling of comfort and spiritual intimacy was everywhere. Between services, we cooked, ate delicious meals, played with Ada's baby, enjoyed chats with Jemima, their exquisite teenage girl, and played the guitar with Hartus, the teenage son. Together with his wife Mary, Ignacio, son of peasants from Jalapa, a quality-control engineer working at a local steel mill, had built a true Jewish home. Judaica was everywhere, within them and without. By the time we left, it was clear that a part of us would always remain. Here, in their own words, are their feelings about our visit, as translated by Allan:

From Ignacio: "The sound of your appreciated voices and those beautiful melodies still vibrate in my mind. You have left us thankful for indelible memories. . . . Don't forget that in the city of Puebla you always have a family and a home where you can come whenever you wish. . . . In Mexico it is very difficult to be accepted in the Orthodox Ashkenazi and Sephardi communities because there is so much racism against the crypto-Jews, which is my background. I need to make aliyah soon, and also my children, Jemima and Hartus, in order that they may serve in the army and study in Israel. The same for the other children in our community."

From Miriam Lior Diaz de Diaz (congregant): "A thousand thanks for having bothered to come to Puebla and to get to know us. I feel that you are my adopted brother and sister; adopted by your Father the Jewish people. All that concerns our people moves and saddens me when we celebrate commemorative dates; sad because of the Holocaust and other such stories. Never forget them. It gives me more desire to move forward with my conversion and go to live in Israel. Though emigrating would also mean suffering, it hurts my children more than me. I have spoken with them and I know they agree, even if we are peasants. I know that Israel is still not a paradise, but no matter. I love it as if it were my first homeland. I hope you can help us realize our most precious dream, the conversion and then going to Israel. I will never forget your faces. You have left joy in our hearts. Our greatest fortune is to have known you, you and other Jews who have shown us their love, warmth, and especially humanity. For me, you were like two jewels that, for a moment, shined only for me. You made me feel like the luckiest woman in the whole world by infusing Beth Shmuel with your strength, vigor, affection, life, joy, and the good fortune to know that we are not alone!"

Looking Back

I often think about Ignacio Castelan Estrada of Puebla. Perhaps he is a thorn in the sides of some rabbis or government officials who prefer to define our tribe in ways that would exclude him and his kind from the full Jewish franchise. But there is no doubt that his passionate energy, focused study, and boundless faith have created and nourished his congregants and enabled them to live full Jewish lives. The surrounding non-Jewish community has also benefited often from his volunteer school where he and his family tutor all who come, helping to erase local illiteracy.

And I often think about Saul Ruiseco's mother in Veracruz, whose eyes met mine in recognition of a shared past.

My own mission is to sing from and about the feminine aspect of the deity in hopes that contemporary Judaism will honor generations of unnamed, largely forgotten Jewish women. I hope my small contribution joins others with this intention. I pray that this work will flow into a larger stream, providing much-needed landfill for some of Torah's white spaces and increasing future participation for all Jews within a balanced, inclusive, fulfilling future.

According to the Zohar creation myth, kindred spirits recognize embers of Self in the broken fragments of other vessels encountered along life's journey. To fulfill our life's personal purpose, we must recognize and then make links with these spirits from our own talents, our own grain. To fulfill our spiritual purpose we must in some way further connect our own fulfillment with our Tribe's destiny. With this wisdom, we act for ourselves, but not only for ourselves. In this way, Ignacio's shining soul in Puebla and Saul's Jewish mother in Veracruz have everything to do with all of us. One destiny for all. Kulanu.

12

Brazil

Searching for Brazilian Marranos
A Remnant Returns
Rabbi Jacques Cukierkorn
with Robert H. Lande

I had long believed that, after five hundred years, the Marranos surely must belong only to history. Their descendants could not have maintained any secret Jewish practices during all these centuries. The possibility that some might be interested in returning to the Jewish faith was too romantic an idea to be anything but a fantasy. But then I discovered one of the most amazing Jewish phenomena of our times.

I was born in Brazil and grew up as part of the large and well-established São Paulo Ashkenazi community. During my childhood I often heard intriguing stories of vestigial Jewish practices among people who claimed to be descendants of the Jews who were forced to convert to Catholicism in the 1490s. But, to my knowledge, no reliable investigation of these claims had ever been made. Was there any way to verify that these claims were authentic? Could the assertions have been concocted to romanticize relatively routine family histories or for any number of other reasons? Were the stories isolated anecdotes, or were they systematic in character and indicative of an important aspect of Jewish history? Most importantly, could any sparks of Jewish souls still be smoldering after all these years?

I enrolled at Hebrew Union College in 1989 to study for rabbinical ordination. One of the requirements was to write a thesis consisting of original research on a Jewish topic. This was my chance to investigate the legends. I embarked on a study of Jews who had been forced to become Christians; I ended up studying Christians who are choosing to return to their Jewish roots.

Origins

The Marranos are a very well known and very tragic part of Jewish history. Forced conversions of Jews started in Spain in the late 1300s and climaxed with the Inquisition in the 1490s in both Spain and Portugal. Many of the Jews came to genuinely embrace Christianity. Others outwardly became Christians but secretly continued to practice Judaism. These came to be known by a variety of names, including secret Jews, crypto-Jews, New Christians, conversos, and Marranos.

Less well known is the subsequent history of the Marranos and their descendants. Because the Inquisition was strongest in Spain and Portugal, it is not surprising that many of those who wished to continue to practice Judaism emigrated to the New World. In 1496, just before they were given the choice of conversion or death, an estimated one-third of the population of Portugal was Jewish. Although the exact figure is not known, it is likely that an even higher percentage of emigrants to the New World were of Jewish descent.

Brazil was discovered by the Portuguese in 1500 and became its colony. Portuguese Marranos, who were among the earliest settlers, prospered there. Tremendous economic opportunities existed for hard-working immigrants, who entered practically every field in Brazil. Moreover, there was relatively little danger that they would be accused of secretly practicing Judaism, since the colony was so remote and sparsely settled.

In 1591, however, the first inquisitor was sent to Brazil to deal with the "problem" of hidden Jewish practices. During the seventeenth century such visits became increasingly frequent, especially in the northeastern provinces. The Inquisition tended to concentrate on the major settlements and to ignore the more sparsely-populated areas.

The remote area of northeastern Brazil known as Rio Grande do Norte was settled by the Portuguese starting in the 1720s, when the most intense Inquisitorial activity was occurring in the Brazilian northeast. This region was noted for its poor soil, dry climate, and hostile Indian population. It seems likely that a major reason it was settled was that it was remote and difficult for the Inquisitorial authorities to reach. It also seems likely that an extremely high percentage of the early settlers were secret Jews.

VISITING VENHAVER

In 1992 I spent a considerable period of time visiting small towns in parts of the northeastern state of Rio Grande do Norte. I interviewed a large number of people about their traditions, history, and way of life. Many were unwilling to talk candidly about their ancestry and customs with a stranger who spoke Portuguese with a São Paulo accent. Some who did refused to be recorded on audio tape, and few would allow me to use my camera or video camera. Many others had no interest in their family traditions. I nevertheless was able to obtain a great deal of fascinating information.

The town of Venhaver, founded in 1750, is 12 miles from the small city of São Miguel and 230 miles from Natal, the state capital and the largest city in the region. It is extremely poor, has no running water, and possesses only the most basic educational and health services. Only the main road is paved.

The origin of the town's name is uncertain, but I heard one intriguing explanation. Secret Jews sometimes used key words or expressions to identify each other, such as calling one other "member of the nation" or *chaver* ("friend" in Hebrew). A legend says that "Venhaver" is a corrupt form of *vem chaver*, which, since *vem* in Portuguese means "come," translates as "come, friend." This would signify that the secret Jews of the area, having found a safe haven, were inviting others to join them.

Of the thirty-two hundred people who live there, approximately half are descended from the original settlers. The rest arrived during the last fifty years. The settler descendants are all Caucasian, unlike the newcomers, who are a mixture of black and white. The settlers say that they almost always married among themselves. I shall refer to the descendants of the original settlers as the Venhaver community.

The newcomers consider the Venhaver community to be a separate group, and call them *os Judeus*, "the Jews," or *os descendants dos Judeus*, "the descendants of the Jews." This is consistent with what the descendants call themselves—either *Judeus* or *gente da nacão* ("people of the nation"). Interestingly, the Venhaver community did not accept me as a Jew. For them, being a Jew meant simply to have been descended from their ancestors.

Members of the Venhaver community are all devout Christians. Yet they continue distinct traditions that can only be Jewish in origin. When I first arrived in the town they refused to discuss these practices. Only after they got to know me did they invite me into their homes and begin to talk more openly. Even then they said that they had no knowledge of the origin of their distinctive practices. They also had no knowledge of what these practices indicated about the community's history.

I was able to discover a fascinating array of customs and behavior, particularly with respect to eating habits, religious practices, and funeral rituals.

Eating Habits

The Venhaver keep a form of kashrut. They do not eat meat from pigs, meat from hunted animals, or seafood. They do not eat meat and dairy in the same meal. They do not, however, have separate meat and dairy dishes.

They only eat meat that they have themselves slaughtered. Their slaughtering technique also is distinctively evocative of kashrut. They slaughter chickens, for example, by cutting their throats with a very sharp knife. They also drain the blood, wash the chickens thoroughly, salt them, and wash them again. They explain that their refusal to eat meat containing blood is because such meat is *carregado* ("charged"). No one could explain exactly what "charged" means, but it seems to have some kind of spiritual meaning.

Another noteworthy custom they related to me is that they do not eat bread during the first week of April. This is, of course, evocative of the Jewish practice of not eating leaven during Passover. Yet they have no association between their practice and the Jewish holiday. Nor is there any other way in which they celebrate Passover. The only explanation I could get is that the bread becomes "charged" during the first week of April.

Religious Practices

Every Friday night, before sundown, the Venhaver woman lights two candles. The candles are lit in the home, but not where they can be seen publicly. When asked about this practice, they say that they are doing it so that the "good spirits" will take care of the house.

Although the members of the Venhaver community are practicing Catholics, they refuse to kneel in church. Their houses often contain pictures of Catholic saints, but crosses are rare. Small bags of earth hang on a few of the house doorposts on the right-hand side. People touch or kiss this vestigial mezuzah when they enter or leave the house. Many front doors also have a Star of David or psalm on their backs. The motivation for both traditions is to "protect" the house from evil spirits that otherwise might haunt it.

In church, the Venhaver community recite the regular Catholic prayers. They also say private prayers in their homes that were handed down from their ancestors. The issue of prayer seems to be a sensitive one, and they refused to tell me the content of these private prayers even though I begged them repeatedly.

I was told that they also have an alternative house of worship besides the local church. The place, which was called *snoga*, was said to be a prayer hall and pilgrimage place up in the mountains. Since the word *snoga* sounds as if it comes from the Portuguese word *sinagoga*, I attempted to persuade them to take me there, but in vain. Its location is remote and secret. The Venhaver people say that they go there only at certain times of the year. They said they go for vigils that can last for an entire day, but refused to disclose the prayers that they use at these times.

They have one other custom that finds no Christian parallel. When parents bless a child, they lay their hands on the child's head or shoulders. This resembles the same Jewish practice to an extraordinary degree.

Funeral Rituals

The Venhaver funeral rituals are another sign of their Jewish origin. The Venhaver people begin making funeral arrangements as soon after death as possible. The corpse is washed and wrapped in a white linen shroud, but no casket is used. An elderly woman explained that they do this because Jesus Christ was buried in a shroud.

The wrapped body is briefly placed in the middle of the main room of the deceased's house, with its feet toward the door. No viewing of the body is permitted. This is contrary to the local Catholic custom of open viewing of the body in its casket.

I was told that both before and during the burial a number of prayers handed down from their ancestors are offered. They would not reveal the contents of any of these prayers.

During the actual burial, the deceased's family and friends help to bury the corpse by throwing handfuls of dirt inside the grave.

After the funeral the deceased's immediate family gathers at home for seven days. During this period they do not work. They light a candle which lasts for this period.

The graves of the Venhaver community are different from those of their neighbors since most do not have crosses. Those that do have crosses that are quite distinct. When members of the community visit graves, they leave stones behind. Sometimes they leave one stone, but sometimes they leave six in the form of a Star of David. No one was able to explain the origin of this custom.

Mixed Feelings

My visits were in part a success. After all, I was able to verify many of the legends I had heard and read. The evidence is overwhelming that these people's ancestors once were practicing Jews.

But there is so much more I would like to know. I came away with the feeling that it would be extremely difficult for any outsider to completely understand their beliefs and practices. A final anecdote illustrates some of the problems that outsiders face when they attempt to get the Venhaver community to talk openly.

I had wondered from the beginning why so many members of the community were reluctant to tell me that they were *Judeus*, or to discuss their ancestors or the origins of their rituals. Others would talk but would only open up to me to a limited extent. For a long time I attributed this only to a normal distrust of outsiders and a long-term habit that had served them well over the centuries.

To my great surprise, however, I was told by my closest friend in the community that many people there were afraid of me. From the media they knew that there had been Nazis outside of Brazil. They also knew that Nazis hated Jews and in the past had killed Jews. When an outsider, who spoke Portuguese with a different accent, came and started asking a lot of questions about Jews, and who observed Jewish customs, what were they to think? Many thought that I might be a Nazi looking to persecute them.

I left with a feeling of regret and sadness that the people in the Venhaver community know essentially nothing about their Jewish past. They have clung to remnants of Jewish practices for centuries but apparently do not know why they have done so. They either do not think about why they engage in particular customs or rituals or rationalize them in terms of Christianity or otherwise.

There was a part of me that ached to be able to tell them that their ancestors had, for five hundred years, clung to certain practices because they had a desperate desire to be Jewish and to pass this Jewishness on to their children. Part of me wanted to help them to vindicate their ancestors' faith and memory and stubbornness. Part of me wanted to be able to help them become truly and unambiguously Jewish.

An Emerging Jewish Marrano Community In Natal

Natal is the capital city of the state of Rio Grande do Norte. It was established in 1599 and has a population of well over half a million people. Only a handful of practicing Jews lived there until just after World War I, when a small synagogue was founded. The community grew until just after World War II, when it began to decline as the Jews left for Israel or larger centers of Brazilian Jewish life. There are now only five families left that qualify as Jews under traditional definitions.

In the 1970s a group of Marranos began to gather. Every member of the group grew up hearing family stories and observing family practices similar to those discussed above. The tiny group grew by word of mouth as members recruited others with similar backgrounds and interests. Eventually it turned into a Jewish havurah (prayer group) that met for member-conducted services in members' homes.

When I heard about this group, I started to correspond with it. But I wanted to see for myself whether the stories its members wrote me were real—stories of their Jewish heritage, of the passing of Jewish traditions from generation to generation (albeit ever more weakly), and most of all, of their return to Judaism. If so, it would be a phenomenon unique in Brazilian history. In 1992 and 1993 I journeyed to Natal, stayed with them, and observed them.

I found a havurah consisting of five traditionally defined Jewish families and twelve Marrano families. It met for religious services regularly and observed all the major holidays, although without a rabbi. During the weeks I stayed there, I functioned as their rabbi and conducted seminars and lectures on a great many facets of Judaism.

During my visits I interviewed every member of the Marrano community. My purpose was to gauge for myself their sincerity and Jewish convictions. I found a vibrant, spiritually Jewish community with an incredible thirst for Jewish knowledge. I do not want to romanticize this havurah—it has had its share of troubles and internal strife. Like almost every Jewish community, it has gone through cycles of decline followed by further growth.

I also began to learn some of the underpinnings of the members' desire to return to Judaism. One of the members, who has been active since almost the beginning, is Joao Fernandes Medeiros Dias, who now often uses the Hebrew name Iohanan ben Imanuel Diya. I will briefly recount his life story, since it is in many ways illustrative of many of the stories I heard from Marranos in Natal (and elsewhere).

Medeiros grew up hearing many stories about his ancestors and observing many practices similar to those in Venhaver. For example, he was taught not to kneel in church, and his family observed many of the dietary habits described earlier.

He developed an intense interest in religious issues and enrolled in a Protestant seminary. He frequently got into arguments with his colleagues, however, over a number of topics. When they told him to observe the Sabbath on Sunday, for example, he would argue that the Bible clearly indicated that Saturday is the true Sabbath.

Medeiros became an ordained minister and in 1970 moved to Rio de Janeiro. Although he was working for the Protestant Churches Council, he met many Jews and began to learn about Judaism. The more he learned, the more he could not reconcile his religious beliefs and family traditions with Christianity. He found a Reform rabbi, Henrique Lemle, who performed a "purification ceremony" to signify his official return to the Jewish people. That ceremony was not a "conversion" ceremony, since its purpose was to ratify his return to the practices of his ancestors.

After his return to Judaism he decided to return to the Northeast so that he could help to bring back others who were, like him, of Marrano descent. He joined the community that was forming in Natal and, due to his religious training, was chosen by its members to be its unofficial spiritual leader.

Medeiros has lived as a Jew ever since and has raised his children in the Jewish faith. One of his daughters lived in Israel for a time, but her quest to become an Israeli citizen failed because she was unable to unequivocally prove maternal descent from Jews for the last five hundred years (a standard that few Jews in the United States could meet). Nor is Medeiros recognized as Jewish by the Brazilian Orthodox community.

Who Will Welcome Them Back?

In 1990 the Brazilian Orthodox establishment sent a rabbi from São Paulo to Natal to check on the community's status. This rabbi asked one of the few Jews in Natal whether the Marranos could meet the standard Orthodox test—whether they could trace their maternal line back five hundred years to unquestioned Jews. When this Jew said that the Marranos could not do this, the rabbi decided that they were of no interest to him. He even refused to speak to a delegation of Marranos that came to plead their case.

The reasons for the Orthodox refusal to accept the Marranos back in the fold, let alone welcome or encourage them, are complex. While halacha (Jewish law) plays a role, Russian and other Jews face less onerous barriers even though their ancestry often is problematic. Since the Brazilian Jewish community has only 175,000 members, perhaps it is in part a fear of being overwhelmed. Scholars estimate that approximately 10 percent of the total population—fifteen million Brazilians—are of Marrano descent, so if even a small percentage were to return to Judaism, they could dominate the local Jewish community.

The Natal phenomenon was the first of its kind to arise in Brazil. But in recent years many similar individuals and groups have begun to emerge, especially in northeastern Brazil. The details of their traditional family practices and the reasons for their individual desires to (re)embrace Judaism vary. But the overall similarities in their stories and quests are uncanny.

The Marrano groups and individuals recently have begun forming a self-help network. They are sharing information and providing mutual moral support. They are trying to help one another become Jewish in knowledge, practice, and spirit.

The only elements of the Brazilian Jewish community that render any significant assistance are isolated individuals, acting alone, and also the small Reform (called "Liberal") movement. The Reform movement makes an effort to help and welcome Marranos by sending them religious books and matzot (matzet) during Passover. But the Reform community in Brazil is too small for this task, has many other items on its agenda, and is, itself, not totally in favor of assisting them.

Recently a United States organization has begun helping the Marranos of Brazil. Kulanu (whose supporters include Orthodox, Conservative, and Reform Jews) is a charitable organization founded in 1994. Its purpose is to locate lost and dispersed remnants of the Jewish people and to assist those who wish to rejoin the Jewish community. It is also providing religious assistance to inquiring Jews and emerging Jews in Mexico, India, Uganda, Ghana, Peru, Brazil and China.

I serve as one of the rabbinic advisors to Kulanu and direct its Brazilian programs. Our activity has been limited due to budgetary considerations. We have, however, been able to help the Marrano network publish a book containing information on Judaism. This book is now being distributed to interested individuals and groups. We have also sent religious and educational materials to Brazilian Marranos.

Perhaps the most important thing that Kulanu is doing for them comes from our attitude. We greet them with a warm welcome back into the Jewish people. We let them know that not everyone in the Jewish community regards them with suspicion, cynicism, and even hostility. If they want to rejoin us, we let them know that we need them. We truly regard them as our long-lost brothers and sisters. We treat them accordingly, and they know it.

Kulanu activists have also begun to give public lectures to inform the American Jewish community about the Marrano situation. It is our hope that as we let our audiences know that these people are sincerely returning to their religion after five hundred years, perhaps American Jews will stop and think that Judaism must indeed be something really special. If a growing number of Brazilians are so eager to reclaim it as their own, perhaps Americans can work to become less likely to loose it. Ultimately, by helping the Brazilian Marranos, we hope to help ourselves.

How Dare We Reject Them?

The Marranos' Jewish claims are genuine and strong. They are the last stubborn remnants of one of the most tragic episodes of Jewish history. Now, an amazing event—dare I say miracle?—is occurring. They want to finish this horrible chapter of history in a positive way, in a way that will represent the triumph of the Jewish spirit over the forces that have tried to destroy us.

How can we reject them? How dare we refuse to welcome them? If this chance to partially rewrite a horrible part of our history passes, how will we live with ourselves? We cannot stand idly by. This must be seen as an incredible opportunity for the renewal of the Jewish people.

How ironic if it turns out that they survived the torments of the Inquisition, and also five hundred years of being forced to practice their Judaism secretly, only to be finally defeated by Jewish indifference.

We Marranos of Brazil
Julio D'Gabriel

The northeast of Brazil was initially populated by "misfits" or "undesirables" (individuals forced into exile by their government), most of whom came from Portugal, while the remainder came from other parts of Europe. There is no doubt that many Marranos and *Novos Cristãos* ("New Christians") came to Brazil with the explorer Cabral. Many of these arrivals are documented, and there is also written evidence of a further influx by the Dutch, French, and Spanish.

So what happened to the Marranos in particular? They strove to maintain contact with one other. There is a great deal of evidence that many Marranos sought refuge in the *Sertão* (the interior, dry, rural area) with the advent of the Inquisition in Brazil after the Portuguese took back the cities of Recife, João Pessoa, Natal, and Fortaleza from the Dutch.

Even today, it is very common to see children and adults in the Sertão with pronounced Dutch ethnic roots (tall, blond, light-colored eyes), and the remnants of customs related to the old Jewish tradition of eating fish on the Sabbath (since there was no guarantee that meat would be kosher, many Marranos ate fish on Shabbat to ensure a kosher meal), a tendency towards the Protestant faith (considered preferable to the panoply and quasi-idolatry of the

Catholic Church), and the use of a Magen David (Star of David) as a good luck token. Though none of these is convincing evidence when taken alone, when combined and added to the practice of killing chickens by cutting their throats and the preservation of the family Old Testament Bible inscribed in Hebrew with the names of ancestors, as well as the many instances of transmission by word of mouth from mother to daughter that they carried the seed of Israel, these lead me to the inescapable belief that these people from the *Sertão* are descendants of Moses.

We have formed the Associacão Religiosa Israelita Marrana here in Brazil with the aim of building a Jewish center to which all Jews can belong. However, due to a severe lack of funds, we are still only a community on paper and in spirit, and without outside help we shall be condemned to remain so.

Those who aspire to return to the religion of their forefathers should not be denied that opportunity. God must surely rejoice in the "return" to His fold of these "lost sheep" who so resolutely insist on being administered the *brit milah* and who want to study for their bar mitzvah. To deny them this right would be nothing less than sacrilege!

Meeting Four Brazilian Marranos

These are the stories of four descendants of Brazilian Marranos active in the Associacão Religiosa Israelita Marrana (ARIM) in Natal.

Ivan Birnbaum

Since childhood I was conscious that my relatives were of Jewish ancestry. My mother, Maria de Carvalho, was a Marrano; my father, Joaquim Bento Birnbaum de Souza, of German-French-Marrano ancestry. I grew up knowing in my mind that I was of

Jewish blood but had very little teaching about Judaism up to 1957, when I entered the Brazilian Navy. From then on I increased my knowledge of Judaism with other Jews I met.

I arrived in Natal in 1975 and discovered a Marrano called João Medeiros who had assembled other Marranos and Jews together, among them Willy Daube and Clara and Kalma Roez. I and my family joined with them, and in 1978 we numbered fifty-two people, including the children. João Medeiros was a lay rabbi, and we would gather at his home. The number of people who attended the Shabbat services and *hagim* (holidays) would vary, naturally, but there would usually be at least thirty-five.

In 1989 a *chaver* (friend) from Canada, Julio D'Gabriel, joined us and brought a new dimension to our community; he was elected president twice for the years 1990 and 1991. Under Julio's leadership we rescued the old building of the original Centro Israelita do Rio Grande do Norte, and the membership increased. Then two new families came to Natal from Belem and introduced new criteria in order to be considered a Jew; the membership vanished, decreasing from fifty-two then, to six now.

To save the community, three former presidents, myself, Julio D'Gabriel, and Roberto Dias, founded the Associacao Religiosa Israelita Marrana to recongregate the members scattered by the prejudices of the new arrivals and bring in new members who wish to join.

Joaquim Galvão

Since childhood, I remember my father speaking of our heritage as descendants of Marranos from Portugal and Holland. He was proud of his genealogy, always seeking his ancestors. We had to read the Old Testament, keep the Mosaic laws, and be selective in our eating habits, shunning the pig, crustaceans, and fish without scales. All meat had to be bloodless.

Around Easter we drank wine and ate crackers without leavening. Saturdays we dressed in our best clothes and went for a stroll. We were not to say "adore" to one another, since one should only adore God! We were not baptized, and during the first week of life the males were circumcised. We kept a Star of David and a psalm behind the entry door.

When I became an adult, following my parents' teachings, I confirmed my ancestry and heritage. I concluded that we were indeed different. Christians considered us atheists and communists. The celebrations we had were our Pesach (Passover), the psalms behind the doorpost was our mezuzah, and the Star of David was our badge of honor.

Today we no longer hide nor improvise; we follow our heritage. We have "returned," as did the prodigal son. It is usual to find the names of my family in the history of the Marranos. No amount of discrimination will turn me or ours from our chosen return. We are here and back to what is ours.

Eder Barosh

Since my childhood I had the consciousness that my family came from ancient Jewish ancestry. I had very little education in Judaism, yet I always knew that I was a Jew descended from Marranos who had come from Portugal.

I was not very concerned about this, but in 1989 I met the Jewish community of Natal, which was open and tolerant. My arrival coincided with the arrival of Julio D'Gabriel and his taking over the presidency, and from him I learned about Judaism in depth for the first time. When the people from Belem arrived, I was expelled from the community along with other members. I founded the Ben Abraham Foundation, dedicated to the memory of the Holocaust. When my firstborn was eight days old I made his brit milah and I am very proud of this. Now I am a member of ARIM and helping to rebuild our community.

Roberto Dias De Oliveria

Since I was a young boy I was aware that I was a Jew. My father, Sinesio Dias de Oliveira, a medical doctor, and my mother, Naisa Pereira Dias de Oliveira, are both of Portuguese-Marrano ancestry. I have received very little education on Judaism, but I have found something very important—the certainty of knowing that I am a Jew.

In 1981–82 I made my first contact with the Hebrew language and studied for two semesters at the Federal University in Natal. In 1989 I was elected president of the Centro Israelita, and I fostered and continued the traditions of being an open and tolerant community. Now I belong to ARIM.

Portrait of a Leader: Helio Daniel Cordeiro
Karen Primack

Helio Daniel Cordeiro, thirty-three, has been called *the* leader of Brazilian Marranos. Founder of the four-year-old Society for the Study of "Marranismo" (the Marrano phenomenon), he corresponds with hundreds of Marranos throughout Brazil, sending information about Marrano history, Jewish traditions, and ways to reenter the Jewish community. Cordeiro himself is a Marrano who was raised with the knowledge of his background, but his family observed no religious practice. When he studied theology in his twenties, Cordeiro's interest in Judaism grew. In 1988, with the help of Rabbi Henry Sobel, an American-born Liberal rabbi in São Paulo, he formally reentered the Jewish community. Together with his wife, Dora, an Ashkenazic Jew, Cordeiro publishes *Israel*, a monthly Jewish magazine, in São Paulo.

Cordeiro likes to remind his audiences that approximately fifteen million people in Brazil—10 percent of the total population—are believed to be of Marrano origin. Although he does not expect most to return to their Jewish roots, he does see his role as a source of information for those interested in exploring their backgrounds. Following prominent articles in the *Los Angeles Times* and a popular Brazilian magazine, he received letters from two hundred Marranos, and followed up by answering their questions and sending printed information. He wrote a booklet based on his responses to questions Marranos frequently ask, and Kulanu approved a $1,000 donation to have the booklet published. He would like to write another book profiling some of the fascinating Marranos he has come to know. Cordeiro's previous publications include an early book on humanism and a recent volume on prominent Brazilian Jews.

"Marranismo" began with the Spanish Inquisition of 1492, when Spanish Jews were given the choice of converting to Christianity, execution, or leaving the country. About 150,000 fled to Portugal, which welcomed them until 1496, when it initiated its own Inquisition, forcing a choice between conversion and death (emigration was not permitted). Some became sincere converts; others outwardly became New Christians, but continued to practice Judaism secretly as Marranos—as have their descendants to this day. When New World opportunities opened for the Portuguese in Brazil, many Marranos made the crossing, although it was still necessary for them to continue to practice Judaism in secret.

Ashkenazic Jews from Eastern Europe emigrated to Brazil in the twentieth century, primarily between the world wars. In Cordeiro's city of residence, São Paulo, there are a hundred thousand "mainstream" Ashkenazic Jews. According to Cordeiro, the Orthodox congregations are unwilling to recognize Marranos or accept them for conversion. The Liberal congregations are more welcoming, but their rabbis are too occupied with congregational affairs to make any major effort toward Marrano outreach. Cordeiro would like to see the hiring of a rabbi whose main responsibility would be to travel to the Marranos in communities throughout

Brazil, educating them in Judaism and officiating at conversions when appropriate.

A Brazilian Genealogist Speaks
Karen Primack

As president of the Jewish Genealogy Society of Brazil, Guilherme Faiguenboim was in the Washington area to attend the 1995 International Seminar on Jewish Genealogy. He paused one evening to address an impromptu meeting of Kulanu supporters.

Faiguenboim reported that nine-tenths of the inquiries made to his society are from non-Jews, and that, while his reference books say much about Jews of Russian, German, and Sephardic descent, he did not have any information about Marrano families.

He soon discovered that a teacher named Valadares, from a humble family in the Brazilian countryside, had a vast knowledge of Marrano genealogy. Valadares, who travels 80 miles to São Paulo every two weeks to read in the society's library, now handles inquiries about Marrano genealogy for the society.

In his talk, Faiguenboim reviewed the history of the Portuguese and Brazilian Inquisitions of the fifteenth and sixteenth centuries. He discovered that in 1496, the year the Inquisition came to Portugal, 30–40 percent of the Portuguese population was Jewish (many had come from Spain in 1492). These Jews were automatically converted to Catholicism by law; there was no expulsion for the first one hundred years. He found that 80 percent of the sugar cane farmers in Brazil had been Jews. The Inquisition in Brazil was responsible for the persecution of forty thousand Jews; persecution included burning, wearing of a masked hood, incarceration, brainwashing, and torture.

According to Faiguenboim, the high illiteracy rate in Brazil today can be traced to the fact that Portuguese and Brazilian Catholicism did not emphasize reading the Bible. It was dangerous to find even the New Testament in your house, he said. The faithful were just supposed to listen to the priest at mass. Factors leading to arrest during the Inquisition in Brazil included owning a Bible, cleaning the house on Friday, and abstaining from pork.

After 1750, with the Inquisition gone, descendants of crypto-Jews in Brazil continued certain customs—giving children biblical names and avoiding church except for birth, marriage, and death ceremonies—even though they did not consider themselves Jewish.

Tracing ancestry is difficult for descendants of Marranos today. Surnames were often changed. For example, when a child was baptized, he received the surname of his godfather. "It's a genealogical mess!" Faiguenboim exclaims.

When people write to him that they have a strong attraction to Judaism and "perhaps" have Jewish ancestors, he advises them to convert according to halacha.

13

Cape Verde

The Jews of Cape Verde
Louise Werlin

The names Lopes, Mendes, Pereira, Cardozo, and Levy sound like the passenger manifest of the *St. Charles*, the ship that brought the first known Jews to New Amsterdam and began American Jewish history. But they are also the names of many people in the country of Cape Verde, off the west coast of Africa.

Cape Verde consists of several islands. When discovered by the Portuguese in 1463 during the Age of Exploration, it was completely uninhabited. It was a Portuguese colony from 1463 to 1975 and was an important port of call, first during the slave trade and later for whaling vessels, especially those from New England.

Most of the people (400,000) are Afro-Portuguese, and many have definite Semitic features, probably inherited from Portuguese Jewish and/or Arab forebears as well as through contacts with North Africa.

Although it is well accepted that many of the original Portuguese settlers were New Christians, and that people of Jewish origin played an important role in Cape Verde's development, the proportion of Jews in the population is not known. There did not seem to be a special category for Jews. They were sometimes categorized as "white" (*blancos*) and sometimes classed with other "oriental" people. At one point the term *Moreno* was used to describe Moors and Jews. Cape Verdeans of Jewish origin, though often aware of their roots, are part of the overall criollo culture. Cape Verde's official language is Portuguese, but most people speak a creole which is close to the Papiamento of Curaçao. The culture is creole (in many ways more similar to that of the Caribbean than of Africa), with the main elements Portuguese and West African.

Because of the poverty of the islands, which suffer from chronic drought, many people have emigrated. There are as many Cape Verdeans in the United States as in Cape Verde, mostly in southern New England.

Most Cape Verdeans are Catholic. Although there is no organized Jewish community and probably no practicing Jew, there is no question that there was an important Jewish presence in Cape Verde. Jews settled in Cape Verde very early. There were Jewish settlements on several islands, and a town on the island of Santo Antão is called Porto Sinagoga. The Portuguese followed the policy of sending convicts and exiles (*lancados*) to Cape Verde. Many of the *lancados*, who dominated Portugal's coastal trade, were of Jewish origin, and a number were settled on the island of Santo Antão after 1548. Other Cape Verdeans trace their ancestry to Jews or Marranos who fled or were expelled from Portugal over the centuries. During the nineteenth and early twentieth centuries additional Jews came to Cape Verde from Morocco.

Considerably more is known about the Cape Verdeans of Moroccan Jewish ancestry than those of Portuguese origin. Most came from the Moroccan cities of Tangier, Rabat, and Mogador (now Essaouria) to trade in hides and pelts or engage in other commercial activities. The majority of the immigrants from Morocco and Gibraltar were single men, and intermarriage with the local Catholic mulatto population was widespread. A number of Cape Verdeans remember their grandparents and the Jewish customs they practiced. The most prominent Cape Verdean with this ancestry is the prime minister, Carlos Alberto Wahnon de Carvalho Veiga, who is the great-grandson of Jews who emigrated from Gibraltar in the mid-nineteenth century. Recently his brother, Jose Tomas Veiga, the foreign minister, visited Israel, with which Cape Verde has opened relations. One of the officials in his party was the director of the research institute, João Levy, also of Moroccan ancestry.

Following Cape Verde's independence from Portugal in 1975, more Cape Verdeans are taking an interest in their history and ancestry. Unfortunately, little has been written down, perhaps because of colonial Portuguese pressure. The only physical evidence of the Jewish presence seems to be the cemeteries with gravestones (mainly of Moroccan-born Jews) that show the evolution of the community; inscriptions occur earliest in Hebrew, then in Portuguese, and finally with crosses. There is currently some interest in restoring the cemeteries, both to help preserve an important part of the country's history and perhaps to help encourage tourism.

While little has been written, there are fascinating oral accounts. Several Cape Verdeans of Moroccan ancestry told writer Carol Castiel of their remembrances of their grandparents, including their Jewish burial services. Several others, of Portuguese background, recounted family stories to me. One man said that he thought his father had been Jewish. The evidence? "He and some other men would get together, cover their heads, and read a language that looked like Arabic. Also, he told me to be skeptical of what the priests told me." Another remembers a family story of a great-grandfather, a New Christian who was forced to become a priest. He mutilated his hand on a sewing machine so as to be unable to conduct the mass and escaped to Cape Verde. Finally, one man told me of relatives who were picked up by German submarines during World War II and deported.

These people and others want to know more about their background; they want scholars to come to Cape Verde to conduct research, and they want to have exchanges with Israelis and American Jews.

These people are not looking to "return to their roots" or become Jewish. What they want, and what should be of interest to the world Jewish community, is to rediscover their past. This should be of special interest to American Jews. As one Cape Verdean told me after I presented him with a copy of Stephen Birmingham's book *The Grandees*, about America's Sephardic elite, "My God, these are all our names!"

An Unusual Society in Cape Verde
M. Mitchell Serels

In the wake of the Oslo Peace Process between Israel and her Arab adversaries, the descendants of Jews in the Republic of Cape Verde have openly reclaimed their identity. An archipelago in the Atlantic Ocean off the coast of Senegal, Cape Verde has had two epochs of Jewish settlement.

From 1460 to 1497 Portuguese Jews settled these barren islands as part of the colonization by Portugal. Their descendants—Lima, Carvalho, Rodrigues, and others—hid their Jewish ancestry behind a façade of Catholic conversion. The only open sign of their Jewish heritage today is a village called Singoga on the island of Santo Antão. Mixed with slaves and slave traders, their clear identity was lost.

In the years from 1850 to 1880, Moroccan Jews, mainly males from Tangier, arrived. Ruth Marcal de Cohen's husband was a descendant of one of them. His family settled in Ribiera Grande, Santo Antão, and opened a merchandising firm. Ruth Cohen, white in complexion, is the grande dame of the island. She remains in the large, green family mansion adjacent to the store, and she entertains guests in a European style.

In the town of Paul, Ildo Benros owns a centuries-old sugar cane press for the production of *grogue*, the same brew the pirates drank. Although aware of his Judaic past, he knows few details. His mother, now in her nineties, is no longer able to transmit her knowledge.

In the capital of Praia on Santiago Island, some of the local Jews have banded together to form the Cape Verde-Israel Friendship Society. The country has now accepted democracy as a way of life. The first democratically elected prime minister is Carlos Wahnon de Carvalho Veiga, of Jewish ancestry. The pro-Cuban, Communist government has been replaced. Although the Chinese and Russian embassies face the parliament building, their influence is lessening, as is the oil money used to ensure the former pro-Arab stand of the Cape Verde government.

The Friendship Society is headed by Dr. Januario Nascimento, of the Auday family of Tangier, founders of the first synagogue there. Often sent on diplomatic missions for his home country, Nascimento is also vice president of the country's Olympic committee, which, this year, sent its first athlete to the games. Abrão Levy is the secretary of the organization, which includes Policario Anahory, brother of the national poet.

I was able to speak at a public meeting organized by the Cape Verde-Israel Friendship Society. Eighty-five people crammed into a room designed to hold seventy. One young woman, during the question-and-answer period, spoke of her family's aversion to pork and wanted to know of other practices which could link her to Judaism.

Among the various objectives of the Friendship Society is the restoration of the three Jewish cemeteries, particularly that of Penha Franca on Santo Antão. Although Antonio Julio Rodrigues carefully keeps the debris off the graves, there is a need for funds to put up a wall around the graves and to properly protect the site.

My Capeverdean Genealogical Account
Donald Wahnon

In a search for my roots, mainly those of Jewish lineage, I dug into my own family records dating back five generations. I also consulted specialized books dealing primarily with Capeverdean as well as Portuguese Jews, and Jews from Morocco and Gibraltar, pamphlets, encyclopedias, and a variety of articles from various sources. I would like to point out the article by Hyman J. Gampeas in a publication of Yeshiva University in New York dealing with name derivations commonly found among Sephardic Jews. It was from this article in particular that I learned that the name Wahnon and its related form Wahnono, common among Sephardic Jews, are of Berber origin.

This assertion makes sense if we note the fact that the Berbers have lived in North Africa, particularly in northern Morocco, since the earliest recorded time. References to them date from 3000 B.C.E. and occur frequently in ancient Egyptian, Greek, and Roman sources. Berbers inhabited the coast of North Africa until the seventh century C.E., when the Arabs conquered North Africa and drove many Berber tribes inland to the Atlas Mountains.

My dear cousin and well-known Capeverdean writer, Luis Romano, of Jewish ancestry on his mother's side, who in the past lived in Morocco, is now living in Natal in the northeastern part of Brazil. He recounts in a publication issued by the University of Rio Grande do Norte a visit he made to Sefru, an entirely Jewish city on the slopes of the Atlas Mountains.

Going back to my direct Wahnon ancestors, they lived in Tetuan, a city and port in the north of Morocco, under the name Guanano and its variants, Wahnono, Wanono, and Wahnon. (Two other variants of the name were used by Jews from Morocco, the Berber-Phoenician Ohnona and the Hebraic form, Ben Hanun.)

Jacob Guanano was born in Tetuan in 1700. His son Haim Guanano, born in Tetuan in 1734, emigrated to Gibraltar in 1751, and was probably the first of the Wahnon lineage to live in Europe. In Gibraltar he married Belida (daughter of Solomon) and had several children, among whom Jacob Guanano (II) or Wahnono or Wahnon, was born in the year 1769.

Jacob Guanano or Wahnon married twice, his second wife being Simy Wahnon. This marriage took place in the year 1784 in

Tetuan, Morocco. They moved back to Gibraltar, where they had several children, including Jonas Wahnon, my great-great-grandfather, who was born in Gibraltar in 1812 and was the first Wahnon to emigrate to the Cape Verde Islands.

According to my sources, a whole colony of Jews had already settled in the Islands in the sixteenth century; they had been persecuted in their native Portugal, despite the opposition of King Philip III of Spain, who was then the country's ruler. Other Jews arrived from Morocco toward the nineteenth century.

The government of Portugal, in an effort to attract Jews back to Portugal, may have sent emissaries to Gibraltar. Jonas Wahnon was one of the Cape Verde-bound emigrants. His wife did not want to accompany him, but he was joined in 1860 by his son Isaac, my great-grandfather, who had been born in Gibraltar in 1843. Jonas Wahnon established himself in the Island of Santo Antão, where he engaged in agriculture.

In Santo Antão, with his Capeverdean wife, Jonas had three more sons and a daughter, whose names were Fernando, born in 1868, Verissimo, born in 1875, Jorge, born in 1878, and Merima. Of these four, I had the good fortune to know Fernando, a prosperous farmer and skilled lawyer, and Jorge, who became a skilled seaman, sometimes transporting Capeverdean immigrants to the shores of New England. Fernando died in Santo Antão at the age of seventy-nine, and Jorge at the age of seventy-eight. As to their father and my great-great-grandfather Jonas Wahnon, he left Cape Verde for Portugal, where he died in 1895.

Jonas Wahnon's first son, Isaac, my great-grandfather, settled in the Island of Santo Vicente, where Mindelo harbor became a busy refueling port for ships traveling between Europe, South America, and Africa. As the owner of the only hotel and restaurant on the island, he had the privilege of hosting some famous people, including Prince Albert of Belgium and John D. Rockefeller.

Isaac Wahnon was married to Rachel Levy Bentubo, also from Gibraltar. It was in Santo Vicente that Isaac and Rachel started a family that grew to fourteen children: eleven females and three males. I was fortunate enough to have known at least seven of these children, including Jacob (III), my grandfather, as well as Jaime, my grand-uncle and maternal grandfather of Carlos Alberto Wahnon Veiga, current prime minister of Cape Verde. It is said that Isaac was a great benefactor and always ready to help those in need, and that it was his custom to personally distribute food and sometimes money to the needy, on a daily basis. He died in 1915 on the island of Santo Vincente at the age of seventy-two.

Jacob Wahnon (III), my grandfather, was the youngest of Isaac and Rachel's three sons. He was born on the island of Santo Vicente in 1884 and died in Lisbon in 1968 at the age of eighty-four. He started working at the young age of fourteen, first as a ship-chandler's assistant and later as a telegrapher for the Western Telegraph Co., an important English submarine cable station based in Mindelo, Santo Vicente. With the passage of time he became a sophisticated and widely traveled businessman. He was very popular, with a passion for sports in general, having excelled in cricket and boxing. It is said that boxing was introduced into Santo Vicente by him. I was very fortunate to have known him, and I still remember his always impressive and very dominant presence.

At the age of twenty, he had a relationship with a Capeverdean girl, my dear grandmother née Amelia Jesus Monteiro, and fathered a son who was named Jonas (II), my father. Subsequently, still in Santo Vicente, Jacob would marry twice, the last time in 1921. Five more children were added from these two marriages: Edna, who died at an early age, Roland, Edgard, David, and Joel, my uncles.

Jonas, my father, was born in 1903 in Mindelo, Santo Vicente. At fourteen he dropped out of school and went to take care of his father's business in the former colony of Portuguese Guinea in West Africa, now Guinea-Bissau. At twenty he returned to Cape Verde, and soon after he fathered a daughter, Edna (II), the oldest of my sisters. About this time he started his own business in Santo Vicente in the field of import-export. In 1926, on a business trip to the island of Brava, Jonas, then twenty-three, met Alice, née Madeira Mascarenhas, my beloved mother, who was a Capeverdean of Portuguese ancestry, and a year later they were married. From this marriage seven children were born, all in Mindelo, Santo Vicente: myself, my brothers Eurico, Aguinaldo, and Antonio, and my sisters Dinora, Maria Alice, and Judith. I was the second of these children; Eurico and Antonio have both passed away.

In the late thirties, my father started a bakery business to which, a few years later, were added very successful biscuit and pasta industries.

Jonas Wahnon was a very bright and honest man, a man of unquestionable integrity. It was this characteristic, together with his love for his country, that gained him the respect of everyone in his native Santo Vicente. Like his father, Jacob, he was an avid sportsman, excelling in tennis, cricket, and gymnastics. He was the cofounder and president of the top soccer club as well as the Tennis Club of Mindelo. He was a Grand Master of the Portuguese Masonic Order, Capeverdean Lodge, which became extinct during the Salazar regime. He also served as president of the local business association. At one point, while Cape Verde was still part of Portugal, he was drafted by the governor for a seat on the provincial council. During his tenure as a council member, his unequivocal dedication to Cape Verde became more evident, not without risks, since the struggle for independence had already started in neighboring Guinea.

For strictly family reasons my father sold his business in Cape Verde and moved to Brazil, where two of my brothers and I were already living, hoping to gather and be near all his family. However, soon after his arrival in Brazil I was informed by the American consulate in Santo Paolo that my petition to immigrate to the United States had been approved, and soon after I was bound for the country of my dreams. A few years later, my father and mother and other members of my family followed.

Jonas Wahnon was very proud of his Jewish ancestry and always talked about Israel and her people with great admiration. He was also a fervent admirer and friend of the United States, having become an American citizen as soon as he completed the required time of residence. He passed away at the age of ninety in Randolph, Massachusetts, where he lived with his wife of sixty-six years, my dear mother Alice.

In August 1994, soon after his death, the city of Mindelo in Santo Vicente, in recognition of his demonstrated dedication, altruism, and faith in the destiny of Cape Verde, honored him by naming a street after him.

As for myself, I am sixty-six years of age, having been born in Mindelo, Santo Vicente, Cape Verde Islands, in the year of 1929. I attended high school in Santo Vicente, but, like my father, had to drop out to help in the family business. At the age of twenty-one, I married Maria Fernanda, née Oliveira Ferro, a Capeverdean woman of Portuguese ancestry. From this marriage four children were born, three girls and one boy: Gloria, Fernanda, Jaime, Capeverdean born, and Susana, Brazilian born.

In Brazil I went back to school, working during the day and studying at night. I completed two technical courses, one in the area of industrial engineering and another in machining technology, which helped in my search for a job upon my arrival in the United States in 1966.

My professional career in the United States exceeded my expectations. From my first job, as a time-study engineer, I was promoted to industrial engineer and later to senior industrial engineer, a position which I held until my retirement in 1990. I became a citizen of the United States in 1972.

And that is a synopsis of the Capeverdean branch of the Wahnon family as I was able to trace it back to its Berber-Jewish origin in Tetuan. It goes back eight generations. If we count my children, grandchildren, and great-grandchildren, eleven generations are covered.

14

The United States

Was Columbus Jewish?
Joseph Hantman

Two countries of Europe have over the years mildly competed for the honor of claiming Christopher Columbus as "theirs"—Italy, because his city of origin was reportedly Genoa, and Spain, because it sponsored his voyage of discovery in 1492. However, historical research indicates that while the above facts are correct, there is little doubt that Columbus's roots were in the Jewish—specifically, Sephardic—people.

In pursuing this thesis, one point must first be acknowledged: Columbus was a practicing Catholic, in fact, a highly visible one. I have visited the small church in the westernmost landfall of the Azores where Columbus is said to have prayed before his fleet headed west.

Without this Catholic identity, it would have been impossible for Columbus to have attended maritime schools in Portugal, to apply for a commission from the king of Portugal, or to have gained access to the Spanish royal couple, Ferdinand and Isabella.

Columbus's voyages are well documented, but his family origins are almost entirely shrouded in mystery. Neither his own writings nor those of his sons or biographers ever clearly define the family's origin. It is known that his father was Domenico Colombo, and his mother, Susana Fontanarossa. There are so many varied places and dates of Columbus's birth that certainty in this area is not possible. It is known that the language spoken and written by Columbus and his family was Spanish and not Italian. The few examples of his writing in Italian indicate a marked deficiency in the use of that language.

It is generally accepted by historians that the mystery of the origins of the Colombo family was intended to hide their Spanish origins. Colombo and Colon are both common, but not exclusively Jewish, names in Italy.

Starting about 1391 in Seville, there was such a great upsurge of anti-Jewish rioting, forced baptisms, and coerced conversions that a large portion of the Jewish population became converts (conversos). Many of them (the Marranos) continued to observe Jewish practices in secret. Many left Spain for other countries, and this was the origin of Italy's Sephardic community. Other Jews had lived in Italy for centuries, going back to the Second Temple period. The original Italian Jewish community was expanded with the fall of the Temple in 70 C.E. and the exile of Judea's leading Jewish families to Rome. Intermarriage has all but dimmed the distinction between the original "Temple Jews" and the Sephardim from Spain, but some families still trace their origin with pride to the captives from Judea.

In Spain and other countries subject to the Inquisition, *limpieza de sangre* ("purity of blood") and *mancha* (the "stain" of Jewish or Moorish blood) constituted a life-threatening fear, and Jewish observance or origin was best hidden. However, language, family customs, music, etc., remained strong among the Jews living in Spain even when Catholicism superseded Judaism in religious practice. This appears to have been the world of the Colombo (Colon) family in Italy.

Columbus took to the sea at an early age. How early varies according to which of his own accounts one reads. It is established that he served as a freebooter (pirate) captaining his own ship in service to various dukes and free states. In turning to the sea, he was following a well-established Jewish practice of the time. Abraham Cresques of Majorca, who became a converso, is called the father of modern cartography. His son Joshua was called the map Jew. Abraham Zacuto (1450–1510), scientist and astronomer, perfected the astrolabe, forerunner of the sextant. He drew up most of the nautical charts in use at the time. The quadrant used to determine a ship's position at sea was known as the quadrant Judaicus. The Alfonsin tables, the preferred astronomical tables of the time, were prepared at an earlier date by two Jewish court astronomers for King Alfonso the Wise. Much of the navigational knowledge had been developed by Jews, and Columbus was in possession of all this data.

While Columbus was an experienced sea captain, his efforts to gain sponsorship for reaching India by a western route were rebuffed by the Portuguese. It is therefore most interesting and significant that his sponsorship and support at the court of Ferdinand and Isabella came primarily from Jewish and converso members of the royal court. At the same time that the royal court was preparing the decree expelling the Jews from Spain, it was also deeply involved in negotiating Columbus's terms and conditions for undertaking the voyage of discovery. Amazingly, many of the courtiers who took part in preparing the expulsion decree and the financing and terms of Columbus's expedition were Jews or conversos. In 1491 and 1492, despite the terrible atmosphere created by the Inquisition, many Jews and conversos still held high governmental posts and remained in favor with the royal couple.

Foremost of them was Don Isaac Abravanel (1437–1508), the most renowned and respected Jewish personage of post-Islamic Christian Spain, who was in charge of all revenue for the crown. He retained his Jewish identity and affiliation despite pleas by the king and queen to become a convert and keep his title, position, and wealth. He went into exile with the Jews of Spain. Today the family name of Abravanel continues in both Sephardic and Ashkenazi communities and is accorded great respect. Together with the converso Santangel, he offered a vast sum to the royal couple to avert the decree of expulsion. Were it not for the personal intervention of Torquemada, the Grand Inquisitor, in an often-described dramatic scene, the efforts of these men might have been successful. Many other conversos high in court circles also befriended and supported Columbus. To judge the feasibility of Columbus's plans, hearings were conducted at Salamanca University. A prominent theologian, scientist, and tutor to the royal prince, Diego de Dieza, reportedly from a converso family, was appointed master of the hearings. Among those testifying was the aforementioned Abraham Zacuto, who, although a Jew, apparently taught at the university. The hearings supported Columbus.

Why this outpouring of support for Columbus among the powerful conversos at court? Did they just perceive his voyage as a worthwhile venture, or did they share a common bond with Columbus? Could they, like Kulanu today, have been hoping to find remnants of the Lost Tribes of Israel in some new land?

When Columbus was in Spain he identified himself as a foreigner, which, indeed, he was. He was fluent in Spanish, and experts have identified it as a Catalan Spanish. However, Spanish linguists indicate that the Spanish spoken and written by Columbus in the 1490s was more typical of what was spoken a hundred years earlier in Spain. In other words, Spanish, as do all languages, continued to evolve in Spain. Those who spoke the language in another land were left with the Spanish of their emigre forebears. It is likely that Columbus's Spanish had more in common with Ladino, the language of the Sephardic Diaspora, than either has with today's Spanish.

While Columbus exhibited great Catholic piety, his associations were almost exclusively with Jews, conversos, or Muslims. The most clear indication of quasi-Jewish identity lies in his writings, including the logs he kept on his voyages. In the prologue and the log of his first journey, he makes reference to the simultaneous departure of the Jews. There are constant references to Moses and

David. He frequently used dates compiled by the Jewish calendar. He refers to the Second Temple as *Casa Secunda*, a Spanish translation of the Hebrew *Beit Shayni*. In his last will he directs his son to use a portion of his fortune for dowries for needy young women of "our lineage." The giving of dowry money was one of the greatest mitzvot among Jews in the Middle Ages and continued to very recent times. Columbus's voyage was postponed by one day. This moved it beyond Tisha B'Av. While Don Isaac Abravanel did not succeed in having the decree canceled, he was able to obtain a day's extension. Jewish tradition has it that activities or enterprises commencing on Tisha B'Av are destined for failure. Tisha B'Av, the ninth day of the Hebrew month of Av, is a fast day commemorating the destruction of the First Temple in 586 B.C.E. and the Second Temple in 70 C.E.

Among Columbus's crews, of course, no Jew would have been permitted, but it is known that there were conversos. Best known of these was Luis de Torres, the interpreter, who was fluent in Hebrew, Aramaic, Latin, Spanish, and Portuguese. He converted a few days before the sailing. Torres was the first European to land in what is now Cuba. Also Master Marco the physician, Master Bernal the apothecary, and Rodrigo Sanchez, nephew of the royal treasurer. The latter's letters to his son, except for those intended to be presented at court, carried in the upper right corner letters which have been deciphered as the Hebrew *Bet Hey* (*BH*). This is a custom still observed by religious people writing in Yiddish or Hebrew; it stands for *B'ezrat HaShem* ("with God's help").

After years of prominence, Columbus's reputation and favor at court declined. There were frequent rumors and allegations that he was a Jew. Franciscan priests among the clergy in the West Indies made this accusation to the cardinal in Spain, but apparently it was not pursued.

In the United States Columbus became a folk hero. October 12 is a national day of recognition in his honor. Statues of the discoverer of America abound, and the Columbus Day parade is a tradition in many cities, particularly among people of Italian descent. The matter of a possibly Jewish Columbus is not part of the ritual.

In the Jewish world there have occasionally been a few flurries of interest. In the United States in the 1880s, in anticipation of the four-hundredth anniversary of Columbus's voyage, Lazarus Straus of the mercantile and financial family, and his diplomat son Oscar Solomon Straus commissioned a study of Columbus and Jewish participation in the discovery of America. They believed that proving such a connection would enhance the status of American Jews as having participated in the building of the United States from earliest times. They assigned this task to an eminent scholar of Spanish and Portuguese Jewish history, Rabbi Meyer Keyserling of Budapest. Much of today's knowledge on the subject stems from Keyserling's study, but his findings left Columbus's origins as vague as they are today. In later years the man now known as the Nazi hunter, Simon Wiesenthal, and the renowned British Jewish historian Cecil Roth both deeply involved themselves in the question of Columbus's identity. They too left unanswered the question of the explorer's Jewishness. But they did restate the possibility as outlined above. There have been recurring but unconfirmed rumors that the Catholic Church at one time considered the beatification of Columbus for having brought Catholicism to America. Perhaps somewhere in the Vatican archives there are answers as to why this action was never pursued.

Today, however, historical revisionists portray another picture of Columbus. Colonizer, enslaver, exploiter are all words the children are bringing from school. In some circles, Columbus's Jewish identity is now fully accepted, though not for commendable reasons, and those who vilify him try to relate his alleged negative traits to his being Jewish. Meanwhile Jewish organizations and publications are no longer seeking Columbus's Jewish connection and are quite content to let the subject drop.

The ironies of Jewish history never cease.

Coming Out of the Marrano Closet
Brian P. Haran

I was terrified at the thought of going before a beth din, a group of rabbis who would question my Jewishness, my sincerity...things that touch very close to home! Little did I know beforehand that one of my "inquisitors," Rabbi Jacques Cukierkorn of Kulanu, would have more than a passing interest in my story and the story of my family.

When I was about twelve, my father told me that we were really a Jewish family. I then realized that my family name, Haran, was not Irish, and that we were somehow special. According to family lore we went to Ireland via Spain. There is a tradition of speaking some Spanish in the family, and quite honestly most of my father's family looked Spanish, if not Mediterranean. I'll probably never know for sure if the Harans actually landed on the west coast of Ireland with the ill-fated Spanish Armada. There were many Marranos with the Spanish fleet. Perhaps they made their way to Ireland with groups of Jews that traveled to the British Isles via Portugal and the Netherlands. The fact remains that we remembered our heritage.

The story of my mother's Viennese family, Dubrasky, is similar to that of my father's family, but somewhat more modern. It was the old story of Middle European pogroms, assimilation, and eventual emigration. One of my uncles even changed his name to hide his Jewishness! In spite of assimilation some customs remained—giving biblical names to the girls, a smattering of Yiddish spoken at home, and a fear of Russian soldiers. They settled in Jewish neighborhoods in the New World at the turn of the century... close to the community but still apart.

My own Jewishness might have simply remained something of a curiosity, but during the mid-1980s a friendship with an Orthodox Jew and his family led me to begin my own studies and worship at home. I began to live my life as a closet Marrano . . . something of a family tradition, I suppose. In September 1993, in fear and trembling, I went to speak with a local rabbi. So I began my public worship and formal studies. The welcoming support that I received from Rabbi Gold was crucial. Who knows whether my Jewish "roots" were simply a part of the Almighty's overall plan for me . . . and perhaps it is so for others as well.

I must point out that however much an ancient tie with Judaism can be a positive force, there is also, in the psyche of the Marrano, a negative that is hard to overcome. Somewhere in the past the direct link with the community was broken. Whatever the circumstances, there was estrangement and assimilation. For many of us it meant physical survival while others perished. To return now carries a certain amount of guilt and perhaps shame that is very difficult to even acknowledge. I don't know if this aspect is often discussed, but I do feel that it may very well be something that should be acknowledged and overcome in a supportive way. Often survivors of wars or natural disasters struggle with feelings of guilt or shame . . . simply because they are survivors. That a portion of our family should remain in hiding, albeit in psychological hiding, is certainly the last thing we should allow to happen.

I'd like to pass along a short story that I hope you'll appreciate. Two brothers inherited an old orchard that had been planted many generations before them. The younger brother was very practical and energetic. He wanted to immediately cut down the old, unproductive trees, plow up the field, and sow grain for a quick harvest. The older brother examined the orchard, which had suffered from years of neglect. A compromise was struck. The brothers would wait a season before cutting down the trees. In the meantime they dedicated some spare time to the old orchard. The following spring they pruned back the trees, nurtured the surrounding soil, and reopened the irrigation ditches for fresh water to reach the trees. Their harvest was abundant beyond expectation. Neighbors were called to share in the harvest. Everyone marveled at the "new" fruit.

Part III

Jewish Roots in Africa

15

Fight for the Honor of the Ethiopian Jewish Community!
Jack and Diane Zeller

Ethiopian Jewry is ancient. In the Bible, Moses marries a Cushite, which is the ancient term for Ethiopian. Isaiah and Zephaniah recognized the Jewish presence in Ethiopia, at a time well before the Babylonian destruction of the First Temple. Jewish soldiers comprised a large part of an Egyptian garrison in proximity to Ethiopia in ancient times preceding the destruction of the First Temple. Jeremiah is saved by an Ethiopian and taken to Egypt. In modern times, in the eighteenth century, the English explorer James Bruce electrified England and the European continent with his description of Ethiopia, including the Falasha community.

We mention this to make a point: Western Jews' forgetfulness about the Ethiopian Jewish community is less than credible. Even the nineteenth-century discovery of the community was prompted by Christian missionaries, who claimed that thousands of Jews had been converted to Protestant sects. The most famous scholar of Ethiopia in Europe, Professor Joseph Halévy, responded to the appeals of his co-religionists in the Alliance Israélite Universelle to determine the truth. He did and described the community in great detail. They were observant, impoverished, virtually enslaved, but proud and Zionistic, and—most important of all—not converted by Protestant missionaries. Still, no Western Jewish relationships came to them until 1904.

In our times we have lived to see the arrival of almost sixty thousand Ethiopian Jews in Israel following the acceptance of the Ethiopian Jewish community as Jews by Chief Rabbi Ovadiah Yosef in 1973. But despite this magnificent change, all is not well.

There are approximately twenty-five thousand Jews in Ethiopia who have been left behind and are in a deep depression. Most of them have some family in Israel, commonly a brother or sister or uncle, and sometimes a parent or child, and they are not allowed to emigrate beyond the rate of one thousand souls per year. This quota, as adopted by both the Ethiopian government and the government of Israel, serves two purposes. For the Ethiopians, it is an appeasement to their Islamic neighbors, and for Israel it is an excuse for limiting the immigration of a community that comes with a low level of literacy and job skills that do not fit into the Jewish Western stereotype.

Approximately four thousand Ethiopian Jews have left Gondar province, their ancient home, and migrated south to Addis Ababa to live as refugees in the capital city and wait for aliyah. They wait in the compound of the North American Conference for Ethiopian Jewry, which is about 200 yards from the Israeli embassy. The Israeli ambassador is instructed to ignore them. Because some of them were crypto-Jews and had to pretend to be Christians from time to time, they have been labeled Christians by the government of Israel and the Jewish Agency. The Chief Rabbinate in Israel, however, considers them Jews who may have strayed. Some receive aid from the American Joint Distribution Committee, but many do not, since they came to Addis Ababa against the express wishes of the Israeli embassy. Still, they do not return to Gondar, since they have sold all their possessions and have nothing but hope to sustain them.

On a recent trip to Israel, we could not believe what we heard from our Ethiopian friends in Neve Carmel, a large absorption center just south of Haifa. They told us about the plight of the Ethiopian Jews waiting in Addis Ababa who were not receiving any regular allowance from the Joint Distribution Committee. The men in these cases would work for 2 burr a day, compared with 5 burr (85 cents) paid to non-Jewish workers. The result: Ethiopian Jews beaten and murdered for competing "unfairly" in the labor market.

We were told that living conditions for the Ethiopian Jews in Addis Ababa were abominable. Up to ten or more in a room that was once—or still is—a latrine, a chicken coop, or a storeroom. We were told that the Joint had vaccinated the late-arriving (1991) Ethiopian Jews only when TV cameras were conveniently present to record the event. Many die prematurely and suffer from malnutrition or untreated illness.

We would encourage you to visit the community in Addis Ababa, but not in Gondar. The Gondar community is scattered, and its members often do better as crypto-Jews than as overt Jews. Those who receive visitors in Gondar are often beaten and robbed after their guests have left. Also, Gondar is somewhat lawless, since there is a rebellion against the government there (and elsewhere). The community in Addis Ababa is safe for visitors, and the Ethiopian Jewish community very much wants American Jews to visit them in the compound. Do not show up unannounced. Ethiopia is a land where a high level of suspicion is the norm—and probably a healthy norm at that. The North American Conference on Ethiopian Jewry (NACOEJ) can arrange for your visit. The office is located at 165 East 56th Street, New York, NY 10022. The telephone number is (212) 752-6340 and their FAX is (212) 980-5294. Their World Wide Web site is http://www.cais.com/nacoej.

When you visit, think about bringing along things that the people can use. There is a large school in the NACOEJ compound, and the children very much need supplies. NACOEJ can advise you about what gifts might be most useful.

Two warnings: be prepared to love and be loved. There is nothing quite like Ethiopian Jewish hospitality. Also, be prepared to take up the exhausting but worthwhile fight for the honor of the Ethiopian Jewish community. Remember, it started with Moses.

16

Are The Balemba "Jewish"?
Karen and Aron Primack

Perhaps "Balemba" will one day be part of the everyday Jewish vocabulary. The people of this tribe in southern Africa, numbering 100,000–150,000, believe they are descended from the ancient Israelites and have, in recent years, stepped up their observance of Jewish practices.

A 1993 article by Immanuel Suttner in the *Jerusalem Report* notes that the tribe's Jewish-like practices were "discovered" in the 1850s by Robert Moffat, a Scottish missionary. The name "Balemba" means "those who refuse to eat unclean things," and the Balemba do not eat animals, such as pigs, that lack split hooves. In addition, they practice circumcision and require that cattle be slaughtered by a circumcised man and that the blood be allowed to drain into the ground. The Balemba also perform ritual washing of the hands before eating. Balemba women do not touch men while they are menstruating, and are considered ritually impure after giving birth.

Although some might ascribe their practices of circumcision and pork prohibition as emanating from Islam, Balemba oral tradition speaks of Abraham and his covenant with the Creator, and of Moses, but not of Muhammad.

Tribal lore tells that the ancestors of the Balemba left Israel after the destruction of the First Temple, wandered southward through

Yemen, and worked their way, never fully assimilating, to their present locations in southern Africa—Zimbabwe, Malawi, Mozambique, and Venda.

Although many Balemba are unaware of or uninterested in their possible Jewish roots, many are becoming increasingly curious. Reform rabbi Wally Blumenthal of Johannesburg, who died in 1987, taught tribe members about Judaism. Modern additions to their practices include the adoption of the Star of David as a symbol, the increased use of cloth skullcaps (use of these by the Balemba was noted thirty years ago by a South African Jew), and the selection of eight days, rather than adolescence, as the age of circumcision.

Balemba are often members of the professional, business, and government class in their respective countries. For example, Ephraim Selamolela, of Venda, who was born on a farm and banished from schooling during apartheid, started out in the taxi business and now owns a shopping center. His four children are all at universities, technical colleges, or private schools. And Matshaya Mathiva, one of the first blacks in South Africa to become a professor, and whose children are all doctors, lawyers, and academics, illustrates the tribe's emphasis on education.

Judaism is a cultural, rather than a religious, affiliation to many Balemba, who have adopted Christianity as well as traditional tribal beliefs. Are they Jews? Who knows? Suttner's assessment skillfully addresses this question:

"Whether that belief [in Jewish descent] has any basis has been a matter for debate among outsiders—churchmen, anthropologists and archaeologists—for 150 years, and the mystery remains unsolved. What's clear, though, is that many of the tribe's customs bear a fascinating resemblance to Judaism, its traditions speak of Abraham and Moses, and more and more of its members today see the link to Jews as part of their identity."

Tudor Parfitt agrees that the Balemba may be of Jewish origin. In his 1992 book *Journey to the Vanished City: The Search for a*

Lost Tribe of Israel, he discusses their possible connections to the Ethiopian Jews, Jews exiled from Saudi Arabia, and Europeans (the Portuguese). But after an exhaustive search and study, he is unable to show a definitive lineage or connection, leaving the answer to the question of whether the Balemba are Jewish still "maybe."

In a study published in the *American Journal of Human Genetics* (11/96), Spurdle and Jenkins showed that the Lemba chromosomal analysis indicates a Semitic origin in more than 50 percent of their Y chromosomes—which is consistent with their oral tradition regarding their ancestry.

Rabbi Eliyahu Avichail conferring with Ophel, Bnei Menashe father of boy about to have a bris in Israel, 1995. Photo by Diane Zeller.

Diane Zeller with Bnei Menashe women in Israel, reading an article about Bnei Menashe in the Kulanu newsletter, 1995. Photo by Jack Zeller.

Bnei Menashe immigrants in Israel, 1995. Photo by Jack Zeller.

Bnei Menashe boy in Israel, 1995. Photo by Jack Zeller.

Bnei Menashe immigrant in Israel, 1995. Photo by Diane Zeller.

Bnei Menashe immigrant in Israel, 1995. Photo by Diane Zeller.

Shinlung Jew in Manipur, India.

Interior of a Bnei Menashe synagogue in Mizoram, India.

Bnei Menashe reception in Manipur, India, to welcome Rabbi Avichail, 1994.

The Kadoorie Synagogue in Oporto, Portugal. Photo by Eytan Berman.

Passover 5752 in Puebla, Mexico. Left to right: Ignacio Castelan Estrada, his wife Mary, sons Abner and Hartus, daughters Ada and Jemima.

Richard A. Kulick and the Jewish community of Puebla, Mexico, at Havdalah service.

Services at a converso havurah in Natal, Brazil. Photo by Jacques Cukierkorn.

Tombstone in a Jewish cemetery in Cape Verde. Fund-raising has begun for restoration.

Members of the Cape Verde-Israel Friendship Society.

Dr. Xu Xin, professor of Jewish Studies in the People's Republic of China. Photo by Aron Primack.

Shi-Ping and son Chao Liang, present-day descendants of Kaifeng Jews. Photo by Ray Kaplan.

שְׁמַע יִשְׂרָאֵל, יְיָ אֱלֹהֵינוּ, יְיָ אֶחָד

Hear O Israel: the Lord our God, the Lord is One

聽着 以色列 主是我們的上帝 主是獨一無二的

Translation of the Shema prayer into Chinese by Denise Yeh Bresler.

Gershom Sizomu, Abayudaya acting rabbi, with his son Moshe. Photo by Lucy Steinitz.

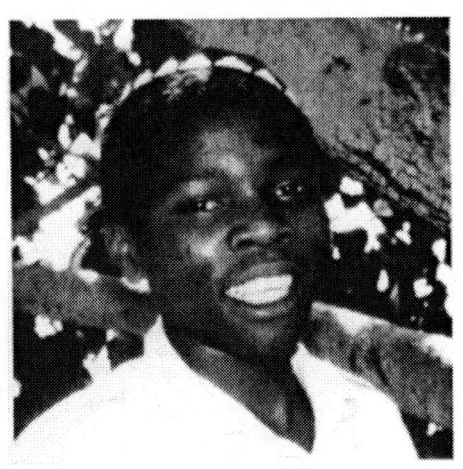

Seth Keki, Abayudaya teenager who often leads services. Photo by Lucy Steinitz.

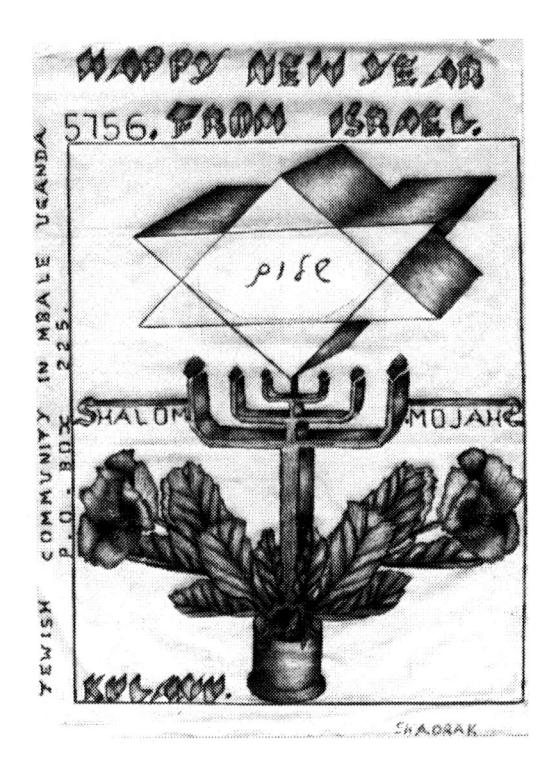

New Year's greeting by Israel ben Shadrak of the Abayudaya Congregation in Mbale, Uganda.

Abayudaya village in eastern Uganda. Photo by Aron Primack.

Abayudaya Torah service, Uganda. Photo by Aron Primack.

Abayudaya Torah service with Gershom Sizomu reading. Photo by Aron Primack.

Rabbi Jacques Cukierkorn with Abayudaya leader Gershom Sizomu, June 1995. Photo by Aron Primack.

Unscrolling of Torah given to the Abayudaya by American visitors in 1995. Photo by Aron Primack.

Women's section of the main Abayudaya synagogue. Photo by Aron Primack.

A meeting between Abayudaya and American Jewish women. Photo by Aron Primack.

Public school children in Gangama, Uganda, two-thirds of whom are Abayudaya. Photo by Aron Primack.

Davening on Sunday morning in Trujillo, Peru.

Rabbi Myron Zuber blesses Pedro, an Incan convert, at his bar mitzvah in Trujillo, Peru.

Members of the Bene Moshe community in Peru, some of whom made aliyah to Israel.

Telugu Jews at synagogue in Andhra Pradesh, India, for Purim.

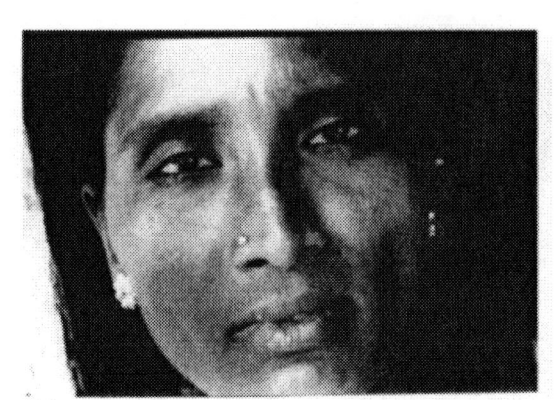

Rebecca Kohari, a member of the Telugu Jewish community in Andhra Pradesh. Photo by Jason Francisco.

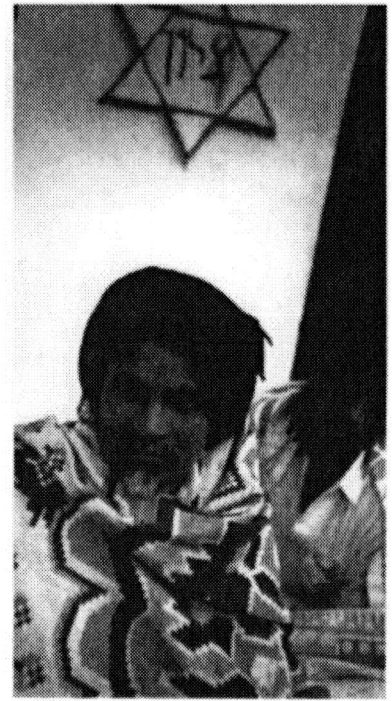

Telugu Jews Moshe Kedari and Abrahim Kafthori. Photo by Jason Francisco.

The Jewish community in Ghana.

17

A Lost Tribe in Nigeria?
Warren Freedman

In 1986 Michael Asher, a thirty-three-year-old English Jew, together with his wife, traversed the Sahara Desert in North Africa from west to east by camel and on foot, a distance of 4,500 miles. His book *Impossible Journey* (published by Penguin in 1988) identifies a Jewish tribe in Nigeria, the Iddao Ishaak, living in the valley of Asakrei.

Asher recounts the incident of meeting with six tribal leaders who, coming out of their leather tents, "looked dangerous, dressed in their long, dark gandourahs, their faces hidden by veils. They carried daggers and axes and wore thick skin sandals. They were inscrutable under their headcloths and came on with the dreadful steadiness of an army. Suddenly Sidi Mohammed [Asher's native guide] said, 'Don't worry: these aren't Tuareg. They are Iddao Ishaak. They are of Jewish origin. They are rich in camels, but they aren't warlike.'"

In a subsequent conversation with these six members of the Jewish tribe, Asher was told about the terrible drought of 1985. The Iddao Ishaak spokesman remarked that "the only thing that saved us was God. . . . The government gave us no help. They still take from us the animal tax for animals we haven't got!"

Part IV
Jews in China

18

Jews Have Been in China a Long, Long Time
Karen Primack

Scholars are divided in their opinions about when the first Jews came to China.

Some think they came in biblical times, and even theorize about one of the Ten Lost Tribes settling between Tibet and Sichuan.

So said Prof. Xu Xin at public lectures in the Washington, D.C., area on November 19 and 20, 1995. Xu is a professor of English and Jewish Studies at Nanjing University in the People's Republic of China.

There is unanimous agreement that Jews have been in China *at least* since the sixth century. One of the earliest pieces of evidence is an eighth-century letter written in Persian Hebrew by a Jewish merchant in China, probably a trader on the Silk Road.

(The Silk Road, which extended from eastern China through Central Asia to the Black Sea and the Mediterranean coast, was a trade route in use for about twelve hundred years. Extending 2,000 miles, through mountains and deserts, it enabled Western goods to be traded for Chinese silk. Jewish merchants traded chiefly in cotton, perfume, and spices.)

In addition, a fragment of a Hebrew prayer was found in northwestern China by British scholars—a prayer written on paper, dated also to the eighth century; this is the earliest report of the use of paper for Hebrew prayers. Also, a ninth-century Arab traveler wrote about his experiences, which included a report of a massacre of Christians, Muslims, and Jews in southern China. Marco Polo (1254?–1324?) also made mention of Jews in China.

Kaifeng Attracts Jews

Up to the eleventh century, these Jews were merchants and traders who traveled back and forth to China, but during the eleventh century, the first group of Jews came to Kaifeng to stay, and they followed their traditions for many hundreds of years. Much literature has been left about them. Although the first arrivals were chiefly single men who had traded on the Silk Road, seventy families with women and children were also among the early Jewish settlers.

Xu reminds his audiences that "China was rich then, and it was a good place to live and to do business." It was the time of the Song Dynasty, whose capital was Kaifeng, a very prosperous international city with a population of 1.5 million.

According to the oral traditions of Kaifeng Jewry, Jews met the Song emperor, who encouraged them to "observe and hand down your religion here," as an inscribed stele (stone pillar) of the time relates. Because he could not pronounce their names, the emperor gave the Jews seven family surnames, which gave them legitimacy. "If you do not have one of these seven family names, you are not considered Jewish," Xu explains. The first synagogue in Kaifeng was built in 1163.

The Jewish community was influenced by Chinese culture, including Confucianism and the Chinese classics, which had to be studied for the imperial examinations, for official appointments, and for social status.

The community grew, and a larger synagogue was built. By 1500 the population peaked at about five thousand. Kaifeng was repeatedly destroyed by the flooding of the Yellow River, which killed many, including Jews. The floods of 1662 alone killed more than 100,000 people; only two hundred-odd Jewish families survived.

The Jews always intermarried in China, for the Jewish community was never large enough to marry among themselves. However, it was the Chinese custom for the wife to take the husband's religion. This enabled Jewish traditions to be maintained for seven centuries.

The sixteenth century saw the beginning of the acculturation of the Jewish community of Kaifeng. Hebrew was not really spoken anymore. Assimilation occurred because Jews spent more time studying for Chinese classics examinations and less time studying Judaism. They also adopted Chinese names. The Jews were known as Hui Hui (meaning "from the West") or by a Chinese expression that translated as "the sect that plucks out sinews," in reference to one of the rules of kashrut.

The Kaifeng community was first discovered by Christian missionaries at the beginning of the seventeenth century. An historic meeting between Jews and a Jesuit missionary took place in June of 1605, and according to Xu, ever since then missionaries and scholars have always sought out the Jews of Kaifeng. At first there was great interest in the Kaifeng Jews among Christians because they believed that this isolated community might still possess an original Torah that had not been altered by the rabbis of the talmudic era to remove references to the coming of Christ.

In 1722, Christian missionaries drew a diagram of the old synagogue; it is now used by the Diaspora Museum in Tel Aviv.

Xu has had a chance to read and examine, to his delight, fifty-nine books written by Kaifeng Jews in the Klau Library of Hebrew Union College in Cincinnati, where he has studied. One of the books, written in both Hebrew and Chinese four hundred years ago, traces ten generations of the Kaifeng Jewish community. In addition, three steles of the fifteenth, sixteenth, and seventeenth centuries, report on the community's history.

The Kaifeng synagogue was repaired or rebuilt at least eleven times until the nineteenth century, when the last rabbi died and Hebrew was no longer taught. (Hebrew had been taught continuously for seven hundred years.)

But, amazingly, "a sense of Jewish identity still persists" in Kaifeng, according to Xu, as today's descendants are "trying to pick up lost traditions" of their ancestors from nine hundred years ago.

The Modern Era

Meanwhile, the nineteenth century saw a westward migration of Jews, especially from Germany, and, between 1820 and 1920, a movement of Sephardi Jews from Mesopotamia eastward to India, Malaysia, and China.

After the Opium Wars of the mid-nineteenth century, in which China was defeated by Britain, China was forced to open its doors to Western society. Among others, the Sassoons arrived in Shanghai, liked it, and brought in their friends and relatives. By 1900 there were seven hundred Jews in Shanghai, along with synagogues, a Jewish cemetery, and ritually slaughtered poultry. In the 1930s the Sassoons donated millions of dollars to help Jewish refugees from Europe.

Pogroms in Poland and Russia in 1905–1917 brought a new migration of Eastern Europeans to Shanghai. By 1930 there were four thousand Ashkenazic Jews there, who survived by setting up small businesses. They established many facilities and a Jewish press. These Jews were early Zionists. According to Xu, Chinese leader Dr. Sun Yat-sen published a letter in 1920 supporting Zionism.

In 1937–39, refugees from Nazi Germany and Austria found all doors closed to them except the doors of Shanghai, the only place in the world that did not require a visa. By 1941, the lives of some twenty thousand refugees had been saved.

Another Jewish community came to Shanghai in 1942: all the faculty and students from the renowned Mir Yeshiva of Poland. Although Shanghai was occupied by the Japanese by then, the Jews were ghettoized and allowed to study and worship. As a result, the faculty and student body of the Mir Yeshiva survived the war intact; after the war they were largely responsible for the continuation of Ashkenazic yeshiva learning in the United States and Israel.

By 1945, the Jewish community of Shanghai numbered thirty thousand, with its own autonomous government presiding over marriages and burials. Today, Xu says, some Chinese still remember their Jewish neighbors.

Another Jewish community settled in Harbin, in northeastern China, after 1898, when it was chosen as headquarters of the East China Railway. Many people were brought in from Russia, including Jewish merchants. In 1903 the Jewish population reached five hundred, in part because the Jews were never discriminated against by the Chinese, as they were by the Russians. Xu notes that when the Russians were defeated in the Russo-Japanese War of 1904, Jewish soldiers who had been forced to serve in the tsar's army stayed on in Harbin and brought their relatives from Russia. By 1908, Harbin's eight thousand Jews enjoyed a better life than they had in Russia. However, the Japanese invasion of northern China in the 1930s resulted in a diminution of the Jewish community in Harbin.

After 1945 most of China's Jews emigrated to America, Canada, Australia, or Israel. By 1950 the majority were gone, and the last synagogue service was held in Shanghai in 1956.

TODAY AND TOMORROW

In China today, the descendants of the Jews of Kaifeng pass remnants of their heritage from generation to generation through oral legends, which enable them to keep a sense of their Jewish roots.

Xu comments that "even today some have a strong sense of Jewish identity" and list "Jew" as their ethnic group in the official government census, although doing this is discouraged (China does not want to encourage ethnic divisions among its huge population.)

Xu estimates that there are four or five hundred descendants of Kaifeng Jews in China today.

Xu also reports that in the last ten years, some Jews have come back to China for business reasons, and those in Hong Kong are not leaving, in the hope that business prospects will remain good after China's takeover of the city in 1997. There are more than a thousand Jewish diplomats and business people today in Beijing, and even more in Shanghai. But there is no synagogue or religious school . . . *yet!*

"Jewish life in China will continue," Xu believes.

19

Xu Xin, an Unusual Man

Karen Primack

Why would a non-Jewish English teacher in the People's Republic of China study Hebrew and Yiddish and Talmud, meet three Presidents of Israel, establish a Jewish Studies program at Nanjing University, edit a Chinese version of the *Encyclopaedia Judaica*, and author a book on the Legends of the Chinese Jews of Kaifeng?

Prof. Xu Xin's personal story is as fascinating as his lectures about Jews in China.

He modestly claims that he was in the right place at the right time—when three events coincided. *One:* Having taught himself English with a gramophone and records from the 1940s and 1950s, he was able to get into a university, and he became a teacher of English in China in 1977. *Two:* The Cultural Revolution was just ending in 1976, finally allowing the reintroduction of Western subjects, including literature, and the dissemination of "outside" news, such as who won Nobel Prizes. *Three:* The Nobel Prize for literature was awarded to Saul Bellow in 1976 and Isaac Bashevis Singer in 1978.

Up to that time, Xu explains, Chinese students in his generation had never learned anything about Judaism except the Bible; Chinese reference books described Hebrew as a dead language. But after excitedly reading Bellow and Singer—and then Malamud,

Roth, Salinger, and others—he decided to specialize in postwar Jewish American literature. And then he studied Judaism "to have a better understanding of these stories."

Another fortuitous event was the arrival in 1985 of an American professor to teach in Nanjing for six months. The professor was a Jew from Chicago. Xu and the professor became fast friends, and the following year he arranged for Xu to teach English composition at Chicago State University, where his students were 95 percent African-American.

During his two years there, Xu lived with a Reconstructionist Jewish family and "had much contact with Jewish culture." They celebrated all the holidays and he attended a bar mitzvah in Milwaukee. Realizing that Judaism is "one of the sources of Western civilization," Xu resolved to teach about Judaism in China.

In 1988, Xu spent ten days in Israel—prior to the time China and Israel had relations—to speak in Jerusalem at the Hebrew University. He emphasizes that his trip was not a secret. The *Jerusalem Post* reported on his talk, and upon arriving in Israel he insisted on having his passport stamped.

Back in China, his students wanted him "to talk about Israel." No fewer than a thousand students showed up at one of his lectures. Xu added modern Hebrew literature (in English translation) to his course list; the course covered the works of Agnon and fifty other writers. He also translated many of their stories and poems into Chinese. He found himself "the sole expert" on modern Hebrew literature in China!

In April of 1989, just two months before the Tienamin Square demonstration, Xu set up the China Judaic Studies Association. Although all its exhibits and lectures had to receive prior official approval, Xu argued that the study of Judaism was a foundation for understanding Western civilization, and he was successful in organizing a major exhibit on Judaic Studies in China, as well as a program studying Yiddish writers of the 1920s.

The Association also organized a Holocaust exhibit in China, which attracted eighty thousand visitors in seven weeks. The exhibit was covered by Chinese TV and press.

Realizing that there was no Judaic reference book available in Chinese, Xu decided to write a Chinese version of the *Encyclopaedia Judaica*. He and a team of forty labored for three years to produce a 900-page, one-volume encyclopedia with sixteen hundred selected entries. Although his salary in China at that time was only $50 per month, he had to promise his publisher that he would come up with $10,000 to meet publication costs. He supplied a $1,000 down payment from his American earnings and raised the additional $10,000 from "donors all over the world."

Xu's academic reputation has been widely recognized both in and outside China. He was invited to participate in meetings on whether China should establish relations with Israel. (He argued that China could play a role in the Mideast conflict; that recognition would improve China's image, since Israel had influence in the United States; and that ties would improve trade relations between the two countries.)

In 1992 he was invited to speak at a Harvard University conference. He returned to Israel in 1993–94, where he met top Israeli government and academic officials and conferred with the Chinese ambassador to Israel. He was invited to do research at Hebrew Union College in Cincinnati in 1995; he took time out over the summer to study Yiddish with YIVO in New York and then put in a semester as a visiting scholar at Harvard.

Xu attributes the interest in Judaism among Chinese students to the fact that both the Jews and the Chinese are ancient, continuous civilizations that have had an important impact on world civilization. And he attributes the lack of anti-Semitism in China to the fact that most Chinese do not have a religion.

He sees university students as the future leaders of his country and feels it is "important to teach them about Judaism." He would like to give a seminar for professors who teach world history and

Western civilization at Chinese universities and colleges so that the story of Jewish civilization can be incorporated into their courses.

A tireless advocate, Xu hopes one day to have a chair of Judaic Studies so that he can teach about Judaism full-time.

He has many plans—his only limiting factor is funding. He is seeking "a few thousand dollars" to sponsor a Chinese student at Hebrew Union College; the college will waive the tuition, but living expenses are needed. He is also seeking $12,000 for research on the history of the Jews of Kaifeng. The knowledgeable museum curator emeritus there recently died, and the families are dying out. His new book, *Legends of the Chinese Jews of Kaifeng*, makes a start, since legends can be an important source of history, but much more research is needed.

Xu has had to become an effective fund-raiser to support his projects. One of his favorite causes is seeking living expenses for Chinese students who want to pursue Judaic scholarship abroad. He notes that only 5 percent of China's population has been to college, and that they are the ones who will have a "big voice" in world affairs. Students in China are curious about Jewish culture. He would like to facilitate their studies in the United States. Membership in the China Judaic Studies Association promotes this and other remarkable work by Xu Xin.

20

A Delightful Introduction to Chinese Jewry
Jack Zeller

Legends of the Chinese Jews of Kaifeng, by Xu Xin with Beverly Friend, illustrated by Ting Chen. Hoboken, N.J.: KTAV Publishing House, 1995.

Chinese and Jewish. To most American Jews this seems an unlikely combination. However, the topic is an old one, going back to the major role of Jews in the silk trade to China that long preceded Marco Polo's visits.

Many sources are available in English, thanks to the efforts of the Sino-Judaic Institute and to the 1992 conference on "Jewish Diasporas in China: Comparative and Historical Perspectives," sponsored by the John K. Fairbank Center for East Asian Research at Harvard University.

Written records are few about the origins of this community, but it is known that in the eighth century the Radhanites, a Persian Jewish community of traders, were well established in the silk business. Most likely, the permanent Jewish communities are a derivative of their activities.

An important source of information is the body of legends passed down from generation to generation by word of mouth. Professor Xu Xin has written a book about legends of the most famous of the cities chosen by Diaspora Jews, Kaifeng. He collected many from meetings with the community's elders, from the famed Wang Yisha (emeritus curator of the Kaifeng Museum, whose legends had not previously been translated into English), and from other scholars who had also visited Kaifeng and interviewed Jewish descendants.

Professor Xu has blended these legends into a single book that provides a historical flow from the Jewish origins in the tenth century to the present. Although the author has taken some artistic license to make the legends readable, he has been very true to their essence because he believes (as do other historians) that legends are an authentic historical form that conveys values and conflicts as well as information.

The reading is delightfully easy and concise. This makes the reader proud of both the civility and dignity of the Jewish and Chinese cultures. For those who have often noted the similarity of behavior of Chinese and Jews, this book provides added impetus and information to casual observations.

Part V

Communities Seeking Conversion

21

Italy

The Case of San Nicandro
Joseph Hantman

There is nothing very unusual about non-Jewish individuals converting to Judaism. Such conversions take place for a variety of reasons, ranging from deep religious conviction to family reasons. However, when communities or groups of non-Jews decide collectively that they wish to be and/or consider themselves Jewish, there is invariably an intriguing story to be told. One such story concerns the converts of San Nicandro, Italy.

Esther and Eleazer Trito live in Israel on a small kibbutz near the town of Birya in the Galilee, not far from the holy city of Safed. Many of their friends and neighbors from the original group that emigrated from Italy to Israel in 1949, and their children and grandchildren, now also live in Ashkelon and Acco. The group is fully observant of Jewish law and tradition and, except for some songs and customs (*minhagim*) traceable to their national origin, are indistinguishable from other Israelis. As with all other non-Ashkenazim, they are categorized as Sephardim. A few years ago, when Israel radio and TV broadcast Pope John Paul's historic visit to Rome's Central Synagogue, where the members of the original group were converted in 1948, they watched with special interest.

Their story began in 1931 in the town of San Nicandro, province of Bari, in southeastern Italy. They were agricultural workers eking out a living on the rocky soil, artisans, and laborers. In the ensuing years, Italy's Fascist government drew closer to Germany, but such matters were outside the world of these isolated people.

The main feature of their lives was their fascination with Donato Manduzzio, a healer, wise man, religious teacher, teller of tales, and singer of songs. Manduzzio was a seeker of meaning and a dreamer. He found in the Bible a truth and an identity which he succeeded in teaching his disciples and instilled in them a sense of shared history and identification with the Israelites. Their isolation was such that only when a traveler passing through the region informed them that in Rome, Florence, and Turin there were communities of descendants of the ancient people did they seek to become part of the existing Jewish community.

The following year the Chief Rabbi of Rome, intrigued by reports about Manduzzio and his "congregation" of new Jews, sent emissaries to inquire into the matter. This led to a constructive relationship between the Jewish establishment in Rome and the flock of Donato Manduzzio. The Jews of San Nicandro constituted an autonomous religious community until 1946, when they were fully integrated into Italian Jewry following circumcision and mikveh ceremonies in Rome.

In 1949, in a joyous departure, the group of about sixty left for Israel carrying little with them except sacks of seed from their small plots which they hoped to plant in new furrows in Israel. So imbued were they with their biblical identity that they truly felt they were going home. Manduzzio (1885–1948), like Moses, never reached the Promised Land, but he is remembered as the patriarch of the Jews of San Nicandro.

The possibility that Donato Manduzzio and his followers were of Spanish Jewish origin cannot be completely ruled out. It is known that in the fifteenth and sixteenth centuries Spanish and Portuguese Jews and secret Jews found refuge in Italy and led Jewish lives in cities such as Livorno, Pitigliano, and Ferrara. In the area of San Nicandro, which was ruled by French Bourbon nobility,

Jews were forcibly converted to Christianity, and some San Nicandro Jews still cherish the possibility that their conversion to Judaism represents a return to centuries-old roots.

22

Uganda

Meet the Abayudaya Jews of Uganda
Aaron Kintu Moses

The history of Abayudaya dates from 1919, when an eastern Uganda governor, Semei Kakungulu, read the Bible and realized nothing but Judaism from his study. He circumcised all his sons and followers and had himself circumcised on the same day. He opened a collective settlement for three thousand of his followers, who declared themselves "Abayudaya," meaning "descendants of Judah" in a native language. According to Samson Mugombe, one of his followers, Kakungulu was influenced by Isaiah 56:1–8 and Ezekiel 47:22–23.

Kakungulu met in Kampala, Uganda's capital, with Yosefu, a Jew believed to have come from Israel, and obtained instruction from him. As a result, the nascent community began observing Pesach, Sukkot, Shabbat, etc. According to Mubale, one of the three thousand followers, ten lashes were given to anyone found violating the Shabbat, such as by lighting a fire thereon.

I'm personally very confident to write that our fathers were very serious concerning their Judaism, given the fact that 1919 was a period when Jews in many countries were persecuted and hunted. Even though they were called "Christ killers," such danger could not threaten their unity.

As for my generation, we are Abayudaya as a tribe and nothing else. We are linked with different customs and traditions from those of our neighbors. We are criticized because of this, and yet we don't have or need any alternative.

During the 'sixties and early 'seventies, when Uganda shared diplomatic ties with the land of Israel, the community received many Israeli visitors, among them Arye Oded, the first secretary of the embassy of Israel to Uganda. He wrote the history of the community and made plans for two of our youths to go for a rabbinical course in one of the yeshivas in Israel, but this plan was frustrated by Idi Amin, who took over in 1971 and the following year declared the expulsion of all Israelis within forty-eight hours.

Presently a few of our members make gradual visits to both the synagogue and the Israeli embassy in Nairobi, but at present no one from the community has ever been to Israel.

Following the Ethiopian airlift to Israel, the Abayudaya gained hope also to migrate and thus fulfill what was said in Isaiah and Ezekiel.

We observe Rosh Hashanah. Tekiah is read by the reader and repeated by the congregation, but we lack the shofar. The service for Rosh Hashanah is read. On Sukkot we build the sukkah, and services for Sukkot are read from the siddur. On Simchat Torah we dance around the synagogue and rejoice for the completion and beginning of the Torah. On Chanukah we light the candles, one every evening, and we sing Chanukah songs taught to us by Douglas King (an English Jew). On Purim, following the fast of Esther, the Megillah is read, and whenever Haman's name is mentioned the congregation shouts "*Akolimirwe*," a native Ugandan word meaning "accursed be he." We celebrate when the Book of Esther, 9:27 is read—"and the Jews vowed to celebrate Purim together with those who join them."

On Tu Beshevat we plant trees at the synagogue and around our homes. On Pesach we make the seder. It was only last year that we received matzot from the Israel embassy in Kenya; otherwise we have been making our local unleavened bread. The searching of the leaven is also done. We eat the bitter herbs, and leavened bread is not found in our homes from the first night (fifteenth of Nissan) through the seven days. We read the Haggadah in both English and Hebrew. On Shavuot we eat fruits, as it is a season of mangoes, oranges, guavas, and jackfruits. Also these are brought to the synagogue and members celebrate the giving of the Torah with joy; the Ten Commandments are read while the congregation is standing. Chag Ha-azmaut is realized, and prayers for the welfare of the State of Israel and the Israel Defense Forces are read.

We have a tape with two compositions, one ours and the other of a London Jew, Douglas King, who visited our community one Chanukah. We also have music from our youth group.

During the past, the congregation lost most of its numbers due to intermarriage. In a meeting of Abayudaya elders, held in August 1989, it was resolved that he who marries outside will be denied the right to be a Muyudaya, a Jew, and I can assure you that we are quite serious with the whole issue; even our young men and women are gaining interest in this. Polygamy has been utterly discouraged.

The other information I can include is that we are facing some small-scale persecution. Words like "*Abayudaya batta Yesu*," meaning "Jews are Christ killers" are always directed toward us. During the Gulf War, Muslims around us were saying, in native language, "Israel will be smashed together with the Abayudaya community." In 1988 our youths organized themselves in a kibbutz program and were making bricks for our new synagogue. They faced torture, imprisonment, extortion, blackmail, and harassment by the local authorities, mounted mainly by Muslims who had planned to confiscate their bricks and convert the synagogue land to the neighboring school authority. But, fortunately, the government in power is behind religious tolerance for all beliefs and, after appeals by our youths to high authorities, this crisis was cooled.

Our knowledge of Judaism is limited due to lack of instruction. We believe with perfect faith that if instructed and with continued efforts to curb isolation, we shall enjoy more experiences in Judaism than at present. No step has been made possible for our group to convert officially. It was only in 1991 when Rabbi Moshe of Nairobi Hebrew Congregation made a formal invitation of the group to go to Nairobi (Kenya), but due to lack of travel documents, this process was not effected and Rabbi Moshe did not stay long in Kenya. I can assure you that we long very much to convert, and any effort to do so is much welcome with great appreciation by members of the community.

Chronology of an Historic Visit

Headed by Rabbi Jacques Cukierkorn, and sponsored by Kulanu, a fourteen-member delegation of American Jews visited the Abayudaya in June 1995. This chronology, traced through Kulanu newsletters, records how the historic meeting took place.

Autumn 1994
Are the Abayudaya Jewish?
Rabbi Jacques Cukierkorn

To the surprise of many congregants, I once preached that I wish I had been born a gentile, so that I could choose, of my own will, to be Jewish—since in my opinion being Jewish is such a wonderful thing.

Apparently, the Abayudaya congregation of Mbale, Uganda, agree with me. They are the most unique of all the Jewish groups I have ever dealt with, because they do not have, nor claim to have, Jewish ancestry. Their connection with Judaism, the Jewish people, and the one and living God is purely spiritual. After studying the Bible, they chose to follow the Jewish religion, because they realized that it is the one that would bring them closer to the Creator.

Answering my original question: No, the Abayudaya are not Jewish. However, they are thoroughly motivated to become full Jews. They have already started living as Jewish a life as they can. They still need a lot of support in educational material, prayerbooks, and other religious objects. The ultimate support they need is a rabbinic conversion, which I would consider officiating upon after careful examination of each individual case.

A first step toward helping the Abayudaya is to make their story known. I believe that if some of us could go to Uganda and document their story and lifestyle, it would be a great push to their cause.

In their search for a Jewish identity, the Abayudaya are a source of inspiration for all of us. They reaffirm the beauty of the Brit, the covenant between God and the Jewish people.

Autumn 1994
Visit the Abayudaya If You Can!
Julia Chamovitz

Something most remarkable happened to me back in the fall of 1992, and I want to share with Kulanu readers some thoughts on my good fortune. While doing undergraduate work in Kenya, I met a group of people called the Abayudaya. This was not just any group of people; the Abayudaya are a group of Jews living in Mbale, Uganda.

Imagine walking into a synagogue made of mud and straw, saying the Shema in Hebrew, English, and Luganda, and sharing a siddur with African women and children.

This is an experience I hope many of you will be able to have on an upcoming Kulanu trip to Uganda. This trip promises to be one of the most meaningful trips of your life. It's hard to put into words the thoughts, love, and excitement you will feel toward the Abayudaya. It is an experience that will move you and make you appreciate what Judaism means to people all over the world.

One of the promises I made to the Abayudaya before I left was that I would help them emerge from isolation from the rest of the Jewish world. The Abayudaya crave information and contacts. We have a responsibility!

Autumn 1994
The Abayudaya Changed My Life
Matthew S. Meyer

The following consists of excerpts from an address Meyer gave at Beth Shalom Congregation in Wilmington, Delaware, in 1992.

A little less than a year ago I stood on this same bimah to talk about why I had decided not to make practicing Judaism a great priority. Well, upon attending Yom Kippur services in Nairobi, Kenya, where I've been studying this past semester, my eyes have been opened to a Jewish community that has inspired me and shaped much of my thinking about all sorts of things in my life. The Shabbat I spent with the Abayudaya community of Mbale, Uganda, a little over a month ago is one that has changed my life. I hope the story I relay to you today will in some way change yours as well.

What both Julia (another American student) and I saw in Uganda was unquestionably a Jewish Friday night service. The service itself was magical. When I heard their *Lecha Dodi* in services, I was quite moved. It was simply one of the most beautiful tunes I had ever heard in a synagogue. I wanted every Hebrew school teacher, every fellow member of the B'nai B'rith Youth Organization, every fellow Jew throughout the world to hear the Abayudaya version of *Lecha Dodi*. It was the magical mix of being Ugandan and Jewish simultaneously that so few Jews in the world have seen previously.

The next day was just as amazing. Julia and I both took part in the Sabbath morning service—I got to have an aliyah, and we both later addressed the congregation. We met with the elders of the community and walked through a second synagogue, of the four total in the community. We celebrated Havdalah together, and Julia taught some Israeli dancing.

As you all know, for an eight-year period in the 1970s, a ruthless man named Idi Amin served as Uganda's head of state. The horrors of Amin have been well documented in terms of Entebbe and Indians being expelled from the country, among other incidents in his reign of terror. Amin also unleashed his reign of terror against the Jews, the Abayudaya. All prayer books were confiscated (many were hidden), their synagogues were leveled, destroyed. The people were given three choices: Muslim, Protestant, or Catholic. As Jews, they were forced into hiding, unable to practice without putting their lives in jeopardy. Under Obote, who followed Amin, they rejoiced. They were allowed to practice, but there was certainly plenty of anti-Semitic feeling.

In 1984, a member of the community traveled twelve hours to Nairobi, having heard there might be a synagogue there. He found the synagogue and explained his story. The Jews of the Orthodox synagogue were indifferent and offered nothing—not even a bed to sleep in. The visitor from Uganda slept outside in a park for two nights.

In 1988, Abayudaya youth developing a kibbutz were beaten and tortured by local groups; there were two other anti-Semitic incidents in 1988–89 committed by local groups and officials, causing many in the Abayudaya community to disperse from living around the synagogue.

These anti-Semitic incidents show the need to bring this community out of isolation. There is anti-Semitism in Mbale, Uganda, because there is a very successful community of about five hundred Jews there, and others have the power to suppress them and get away with it. I thought I learned in Hebrew school that we now have organizations to look out for these things, and that as long as world Jewry keeps its eyes and ears open, there can never be another Holocaust. The need to bring the community out of isolation is probably the single most important thing bringing me before you today.

Next, it is necessary for me to address whether or not these people are actually Jews. Basically, a community leader in Mbale in 1919, Semei Kakungulu, rejected Christianity, learned about Judaism, circumcised himself, and proclaimed himself a converted Jew. He later trained others. That is the foundation of the Abayudaya Jewish community. Now, my dad has been bugging me that such a conversion would not hold up in any Jewish court of law. But months ago, my mom told me how she believes we are descendants of a group of people called the Khazars from Eastern Europe who were self-proclaimed converts to Judaism in the eleventh century. So how am I any more Jewish than Gershom (an Abayudaya), who knows far more than I about the religion itself, and practices far more frequently than I do?

Regardless, if we don't consider the Abayudaya community Jewish, it is merely a technicality in my mind. Let's just send a rabbi there to convert them. If any of you were there rather than here for this Shabbat, hearing the same Haftarah that Dave read for us today, hearing the day read according to the lunar calendar, and hearing a sermon on the morning's passage of the Torah, you would have little doubt that the Abayudaya are Jewish.

I have shared with you only a fraction of the details and stories of one of the most amazing experiences of my life. If you are more interested, please talk to me. Or even better, go and see for yourself one of the most phenomenal and unknown Jewish communities in the world, the Abayudaya of Mbale, Uganda.

Autumn 1994
The Amazing Abayudaya
David Levine

The author served as a Peace Corps Volunteer near Mbale, Uganda, through July 1993.

I attended Shabbat services with the Abayudaya a number of times and tried to raise money for the completion of their synagogue.

The Abayudayas' devotion to their faith is truly amazing, considering the isolation from the rest of the Jewish world that they face and the persecution that they face—though this is less pronounced than it may have been during Idi Amin's time.

The Abayudaya are seeking ways of furthering their religious education and are hoping for the prospect of conversion and acceptance by organized Jewry. Though the Abayudaya may not be officially converted or as steeped in tradition (through centuries of Jewish practice) as other groups, their story should be told for their steadfastness in their belief in Judaism, their eagerness to learn more, to become converted to Judaism, and to get in contact with the worldwide Jewish community.

They deserve our attention. Anything we can do to relieve their isolation will help them become stronger in their faith. Any assistance we can bring to them will be received with a sincerity and joy that will surpass expectations.

Winter 1994–95
Come with Us to Uganda!
Rabbi Jacques Cukierkorn

I am very excited because our trip to visit the Abayudaya Congregation in Uganda is approaching rapidly. I know this is going to be a memorable trip. I have been communicating with the Abayudaya, and they are waiting eagerly for us.

Trying to organize a trip to Africa is certainly one of the most challenging things I have ever attempted! Having spent several hours on the phone with Kulanu members and tour operators, I have finally arrived at definitive plans for our trip.

We will depart the evening of June 12, 1995, from JFK Airport, New York, via Sabena Airlines and arrive in Brussels, Belgium, the next morning. On that evening we will fly directly to Entebbe Airport, Uganda, arriving the morning of June 14. We will spend that day and night in Kampala, the capital, resting and/or sightseeing. On the morning of June 15 we will depart, via minivan and driver, for the three-hour road trip to Mbale, the town that is home to the Abayudaya. We will remain there for five days, staying with families or, if you require running water and electricity, in a local guest house or hotel.

While in Mbale we will spend a Shabbat with the Abayudaya and also use our time to better acquaint ourselves with them and their practices. And we will be teaching them some basic concepts of Judaism. I am hoping that each Kulanu participant will take responsibility to lead a teaching session on some facet of Judaism. We would like to set up a continuous learning program that can be accomplished through correspondence, to prepare those who are interested in formal conversion to Judaism.

I am hopeful that Matt Meyer, an American living in Kenya who is familiar with the Abayudaya, will join us in Uganda. He is a very knowledgeable and resourceful young man, and I feel he will greatly facilitate our stay in Uganda.

We will be bringing the community religious articles and other gifts.

There is a possibility that Lisa Kaufman, a young film maker from New York, will be joining us to produce a documentary on the unique story of the Abayudaya, and Kulanu's work with the Abayudaya. She is seeking funding, and is optimistic that the film will become a reality.

There is also the possibility for a hike up Mount Elgon, an extinct volcano right in the Abayudayas' backyard. It has the largest external surface area of any single mountain in the world.

We will return to Kampala June 20, with another hotel overnight.

Spring 1995
Mission Prepares Departure to Uganda
Karen Primack

As we go to press, participants on Kulanu's study/teaching mission to Uganda are just days away from departure. Rabbi Jacques Cukierkorn will lead the group of fifteen to visit the Abayudaya Congregation at Mbale, in eastern Uganda.

At a recent pre-trip meeting, Rabbi Cukierkorn commented that it was auspicious that the group was preparing to assist in training new Jews as the world was celebrating the fiftieth anniversary of the Nazi surrender and the end of the Second World War.

The Abayudaya, a group of about five hundred indigenous Africans of the Baganda tribe, embraced Judaism in 1919 and have been leading Jewish lives ever since.

The purpose of the trip is twofold. First, it will study the form of practice this congregation has developed in relative isolation over the decades, as it was taught by occasional Jewish travelers who happened to pass through Mbale. It is already known, for example, that the Abayudaya have set familiar Jewish prayers and songs to traditional African rhythms and melodies.

Second, it will fulfill the congregation's desire to learn more about Judaism. Each member of the mission will be prepared to impart some facet of Jewish religion and culture to the African hosts. Topics range from holiday observances and lifecycle events to history, music, and Talmud.

Rabbi Cukierkorn summed up the mission: "We will learn from them and try to teach them a little." He noted that this would be the first of many contacts, to "assess what they know and what they don't, and to call world Jewry's attention to their story."

The Kulanu representatives will also deliver educational materials and gifts to the Abayudaya, including children's books on Hebrew language and Jewish history and a student Torah scroll.

The Kulanu representatives are residents of New York City, Baltimore and Silver Spring, Maryland, and Alexandria, Virginia. Participants are Orthodox, Conservative, and Reform Jews, and include lawyers, social workers, a physician, students, and retirees.

For all their devotion to Jewish practice, the Abayudaya have never been formally converted to Judaism, and this is their most basic desire. Rabbi Cukierkorn hopes to plan a course of study that, over a year or two, might lead to conversion. The visitors will brief the congregation on the various forms Judaism takes across the globe and explain the options for conversion to the various denominations of Judaism.

Rabbi Cukierkorn seeks the participation of other rabbis interested in assisting the Abayudaya in any capacity.

June 1995
Sweet Anticipation in Uganda
Matthew S. Meyer

Jokes and laughter flew like an eagle in the hut next to Moses Synagogue on Wednesday, June 14, 1995. Enos tried to do a little Hebrew improvisation. One of about five hundred native Africans practicing Judaism in a village outside Mbale, Uganda, the young boy forgot his lines. Gershom Sizomu, the youth leader who wrote the play about the community's founder, sighed in frustration. Everyone laughed and Gershom smiled, a little nervously. Enos tried to perfect his Hebrew. He had performed the play many times before for his community. But today the visitors were coming, and the practice was not a regular one. June 14, 1995, was not a regular day for the Abayudaya.

On the morning of Wednesday, June 14, I approached the Mbale Total Petrol station as I had on so many previous occasions, eager to start a visit with my friends in Uganda, the Abayudaya community of Jews. Nehemiah Jabingo, a gas attendant and treasurer of the Abayudaya, peered at me through the glass windows of the station. The contrast of his bright white eyeballs and his dark black face struck me. His eyes fixed on mine as we jogged toward one another, simultaneously our lips stretched into wide smiles and we embraced as old friends do. "Shalom, shalom!" Nehemiah said. But his enthusiasm and excitement, a normal reaction the Abayudaya have when receiving visitors, hastily waned. He was nervous, and I could tell. Today, things were different.

"When are they coming?" I shrugged and shook my head. "Well, Joab went to pick them up in Kampala." (Joab Jonadab Keki is the community's chairman.) "They should come back today," he added, "maybe at two in the afternoon. Maybe even this morning by eleven." There was a stilted pause. Nehemiah bought me a Coke and asked, "Do you think they are really coming?"

"I was about to ask you the same thing," I said. I sat and talked with Nehemiah for a few minutes. "When they come," I added, "tell them I am at the shop on Kumi Road." It was nearly nine o'clock. In two hours they would arrive, I thought.

The day was to be an historic one for the Abayudaya. Fifteen American Jews from Kulanu were about to visit. The community, visited previously by about twenty Jews from outside Uganda in all of its seventy-year history, was about to have fifteen American Jews visiting for days, maybe even weeks. A rabbi would daven in Moses Synagogue on Nabugoye Hill. Individuals within the Abayudaya could test their thoughts and theories on the Torah and Jewish practice on fifteen others as they had on me. And the community, for better or worse, would be transformed forever. And that's okay, I thought, staring at the beautifully majestic Wanale

Mountain, its vast face looking down upon the town as a father would a child. I knew what the Abayudaya did not. The Americans were about to see Judaism practiced on the hills of Wanale as they had never seen it practiced before.

I stopped and turned back to see Nehemiah smiling toward me as I walked away. It is amazing how they make faraway visitors feel so at home. No, maybe it would not be okay, I thought. Two and a half years ago I accidentally landed on a spiritual gold mine, an amazing community with no electricity and no running water that had a wealth so many of us, driving the finest cars and making good money back home, do not have. I wanted others to see, to learn. I longed for the day when a rabbi could come and see the Abayudaya, who lived kosher lives, had bar and bat mitzvahs, and kept the Sabbath very, very holy. I longed for the day when other Jews could hear the electricity in Moses Synagogue when the guitar started to play and the harmonies of the Abayudaya's *Lecha Dodi*, welcoming the Sabbath Queen. I also knew they longed for this day, the day when they could learn our *Lecha Dodi* and learn how we practiced our Judaism. But would theirs disappear? Might the wealth be lost?

I had met Gershom two and a half years earlier in the Nairobi synagogue. He had told me about the community. He had shown me some pictures and invited me to visit. To his surprise, six weeks later, Julia Chamovitz and I accepted his offer and went to Mbale, Uganda, for Shabbat. They celebrated us from the moment we arrived at the Mbale Total Petrol Station until we left. We sang and danced, we taught a little and learned a lot. And after Havdalah, amidst Julia's and my excitement, came a plea, to aid the community that Abayudaya leaders saw deteriorating before their eyes. A community practicing Judaism in the isolation of the villages of Uganda once numbered two thousand. Now there were about five hundred. The Jewish resources were far too few to feed the Abayudayas' hunger to learn and practice Jewish ways. They had enough food to eat, but hoped their spirit would one day soar as

Jews would recognize them as equal partners around the world. Bringing a rabbi and many visitors was part of that process.

After Havdalah they read to Julia and me a list of specific questions about marriage and funeral rituals, as well as about the laws of kashrut. Sitting in a mud hut in eastern Uganda, listening to Gershom read his list that pushed my knowledge of Judaism to its limits and beyond, I thought, "This is when my mom would tell me I should have paid more attention in Hebrew school." "Let's make a list," Julia suggested, and we did. A synagogue, a Torah, siddurim for all in synagogue, and even a rabbi. Toward the end of our meeting, Julia and I looked at one another and laughed. We guaranteed nothing. We could not mislead this group of kind and generous people. These were distant dreams.

I arrived home in December 1992. The mere size and material beauty of my synagogue at home, in Wilmington, Delaware, overwhelmed me. I knew the synagogue to be humble by American standards, but to me it stood as an object of material beauty, with its beautiful Torah scrolls and padded seats, the huge sanctuary and fabulous stained-glass windows. And yet, more and more, I found congregants absorbed with the beauty. "Do we go to synagogue to practice Judaism or to listen to nice organ music and gaze at the luxurious windows?" A question I could not answer. A question I cannot answer. I began to realize how much I had learned from my Mbale Shabbat.

The Abayudaya wanted more Jews to come and teach. I wanted more Jews to go and learn. I wrote some letters. I sent out tapes and pictures and even did a slide show. Most laughed at me, several laughed with me, and a few said, "I must go." One was a rabbinical student in Cincinnati. His name was Cukierkorn, and he had a cool Brazilian accent, as I discovered when we spoke on the phone about his dissertation on lost Jewish groups. He had a plan for the Abayudaya that could one day lead to their official conversion. And he wanted to go. Brown University Hillel raised money to build a synagogue in Mbale, and scores of people, including many congregants from home, sent siddurim. My mother worked tirelessly to find a Torah. She found several. In the fall of 1994, shortly after graduating university, I moved to Nairobi, Kenya. In November, I brought the Abayudaya their first Torah ever, donated by Beth Shalom of Wilmington, Delaware.

Two years earlier, following my first visit, we traded audio tapes with the Abayudaya. They gave me their fantastic music. In exchange, several friends of mine recorded Hebrew songs and sent tapes to the Abayudaya. It was a wonderful exchange, I thought, and I made sure they received more music than I did. When I returned for Shabbat in November 1994, their synagogue service consisted primarily of American versions of Hebrew songs. The beautiful harmonies and melodies that had planted my heart's seeds firmly in the soil of Nabugoye Hill were gone from the weekly service at Moses Synagogue. I struggled to explain to them the value of their songs over ours. They saw the beauty of the American *Lecha Dodi* as I saw theirs. My attempts to aid a community had dented it. Would the American visitors be any different in accelerating the regressive process I had begun?

On the Shabbat in November 1994, as we walked the many-mile journey to shul carrying the bag holding the community's Torah, Joab told me he had received a letter from Rabbi Jacques Cukierkorn. He wanted to bring a group of Americans from a new organization named Kulanu. A little less than eight months later, Nehemiah and I stood outside, nervously looking into one another's eyes, both in disbelief at what was about to transpire. And then we waited. I finished my Coke and walked to the Abayudaya Community Store on Kumi Road. Gershom's younger brother, Seth, stood alone in the store. He saw me and embraced me, "Shalom, Matty Meyer, SHALOM!!" he said. We smiled. Then Gershom arrived, as did his elder brother, Aaron Kintu Moses.

After a brief greeting, Gershom exclaimed, "I think he will convert us!" I laughed and shook my head. The Abayudaya's dedication and commitment to Judaism inspired me. Gershom wanted to be a Jew, no questions asked. And so did Aaron. Like many in the congregation, Aaron had suffered for practicing his Jewish beliefs. In 1989, a local official demanded that he and others in the community leave the sukkah where they were sleeping. The local police paraded many from the community across town, shirtless and at gun point, and forced them to pay a fine. Such hostility and hatred have been a part of Abayudaya life through the years. "It is part of being a Jew, isn't it?" Uri once asked me.

At noon, we all began to feel impatient. Aaron wore a wide smile and said, "I think this is a joke. No rabbi is coming. No one is coming. We are sitting here for nothing. Waiting for what?" There was nervous laughter, for Seth, Aaron, Gershom, and I knew, deep in our hearts, that Aaron was probably right. "Well, let us just wait and see," Gershom concluded. "We must take what God delivers to us." So we waited.

After two tea breaks, two naps, and many hours of waiting, I turned to Gershom. "Six o'clock," he said. Seth had left to go home. The sun began to dip beneath the horizon. It was time to start the three-mile walk back to Abayudaya headquarters on Nabugoye Hill. We did not want to leave. The three of us had been together two and a half years earlier on a Havdalah evening when we had decided to find a rabbi to visit the Abayudaya. And there we stood, years later, Aaron, Gershom, and I, our hopes dashed. What had happened?

Two and a half years earlier, Joab also sat with us as we mapped out a dream future for the Abayudaya. A central plot to the dream of the Abayudaya community was the arrival of a rabbi in Mbale. At that very moment, as we began our journey through the hills of Mbale, Joab and the community were on Nabugoye Hill at Moses Synagogue, greeting the visitors with song and joy. When we arrived at the headquarters, the guests were gone, but excitement beamed from all corners. Joab eagerly told us every detail of the group's journey from Entebbe. We listened in disbelief as he told us how the American visitors had ascended Nabugoye Hill and how the Abayudaya had greeted them in song.

As Gershom, Aaron, and I gazed at one another, doubting that the visitors had actually stood on Nabugoye Hill, we began to prepare for the coming days' events. A rare hastiness, even slight panic, came across the faces of the community's leaders. These were the most important visitors the community had ever hosted. It was time to rearrange and reconstruct the tentative schedule the Abayudaya had written. They knew that the planning needed to be extensive.

We had twelve hours until the Kulanu visitors returned to the village from the hotel where they were staying. The rehearsal began. I was the sample visitor. Each member stood up and gave a sample speech. There were a few sample songs. All went well until little Enos rose and began to do his play in Hebrew on the founding of the Abayudaya community. I did not understand a word, but Gershom did and his face indicated anxiety. Everyone laughed, and Gershom smiled, a little nervously. Enos struggled through the Hebrew. Gershom had written the play months ago for the youths. He had worked with them to get the Hebrew just right. "I always nod appreciatively," I told them. "I do not know what you are saying." But if the Hebrew is wrong, many of these visitors would know. Gershom knew it, too. This was the first time his play would be performed before a critical audience. It was important to Gershom as a teacher that the Hebrew be read correctly when Enos stood up with an open Bible.

The visitors arrived the next morning. They all formed immediate bonds with the community, whether it was Rhoda, who thrived on her intense philosophical discussions with Gershom, Sarah, and others, or Bill, who spent his days trying to teach adobe-brick construction techniques as developed by Native Americans. The next day Enos did not miss a line, but someone forgot to bring the Bible, and the audience we feared would be so critical reacted sympathetically, much as Enos's brother and sister Abayudaya do. Gershom tried to stall while Enos ran to get the Bible. The Old Testament is the foundation of Abayudaya community life. There was a silent delay that slowly evolved into wide grins.

I saw Nehemiah seated next to one of the Americans, his whole face smiling freely. My eyes drifted out one of the windows of Moses Synagogue, out across many hills and valleys to where the plateau on top of Wanale met the lone cloud in the sky. There are things I cannot understand, I thought. The mountains meeting the clouds, and people meeting people. I feared the future and thought back to the past. But above all, as Enos scampered back into Moses Synagogue, I cherished the present.

* * *

Two months later I stood underneath the iron sheet that is the roof of the community hut on Nabugoye Hill. The rain poured down from the sky, and the sun shined through it. My brother Jeremy stood at my side, having flown to East Africa to visit me. We stared into the slopes of Wanale, as a double rainbow appeared above it, stretching nearly from one horizon to another. "Wow, this is beautiful," Jeremy said as I stepped out into the rain. "It's more than that," I told him. "It's a dream." And I pictured all of them, Jacques, Karen, Aron, Elaine, Irwin, Lucy, Janet, Bill, Sherri, Joan, the two Joyces, Rhoda, Carolyn, and Lisa davening behind me with Gershom, Sarah, Israel, Esther, Nehemiah, Rachel, Naomi . . .

Summer 1995
Visiting the Ugandan Miracle
Karen Primack

We are at a hilltop village in eastern Uganda, with breathtaking panoramic views, miles from the comforts of electricity and plumbing. A young African woman named Esther, upon receiving a gift of a scarf from a Western visitor, quietly recites the traditional Hebrew blessing for new apparel, thanking God for clothing the naked (. . . *malbish arumim*).

Even with meticulous preparation—reviewing correspondence from the community, interviews with other visitors, a traveler's home video, a tape recording of their Hebrew and African renditions of traditional liturgy—I was not prepared for the Abayudaya.

I knew that this community of five hundred had been leading Jewish lives since 1919, when their leader embraced Judaism. I knew that they didn't work on Shabbat, that they celebrated all the major and minor holidays, that they davened a complete Shabbat service, Torah reading and *drash* included. And I knew they were seeking formal conversion to Judaism. What I did not appreciate was their deep understanding of and commitment to Judaism.

I was part of Kulanu's five-day study/teaching mission to Uganda, a delegation of fifteen Orthodox, Conservative, Reform, and Reconstructionist Jews led by Rabbi Jacques Cukierkorn.

We arrived late one afternoon after a long but scenic drive from Entebbe Airport, passing green hills lush with mango trees, cassava, sugar cane, banana trees, corn, and millet. We stopped in Jinja to see the source of the Nile River in Lake Victoria, and again near Tororo to admire a family of baboons watching the sparse traffic at the roadside. We were in a van driven by a Muslim named Kikomeko Muhammed.

At our destination, the village of Gangama, we were joyously greeted by fifty Africans singing *Hevenu Shalom Aleichem* and *Hava Nagila* accompanied by a guitar and the ululations of women. We tried to ululate back, but we could only laugh and sing and just share the emotional moment.

We all piled into the new, almost-completed synagogue, financed in part by Brown University Hillel. The building's dirt floor is not yet paved, and the open-air windows are not yet paned or shuttered. Balloons decorated the ark, where a simple white curtain hung. A brief welcome ceremony featured more songs and introductions. In his greeting, Cukierkorn commented on the congregation's singing of *Hiney Ma Tov*, which translates "How good to sit as brethren together." He said, "All of us from Kulanu are your brothers in spirit because we are one in faith, one in hope, and one in destiny." Simultaneous translation into the local language, Luganda, was provided, and we soon learned that the Luganda word for "Jews" is *Abayudaya*.

Our hosts treated us to a feast of homemade bean samousas (Indian filled pastry triangles), hard-boiled eggs, and orange sodas as the sun set over nearby Mount Elgon.

Our delegation included three graduate students in film at Columbia University who had received a partial equipment grant from Robert Halmey of Hallmark Entertainment to cover "the interaction between American Jews and the Abayudaya community." They will be seeking further funding to complete the project. In addition one colleague, Lucy Steinitz of Baltimore, took thorough notes throughout the visit in preparation for a cover article on our trip for the *Baltimore Jewish Times*.

A Song Called "We Shan't Give Up"

On our second day, we visited the local "public" school (fees are charged) and witnessed 260 students in uniform, aged six to sixteen, standing in lines singing a medley of songs that included *David Melech Yisrael*. We were told that 180 of the pupils were Abayudaya.

Next, at an assembly in the main synagogue (there are four in all), a small choir of young adults and a talented soloist, the diminutive thirteen-year-old Rachel, sang a song called "You Are Welcome." This was followed by the Abayudaya "motto song," which features the refrain "We shan't give up," arranged with words from the Twenty-third Psalm, in an infectious African rhythm.

After further introductions of Abayudaya community and youth council officers and local teachers who had come for the ceremony, the congregation staged a Shabbat service (it was Thursday) at our request so that filming could be done.

The service was reminiscent of those in many American shuls, except that cocks were crowing in the background. The leaders were fluent in Hebrew and knowledgeable about davening. Women and older men joined in more often when a psalm was sung in the vernacular, Luganda. In his *drash* about chapter 12 of Numbers, the chairman of the congregation, Joab Jonadab ("JJ") Keki, pointed out that Moses was chosen as God's leader over Aaron and Miriam, even though he, was younger than they. He then commented, partly in jest, that both he, at thirty-four, and Rabbi Cukierkorn, at twenty-eight, were relatively young but served as leaders.

Abayudaya men wear attractive kippot with six-pointed stars knitted in. They look remarkably like the headgear worn by Muslims—not surprising since they are knitted by one of the Abayudaya's Muslim neighbors. The Abayudaya are on very good terms with all their neighbors, Christian and Muslim. Muhammed, our driver, had known the Abayudaya previously and attended many of the sessions with the Kulanu delegates.

Moving Discussion at the Flat Rock

After a lunch of sweet bananas, pineapple, and bean samousas, the leaders of the congregation and of the Kulanu delegation settled down on a flat rock for a frank discussion about Abayudaya beliefs and motives.

The Abayudaya have a certification of registration from the Uganda government as a nongovernmental organization formed for the "propagation of Judaism" and other charitable purposes.

In response to Cukierkorn's question, "Why do you want to be a Jew?" Aaron Kintu Moses, secretary of the community, voiced the opinion that Jewish traditions are very preferable to the African traditions practiced around them, such as female circumcision, demeaning dances done in the nude by older males as a circumcision ritual, and the indiscriminate ritual slaughter of animals. He said that embracing Judaism is in part a way to reject the "harsh" environment.

Cukierkorn continued the exchange, referring to periodic outbreaks of Ugandan anti-Semitism: "I assume Uganda is not the best place in the world to be Jewish. Why would you want to take upon yourself such troubles? Judaism doesn't say that to go to Heaven, to be saved, you have to be a Jew. If you are a good person, that's enough."

Keki reminded the listeners that he had been born into Judaism, since his father had been a follower of Semei Kakungulu, the Baganda warrior leader who had embraced Judaism seventy-five years before. "I was raised Jewish; it was already in my environment. Now I realize that someone might question my Judaism. I read in the Bible that it is possible to convert to Judaism and that God treats those who convert as Jews." He also cited Isaiah 56 concerning the acceptance by God of the mitzvot of strangers and the ingathering of the dispersed of Israel.

Cukierkorn: "What do you hope to gain?"

Keki: "When you die there is eternal life."

Gershom Sizomu, twenty-four, who leads most of the services, observed, "In Jewish observances there is civilization. If you practice Judaism you become civilized. Shabbat is a benefit, too. If you rest, there is refreshment for your body.

"The Bible shows that God loves Israel very much, more than any nation and language in the world.

"Another benefit is that precious instrument, the Torah. To be Jewish is to submit to the Torah. There is no physical benefit that you get from observing Shabbat directly. But we hope that in the world-to-come we shall have a share in the good that God will bestow on His people, and we shall share it together. We shall also be called God's people. That's why we have chosen not to miss that."

Cukierkorn: "Would you want to move to Israel?"

Sizomu: "I can only speak for myself. The land of Israel is significant in the eyes of every Jew because it is the land of freedom. It is the land in which the Jew gains his freedom to observe the mitzvot. Given the fact that the land of Israel was so, so important that the whole Bnei Yisrael who came out from Egypt didn't even have entrance there—because of their misconduct they had to die in the wilderness—if I got the chance to go to the land of Israel, that would give me a lot of joy."

Keki: "When we became Abayudaya in 1919, there was no State of Israel, but our founder knew there would be an Israel, and he talked about going."

Sizomu: "I love Judaism because it is a religion of people who are hated all over the world without reason, people who are just blackened, smeared. Any person who is sensible sympathizes with a person who is hated and mistreated without cause. As we sympathize we are called Jews, and we want to be Jews."

During the reign of Idi Amin, who was president of Uganda in the 1970s, Jews were forbidden to attend services and most of the Abayudaya synagogues were destroyed. Sizomu muses, "I think if Amin's power had continued ten years more, the community would not have survived. But God saved it." The community has experienced more recent problems with local politicians, who harass its members as "God-killers," and in 1988 four of its leaders were imprisoned. Although the harassment is "because of being Jews," Keki judges the ulterior motive to be seizure of their lands.

In response to Cukierkorn's questions about the feasibility of being converted to Judaism, Sizomu says, "We have survived because we were not willing to give up. If Jews came here and told us to stop being Jews, we can refuse because we are not willing to give this up. It is part of us.

"Persecution can come again, but now we shan't perish in isolation. Once we are given recognition, if a force was directed against us, Kulanu could get concerned. If we perish, Kulanu can at least write something—it would not be like dying like a snake in the grass."

Another young leader, Israel Ben Shadruk, noted, "Our beginning wasn't precipitated by a Jew from the outside, but from discovery in the Bible that the Jew is the only person who is loved by God, even though he is persecuted everywhere and called Jesus-killer. From that discovery we have decided to be Jews and read directly from the books. If they say, don't cook on the Sabbath, we don't cook.

"Though we are not recognized anywhere, if they refuse to convert us officially and recognize us around the world, we will still remain Jews and observe accordingly.

"I didn't see my first letter from an outside Jew until 1987. But I had heard stories about other Jewish communities outside and I kept my faith. But Kulanu has come and brought us encouragement so that I believe God cannot leave us. People can tell us, No, we shall not convert you. Still, the time will come that God will rescue us and we shall be converted."

Sarah Kaliesubula added another dimension: "Because I am a Jew, I am an example. We are obligated by God with a responsibility. Torah was given to Jews. We are not strong nor rich, but we have hope that God will help us, will convert us."

Sizomu summed up their position: "A person can observe Judaism, and if not converted, he can keep on observing. But we want world Jewry to have concern over us so that we have concern over them. We want to be united, to be in one circle with all the Jews of the world."

Those frank exchanges at the flat rock will stay with all of us for a long time.

At an afternoon assembly, Aaron Kintu Moses reviewed the history of the Abayudaya, beginning with Semei Kakungulu's realization of Judaism from reading the Bible in 1919. As Kintu Moses sees it, "Kakungulu presented it and the people seized it with both hands. The Bible provided clear teachings about peace, unity, freedom, and so many other things. His followers wanted to live as Jews; they circumcised themselves and their sons, and observed the Shabbat. We follow these traditions that make us enjoy Judaism—the leisure we enjoy on Shabbat, the unity we experience during services, the Hebrew language, the original language of the Bible, and the Torah, the book of substance.

"But," he continued, "much as we enjoy our practices, we are limited by the fact that we cannot perform them properly in isolation. The persecution we face and the low level of education that we possess lead us to worry that acceptance of our community by world Jewry is necessary, and we hope that Rabbi Cukierkorn and the Kulanu delegation will take that position."

"You Are An Inspiration For All Of Us"

Cukierkorn responded: "We have brought you some small gifts. You have given us something much more valuable. The love you have for Judaism, the concern you have, is unparalleled. Very seldom have I seen it. I do feel you care tremendously about your relationship to God, and we are committed to making your case known. You are an inspiration for all of us."

The Kulanu delegation closed the assembly with the presentations of gifts donated by Kulanu and individuals and groups in America—a student Torah, books, Jewish educational materials, musical tapes, ritual objects, housewares, toys—received by the Abayudaya with joyous songs, applause, and, of course, ululations.

The next order of business was a tour of another synagogue at Namanyouyi, a sister village a few miles from the main synagogue. In the modest mud structure decorated with wall drawings of Jewish designs, Israel Ben Shadruk demonstrated his drumming technique as he explained that the sounds were used as a shofar (the synagogue has none) and as notification that Shabbat has come. As we walked around, village women warmly admitted us to their simple mud huts, generally consisting of three small rooms with clothes hanging on wall nails, sparse furniture, and an outdoor cooking area. It is not unusual for them to walk a mile or so through corn fields to fetch water from a spring or well.

The Kulanu delegation held a nightly "debriefing" session at our hotel in Mbale. That night, upon considering the hardships of the seventy to one hundred orphans in the Abayudaya community, we immediately established an Orphans Education Fund to help with school fees and expenses.

For Shabbat most of the Americans decided to move from the hotel, a fifteen-minute drive from the synagogue, to sleep on mats in snug quarters in small Abayudaya guest houses with mud walls and tin roofs. In a separate, smoky kitchen space, Abayudaya women were cooking over open coal fires, anxious to finish before the Sabbath was ushered in.

On Shabbat evening and morning it was Cukierkorn's turn to lead services and read the Torah, although the congregation recited the Prayer for the Country (Uganda) in Luganda. At the service Matt Meyer, a young American working in Kenya, delivered a stirring impromptu address. Meyer, who first met the Abayudaya over two years ago when he was a student on a Brown University semester in Nairobi, spoke about the gains the Abayudaya have made in achieving construction of a synagogue, possession of a Torah, and recognition by world Jewry.

At various points throughout the five-day mission, the visitors gave presentations on different topics. Aron Primack, a Silver Spring physician who had studied Swahili (another language used in Uganda) in the past, compared Swahili sayings with sayings from Pirkei Avot. (The following day, he was asked by the Abayudaya leaders to give an impromptu talk on family planning.) Irwin Berg, a New York attorney, spoke on early Jewish history. Bill Katzenstein, a retiree, assisted with construction projects. A session on halacha relating to women was led by Rhoda Posner, a Jewish Family Services worker from Baltimore. My own talk was on the various branches of Judaism as practiced today.

When it was the Africans' turn to bestow gifts, no one was disappointed. Kulanu was presented with an Abayudaya bimah decoration, a menorah sculpture made by one of the congregants. Cukierkorn was given a plaque, and some other individuals were presented with baskets made by Abayudaya women. And, as a personal gift, Esther Kaliesubula (see the opening paragraph) gave me a small straw tote basket, which I cherish.

Cukierkorn's final official act was a moving one—unscrolling the new Torah around the entire congregation, encircling the Africans and Americans together.

Our farewells were tearful. But I am confident that the isolation is over. I know there will be future trips by Kulanu visitors and other Jews around the world who want to get to know these remarkable people. There will be media attention. And Kulanu hopes to raise funds to send a rabbi or Judaic teacher to stay with the community for several months.

Even though I had prepared my talk on pluralism in Judaism before I left the United States, I meant these words I spoke at the conclusion of my talk even more than I had anticipated:

"I hope, as you become more Jewish, you are able to accomplish something that most communities are unable to accomplish—that you can somehow accommodate your differences and still accept each other as equals. If you do, it will be a miracle, but not your first miracle. Your very existence is, to us visitors, a miracle."

Summer 1995
Women-to-Women in Uganda
Rhoda Posner

Three of us were sitting on the rocks under the trees overlooking the valley on a Shabbat afternoon. We (Lucy Steinitz, Janet Kurland, and I) were staff members of Jewish Family Services in Baltimore and members of the Kulanu delegation to Uganda in June to visit the Abayudaya, indigenous Africans who have been practicing Judaism since 1919, when their leader embraced the religion. We were joined by twenty or twenty-five Abayudaya women and a scattering of babies to talk about issues, Jewish women to Jewish women. Sarah Nalunkunia served as the translator from English to Luganda.

Arrayed before us was a group of women, most in *besutis* (their traditional dress with puffy sleeves), and with their heads covered by colorful scarves. They were of varying ages, from early teens to senior citizens, and appeared to sit with the most senior and respected women closer to us and the others farther away. The children freely wandered back and forth from one woman to another.

We opened the discussion by saying how much we were enjoying our visit. We said that we knew that women sometimes didn't speak as freely when there were men present and that they might have several questions that they wanted to discuss. The women laughed readily at this, acknowledging their understanding that women-to-women we could relate differently. We told them that we, too, were mothers and, in one case, a grandmother, and that we were open to any questions they might ask—they did not need to feel shy.

After hesitation, one of them asked us to start talking in order to stimulate the discussion. We briefly talked about the importance of the home in Judaism, the role of women in the traditional home, and the three mitzvahs given primarily to women: to light candles, bake challah, and go to mikveh. This introduction led to more questions and a discussion.

One woman's concern was with lighting candles. It appears that they keep candles burning for their dead for seven days. However, the candles are short, and they find it hard to keep them burning so long. They were amazed that we, in the United States, use a candle that burns for seven days.

They asked what to do if one prays for something and doesn't get it. They wanted to know what to do if one makes an oath and then can't keep it. They had several questions about when and how one can cook on the Sabbath. They had several questions about what to do if they don't have the money to do what is required because Uganda is very poor.

They shared with us the ceremonies that they use for baby naming and bat mitzvah, and one of the younger women described her recent bat mitzvah. They asked questions about when women are allowed into the synagogue; it is their custom for women not to enter when they are menstruating.

In discussing the need for education among women, we learned that almost all could read Luganda, about five could read English, and two said they could haltingly read some Hebrew.

Our answers to them tried to acknowledge their struggle and their efforts, to encourage learning and preservation of their uniqueness as a culture, to empower them to be active partners in their community's decision-making process, and to develop rituals to meet their own needs when none exist.

We were impressed by the ambiance of the session—the easy manner in which they talked and laughed, the children weaving in and out among their mothers, grandmothers, and aunts, and the babies being nursed. Those who had a long walk home and needed to make it back before dark excused themselves and left early.

Their final question was whether it was okay to tell the men what we had talked about. We assured them it was. One of the male leaders had previously shared with us the struggle they have had in trying to go against the dominant culture in the area by allowing the women to eat meat (as men do) and to learn.

The discussion with the women alone was much different from the formal ones at which both men and women were present but mostly the men participated. While the men seemed primarily interested in interpretations of the Bible and in the rituals and halacha of Judaism, the women wanted to know about the practicalities of applying these things in their complex lives.

The best summary was offered by Sarah's comment that we are really not so different. It did appear that, from halfway around the world and from different racial and cultural backgrounds, a group of women had gotten together to talk about mutual concerns.

Summer 1995
Abayudaya, Remember Who You Are!
Matthew S. Meyer

Meyer spoke these words at Shabbat services in Mbale, Uganda, on June 17, 1995.

Two and a half years ago, after Julie (Chamovitz) and I sat through Shabbat morning services in a synagogue right over there that's now a carpentry workshop, your community gave us a chance to say a few things. And today I want to repeat many of the things we said on that day, and I also want to add a few new things.

The first thing I want to say is, I want to thank everyone for coming here. There are a lot of people. And while it's not a very hot day, I can see by the sweat on many of your faces as you walk in that you've had a long, long trip. I feel very honored by your presence.

Two and a half years ago, when I met with Gershom and Aaron and Joab with Julia, we talked about getting four things here. First, a new synagogue, and we've done that. The second was a Torah. Third was a rabbi. And fourth was improving general knowledge around the world about the Abayudaya.

Now, when I say these things, it might seem like, in the past two and a half years, everything has changed. In my mind, very little has changed, because the changes in this community are changes that should come from the inside and not the outside. If you have a Torah or you don't have a Torah, you're still the Abayudaya. And I cannot say for sure, but I would think that many people would tell you that Judaism is not in the synagogue or the mikveh or the Torah, but in the heart.

So, as there continue to be changes in this community, I want you to remember who you are.

There's also a theme that has been running the past two and a half years of my relationship with this community. I met Gershom in the Nairobi synagogue in 1992. He came here and he told you that Julia, a young American woman, and myself, a young American man, were coming. And he tells me at least that people thought he was crazy; they didn't believe him.

And then I came here and Julia came here, and we went back to America, and we told people. And so many of them didn't believe us. They thought we were crazy. But a few of them did believe us, and they came. They're here today. And one thing I want the hosts to realize is that many of the people here are very prominent leaders in their respective communities. And, simply by their coming here, they put their reputations on the line. And the people here are willing to be called crazy and willing to be laughed at back home for something they believe in.

So I just want to thank both the hosts as well as the visitors, because two and a half years ago, five of us sitting in a small room had this crazy dream. And over the past forty-eight hours, before my eyes, I've seen these dreams coming true. So I thank all of you.

Last night, after everyone tried to go to sleep, a group of us were talking about fruit. As I lay in bed early this morning, all that came to my head was, *tumelima, tumelima, tumelima, matunda zimeiba*—"we have farmed, we have farmed, we have farmed; the fruits, they are ready." *Tukule.* "Let's eat!" *Sasa tugende tubiende kulimate.* "Now let us go and dig more for us to eat."

I just wanted to take this opportunity to speak to all of you and to say, from me, thank you very much.

Autumn 1995
Let's Be Activists for the Abayudaya
Rabbi Jacques Cukierkorn

Kulanu's visit with the Abayudaya Congregation in Uganda last June continues to be a great success. I say "continues" because the interest it generated has not abated.

I, personally, as well as other trip participants, have been interviewed. Our mission was featured on National Public Radio and Israeli television. Avi V. Stieglitz wrote a story for the Jewish Telegraphic Agency that appeared in several Jewish newspapers.

The most exciting coverage has come from the *Baltimore Jewish Times*. Not only did it publish a six-page cover story by Dr. Lucy Steinitz, with eight pictures; it also printed a follow-up letter to the editor by trip participant Janet Kurland and ran a very favorable editorial about the Abayudaya!

As a result, Kulanu has gained a tremendous amount of positive attention. Let us not forget, however, that people have short memories, and that the Abayudaya's needs are many. Here are a few suggestions for individuals and groups interested in helping this remarkable community:

(1) Educational needs. The Abayudaya chairman wrote to me that there are over a hundred orphan children who lack the funds to go to school. It costs $36 per year to send a child to school. There are also a few Abayudaya who would like to attend university. That will cost about $2,000 per student per year for tuition alone.

(2) Pen-pal program. Irwin Berg is trying to establish a pen-pal exchange between Abayudaya children and North American Jewish children. We should try to promote this idea in our synagogues and communities.

(3) Lectures and articles. We should try to promote the Abayudaya cause by arranging lectures in our synagogues, Jewish community centers, and federations. Only this way will the Abayudaya cause gain its due recognition. We should also make our rabbis, lay leaders, and other Jewish professionals aware. And we should try to bring their story to local and national Jewish publications.

(4) Travel to Uganda. Many people have already asked me to lead a second mission to the Abayudaya. I believe that would be very productive, especially if the mission were to be formed of lay

and religious leaders who could, upon returning, have a greater impact on their local congregations and communities. Even without a group mission, however, knowledgeable Jewish individuals and families willing to give and receive knowledge from the Abayudaya will always be welcome there.

(5) Fund-raising. It says in the Talmud, "When there is no Torah, there is no flour; and when there is no flour, there is no Torah." In other words, in order to attain our objectives we need money. We encourage the formation of Kulanu chapters across the United States and around the world to engage in education about and fund-raising for the Abayudaya. We hope to produce cassettes of Abayudaya music (settings of Jewish liturgy to African melodies and rhythms). A few hand-made kippot, knitted by the Abayudaya and their friendly Muslim neighbors, have been sold. Rabbi Hershy Worch has suggested setting up looms so they can weave tallitot. The Abayudaya themselves have some ideas, which mainly focus on their local economy, such as setting up a film-developing lab.

(6) Spreading the word. We should increase our lobbying efforts on their behalf. Make your rabbi, federation executives, friends, and family aware of the Abayudaya cause. I also believe we should open contacts with the closest Jewish community to the Abayudaya, in Nairobi, Kenya. They are the ones who could help the most. Perhaps the second Kulanu mission to Uganda should visit and confer with the Nairobi congregation about joining with Kulanu in this endeavor.

I know my list is demanding. Let us remember the saying in Pirkei Avot, "It's not incumbent upon you to finish the job, but neither are you free to desist from it." So, let's take it upon ourselves to do a little on behalf of our Abayudaya brothers and sisters, who are in so much need.

Mikvehs and Cholent in Uganda
Rabbi J. Hershy Worch

It is difficult for me to describe in words without hyperbole my own reaction to the faith and conviction of the Abayudaya. Here are the remnants of a people, reduced in every way but their indomitable spirit, looking to the world as the last means of preserving the threads of worship and joy in the One God, the Living God, the Jewish God.

"Reduced," I say, because it is not at all clear to me that we are not already too late. Were we to take a beth din there tomorrow, and were we to educate them in the practice of Judaism, and were we to convert them en masse according to the halacha, can they ever be a viable community of Jews? They are already so reduced in numbers, so reduced in means and circumstances.

The Jews of Yemen on the Arabian Peninsula may indeed have been poor, but they had a Jewish culture nearly three thousand years old. Rabbis, yeshivot, traditions and infrastructure. Scribes, *dayanim*, *chazanim*, *paytanim*, makers of tefillin and parchment, *shochtim*, cheder teachers, and all the accouterments of a Jewish society designed to last until the coming of the Messiah.

READY TO DIE FOR THEIR RELIGION

Semei Kakungulu, who died in 1928, left the Abayudaya with 20-acre plots of arable earth, scattered hither and thither in Mbale district, and the vision of a glorious ideal, Judaism. For the awareness of the existence of these people to have manifested and registered itself in our consciousness the way it has done, they have already had to travel an immense distance.

The long and short of their story is this:

They are ready to die for the sole reward of being Jewish.

They are willing to die out rather than intermarry with their neighbors.

They are ready to let go of all they have received in the oral tradition of their own elders in order to be accepted into the family of the Jewish people.

According to the halacha as it is understood and administered today, if a group of people considers itself Jewish and is willing to die for this belief, even though they are not Jews halachically, we are all under an obligation to do whatever we can for them.

The Abayudaya have a uniquely African culture of music, food, and clothing. They have a very fragile clan network based upon family ties and leadership hierarchies. It would be cruel and ill-advised to threaten their existence by removing the youngest and fittest, or interrupting their lives in any major way. To introduce someone into their community as teacher and guide who is insensitive to the beauty and fragility of the Abayudaya tradition would be an even bigger crime.

The first and most important job is to provide the Abayudaya with means to improve their health, living standards, and comfort level, as well as to create their own wealth.

OF BRICKS AND MIKVEHS

For days we talked about the mikveh. How many cubic yards of earth would need moving? What type of brick might be used to line the pit? How best to cover the finished mikveh, and how to capture the rainwater?

This is rural Uganda; bricks are made from the wet clay earth you walk on. Air-dried beneath banana leaves in the sun, then stacked in kiln-shaped piles, they are fired in the open air. Families gather to chop firewood and make bricks. Fathers and sons squat for tedious days and nights, stoking and tending, coughing by turns and dreaming of their brick-house. The outside layer of bricks rarely survives the firing process; the rains come and reduce them first to mud and then to the red dust of Africa. Bricks from the center of the stack may have the properties that we, in developed countries, associate with building bricks. They will have been adequately baked. Most, though, will not carry much weight before crumbling, decaying rapidly in water.

The Abayudaya village at Gangama sits on a hill. Drilling down, through to the water-table might involve 50, perhaps more, meters of boring at $50 to $80 a meter, perhaps more.

If the mikveh is to be one of stagnant water, how would hygienic standards be maintained? In a village without running water, what bathing facilities could be realistically designed alongside the mikveh, that might prevent contamination? How many pits would have to be dug?

The more we talked about these problems, the more complex, difficult, and unattainable appeared the solutions. The people understand exactly the ramifications of having a kosher mikveh, and how impossible it would be to achieve recognition as a Jewish community without one. They had only been waiting to be shown how to build it when I arrived.

Old Mishael sat listening. He understood nothing of our conversation, belonging as he does to the generation of Abayudaya who refused primary and secondary education in Christian mission schools. The self-educated Abayudaya, generally, can speak, read, and write six local languages and Swahili, but the youth have English and Hebrew as well. Mishael is mostly blind; cataracts, viral infection, improper nutrition, who knows? On the morning of my departure I gave him 40 pounds sterling to have his eyes examined by an optician. Did he use it for that purpose? Who knows? Perhaps he has some need more pressing than mere eyesight? I cannot fathom the poverty of these people. Every time I think I have its measure, I stumble over a new, previously unthinkable possibility.

Mishael knows the Hebrew Scriptures. A lifetime of study has made the Bible as familiar to him as the footpaths of his mountainside. When Mishael asked me a question, I reached automatically for my Chumash with Rashi commentary.

The first time I found him learning in the synagogue, he was making hard work of reading the Hebrew Bible text. At first I thought his reading skills might be poor, but wondered why the young men hung on to his every stuttered word. It was his eyesight that was failing, not his language skill. It is his chief joy in life to learn the Chumash. Oh, how he knows it! The very first question he put to me was this:

Quoting the text from Genesis, "God said, Let us make man."

He asked, "Who was God talking to, and why ask their permission?"

I showed him the answer in the eleventh-century *perush* (commentary) of Rashi, the most influential and favorite scholar of the Franco-German school, whose commentary is printed in virtually every scholastic edition of the Bible. If I had endowed Mishael with millions, or invested him with the power of prophecy, he could not have been better rewarded. What a smile! To think that he had a thought run through his head like the one Rashi thought!

"Tell it to me again," he said. "Tell it to me one more time."

I soon grew to appreciate the speed of his mind, his wit and erudition. It was easy to forget we were in the heart of postcolonial, post-Idi Amin, AIDS-epicenter Africa, that this man had no idea what a cheder room with a pot-bellied stove smelled like. That he had never seen or heard a shofar blowing, tasted Kiddush wine, challah bread, or seen a Seder plate.

Aaron Kintu Moses, sitting next to me, took the duty of translator. He explained to Mishael the essence of our discussions about the mikveh, responding at length to Mishael's questions about my specifications for the mikveh. I was paying only minimal attention to their conversation when I heard Mishael's characteristic laugh, followed by rapid speech and excited gesticulations.

"Mishael says he can lead us to a place near here where there is a mikveh just like the one of which you speak," Aaron told me.

"Let's go," I said, getting to my feet.

It was uncanny to watch Mishael, the blind old man, complete with white stick, leading us barefoot down the hill. Through farms and small holdings, clusters of mud huts and dense prickly bushes. We came across some children preparing bundles of firewood. Brandishing wicked-looking machetes, called pangas, they were stripping the foliage from a freshly felled tree. We looked at it with dismay. A beautiful jackfruit tree, cut down for firewood. The ground was strewn with unripe fruit, useless, wasted, and testament to the most ignorant and foolish of sub-Saharan agrarian policy. Our small company of Abayudaya men turned away in disgust; there was nothing to say.

We continued tramping through the increasingly taller grass. We hopped and skipped over a small stream of water hidden in the thick underbrush around our feet. Mishael knew exactly where we were going. He stopped suddenly, pointing with his stick to a tall thicket of elephant grass and reeds.

"This is where Kakungulu dipped my mother," he said. "He had his workers dig this pool right here for that purpose."

Aaron, Joab, Gershom, Samson, and others began pulling the foliage out by its roots. Two of them ran off, returning swiftly with pangas borrowed from the tree-felling children. There was growing excitement as we found water. Mishael shouted encouragement to the young men hacking away at the junglelike growth around the mikveh. And, lo, there it was—undeniable, irrefutable, almost inconceivable—a bubbling spring of natural, living water, about eight feet across, the ultimate mikveh.

Shabbos Cholent In Uganda?

It was more than three hours past midnight on a Friday night. I was in Africa, a few minutes north of the equator, close to the source of the river Nile. I was sitting on a wicker chair with my friends the Abayudaya. As I told a story, all around me on the red earthen floor, they were taut with listening. The oldest and youngest of the group snored softly on their bamboo mats. I finished my story.

The dark was overwhelming, palpable; I could not make out a hand in front of my face. It was time for us to retire, to rest, to sleep. But we were much too excited.

"Shall we dance?" I asked. For an answer there came a swish, a rustling of clothing, shuffling feet, and we were dancing. Mine were the only feet in shoes that night as we all danced and danced.

I began singing a simple melody I remembered from my childhood. I had heard it from the Sekulener Rebbe thirty, maybe more, years ago. We held hands and stomped our feet, singing quietly, "*U'vyoim Ha'Shabbos, Shabbos Koidesh, sissu v'simchu . . .*"

A little to one side stood the women, Mamma Debra, Mamma Naom, Mamma Erina, and other intrepid mothers of the tribe, swaying, listening, humming, with their fingers interlaced, their heads nodding.

These women, the tribal mothers, fast too much. If one has a bad dream she declares a fast. When prayers must be answered—a child is sick, a crop is failing—they fast, days and weeks. And perhaps I am too judgmental, but I gave them a rabbinical ruling: Fasts may be subsumed by cash. A few shillings donated to charity is equal to one day of fasting.

I had thought of telling them about the popular European Jewish sublimation, *chai*, the number eighteen, but I stopped myself just in time. There are nearly one thousand Ugandan shillings to the dollar, but eighteen is much too much to suggest as a *pidyon* (redemption) to these holy women who survive by subsistence-farming.

Eventually we slept. In the morning we prayed and I read the Torah. They asked me to speak yet again after davening, but I had already explained the Torah portion as I went through it. "Any rabbi," quipped I, "can speechify at the drop of a hat. But only a truly great rabbi knows when to be quiet."

Actually, I was aware all the time that most of the congregation had walked since dawn to reach the central synagogue where the services were being held that day. None of them had eaten or had anything to drink. I suggested we meet again to talk after lunch.

Only five or six people could eat at one time, there being only five or six plates on which to serve food to the sixty or seventy people gathered there. The elderly and very young were fed first. When Sarah, the reigning baalebusteh, served the cholent which I had so painstakingly prepared, it was greeted with hostility and suspicion. What kind of Shabbos-goy was I, cooking on Shabbos, they wanted to know. What kind of fraudulent Judaism was I trying to sell them here in Uganda, they demanded.

You should have seen the grins on the faces of the young leaders of the community as they showed their elders the Shabbos-oven I had built into the packed earth floor of my bedroom, a shining smile that went from ear to ear. Eighty years they have waited for my cholent, can you imagine, the first hot food on a Shabbos morning for eighty years! Prometheus had no such thrill. Perhaps Moses, watching the Israelites licking their fingers over manna in the wilderness, may have had such naches, maybe.

Most people know nothing about cholent, and those who do probably consider it no more than an odd quirk in the Jewish diet, something akin to gefilte fish or latkes.

To a hushed audience I explained the significance of the food they were eating. How rabbinical Judaism, the halacha, the Talmud well nigh demand hot food on Shabbos morning. This is how we Orthodox Jews may be distinguished from Karaites, Samaritans, and other fundamentalists who rejected the Oral Torah. The hushed silence broke into thunderous applause.

On Friday I had been driven into town. First I bought a new cooking pot with lid and a ladle, wondering all the while how I might *toivel* it (immerse it in a mikveh). The pot resembled something you might buy in a hardware store. It had been made in someone's backyard from salvaged materials. Hub caps, engine blocks, bulldozers—who knows what goes to make up a brand-new cooking utensil in that part of the world? It was unusable in its pristine state. The inside was scoured crudely as though turned on a lathe and hollowed with a blunt instrument. I decided to glaze it as I might a new cast-iron skillet. I went looking for some peanut oil or any kosher edible oil that can withstand high temperatures before igniting. The smallest quantity I could purchase of oil of whose kashrut I was sure came in ten-liter cans.

Mohammed, my guide, driver, and protektsia, businessman and politician (honorably defeated in his 1994 campaign for a parliamentary seat), helped me avoid those beans on sale that had been sprayed with chemicals and were for planting only. He showed me the unsprayed, healthier-looking ones that might be used safely for eating. I found good kidney beans, red and white, black-eyed peas, and other local varieties of legume.

Onions, garlic, salt, pepper, cloves, cumin, and other more esoteric ingredients made up the remainder of my shopping list. I had bottled water purchased in Entebbe on the way from the airport and a bottle of Carmel grape juice, which had traveled rather well from Manchester, England. Two huge loaves of rye bread I had commissioned at the vegan village of Salem-Cologne, where I was renting a grass-thatched hut. I was about ready to begin cooking for Shabbos!

I wanted to avoid getting in the way of the women hard at work in the smoky communal kitchen, so I was given a small portable stove made from condensed-milk tins. It was an ingenious contraption, standing perhaps eight inches off the ground, and fueled by charcoal purchased from the charcoal maker down the road. The main problem with this particular purchase was finding a plastic sack in which to take my charcoal home. Nothing is simple or swift in rural Uganda, where untreated water must be carried on someone's head nearly two miles from a waterhole shared by umpteen villages after waiting in line all morning to fill the jerry-can.

Once the pot was bake-glazed with cooking oil, after I had extinguished the blaze and waited for all the components to cool off again, I boiled some water in it. Then I borrowed a hammer and closed off all the tiny holes leaking the precious water from my new cooking pot. Locals told me that they use grains of soft rice to plug such holes, but my less elegant and more violent solution had quite solved the mikveh problem, once and for all. A pot made by a Jew does not require immersion in a mikveh, and by that time I was sure the pot was my own creation!

After lunch on Shabbos afternoon I met with all the women who had come for the halacha learning. That was when I told them about giving tzedakah (charity) in lieu of fasting. They asked me for the halacha concerning marriages between consanguine cousins of the first remove. I described a chuppa marriage ceremony, the spiderweb-spinning, circling of the bridegroom by the veiled bride, who is led by her mother holding candles. The placing of the ring, the reading of the ketubah (traditional marriage contract), the seven benedictions, and the smashing of the glass beneath the foot of the bridegroom.

There was much deep sighing and wistful remembering as I spoke. Abayudaya women have no wedding rings or jewelry made of precious metal, yet they have romance. They live in mud huts and dream of sufficient candles to light their Friday nights, when most actually make do with smoking naphtha lamps and crude wicks which reek and blacken the ceiling. I am referring to those affluent Abayudaya who can afford to light lamps at night.

"Please," they whispered, "send us someone who will teach us how to use the mikveh properly." They discussed the halachic difficulties around the care of their beautiful wiry black hair on Shabbos. When hair cannot be brushed without pulling out hair, it may not be brushed on Shabbos. At that gathering they decided to adopt a special Shabbos hairstyle, which would be arranged on Friday into tiny plaits and ribbons, obviating the need for combing on Shabbos altogether.

And all the time I was thinking in Yiddish: *"Wer kan schatzen a Yid?"* ("Who can take the measure of a Jew?")

Personally, I feel moved to tears by the Abayudaya. Some part of my heart remains with them in Uganda.

Let's Send Abayudaya Orphans to School
Karen Primack and Matthew S. Meyer

Joab Jonadab Keki, chairman of the Abayudaya Congregation in Mbale, Uganda, recently reported that Kulanu funding has enabled a substantial number of children without means, many of whom are orphans, to attend school.

In the school year 1995–96 a total of eighty-two children of primary school age received partial tuition assistance of $6.25 each (out of a total tuition of $12 per student). In addition, eleven senior school students received $37.50 each; complete tuition at this level is $55 per student.

We are told that many, many children who would otherwise be out of school are schooling because of Kulanu's Lorna Margolis and Clara Shair Orphans Education Fund. There is a whole back-to-school movement, where older children who never thought they would have a chance to go to school are going back. As the reader can probably guess, when money is low the girls are dropped from school before the boys; but a very large number of the beneficiaries are female.

Twelve-year-old Selina Mwamula is one of the orphans being assisted by Kulanu's Margolis-Shair Abayudaya Orphans Education Fund. A student in Standard 3 at Nabweya Primary School in Mbale District, Uganda, Selina enjoys net ball (girls' basketball) and names science as her favorite school subject. Each day she carries vegetables she grows into town to sell them for some money for her family. We are told, "She is in school because of Kulanu."

Contributors can be proud of enabling a total of ninety-three Abayudaya children to go to school. On the other hand, much remains undone. Our goal is to pay total tuition for every child whose family or guardian cannot afford it.

Also, we have been advised that our Fund did not enable any of these students to buy needed uniforms and books. A further goal of Kulanu is to supply these as well as tuition.

For about $20, a primary school student can be set for the year. The figure would be closer to $70 for a senior school student. By U.S. standards, school tuition is certainly not costly, but by Ugandan standards it is extremely expensive.

The Margolis-Shair Fund is also enabling one student to attend college in Uganda. Hopefully, two or more students will be eligible for college in the near future. Most of the tuition and supplies for one student are covered by our contribution of $2,000 per year.

Readers are invited to earmark their tax-deductible Kulanu contributions for this education fund. Your donation is tantamount to "adopting" a student. For a contribution of $200, you can make a difference in the lives of ten youngsters. What an opportunity!

Two Fascinating Books About Ugandan Jewry
Irwin M. Berg

SEMEI KAKUNGULU: JEWISH WARRIOR?

Michael Twaddle. *Kakungulu and the Creation of Uganda.* Ohio University Press, 1993.

I first heard of Semei Kakungulu when reading the Kulanu newsletter of Winter 1994–95, which described him as a "local warrior and governor" who "studied and meditated on the Old Testament, adopted the observance of all Moses' commandments, including circumcision, and suggested this observance [for] all his [formerly Christian] followers." As a student of Jewish history, I knew that such a person was rare—although not unknown—and I was much intrigued.

This summer I visited the Abayudaya, the descendants of the followers of Semei Kakungulu. I met and spoke to Africans who are passionate about their commitment to Judaism, and I also met two descendants of Kakungulu. My interest in this "local warrior and governor" soared.

After learning that a book had been written about him, I purchased a copy at a bookstore in Kampala, Uganda. Later, I saw the same book being offered for sale at the airport bookstore in Entebbe. Before I read the first page, I knew that Kakungulu was an important and famous, as well as a unique, person.

I have no background in Ugandan political or religious history. Therefore, this article cannot be a critique or even a review of Michael Twaddle's book. Nor is this a summary of the book, because the author was primarily interested in Kakungulu's contribution to the creation of Uganda. This article reflects my interest—the historical, social, and religious forces as developed by Twaddle which induced Kakungulu to lead a Jewish life and to create a community of followers to carry on after his death.

Kakungulu (1869–1928) was a warrior and statesman of the powerful Baganda tribe. In the 1880s he was converted to Christianity by a Protestant missionary who taught him how to read the Bible in Swahili. Because he commanded many warriors, had connections to the Bugandan court, and was a Protestant, the British gave Kakungulu their support. He responded by conquering and bringing into the British sphere of influence two areas outside the Bugandan Empire, Bukedi and Busoga. These areas were between the Nile River's source in Lake Victoria and Mount Elgon, on the Kenyan border.

Kakungulu believed that the British would allow him to become the king of Bukedi and Busoga, but the British preferred to rule these areas through civil servants in their pay and under their control. The British limited Kakungulu to a 20-square-mile area in and around what has now become Mbale, Uganda. The people who inhabited this area were of the Bagesu tribe—rivals to Baganda. Nevertheless, Kakungulu, with the help of his Baganda followers—now much reduced in numbers—was able to maintain control so long as he received British support.

Beginning about 1900, a slow but continuous mutual disenchantment arose between Kakungulu and the British. In 1913, Kakungulu became a Malakite Christian. This was a movement, described by the British as a "cult," which was "a mixture of Judaism, Christianity, and Christian Science." Many who joined the religion of Malaki where Kakungulu was in control were Baganda.

While a Malakite, Kakungulu came to the conclusion that the Christian missionaries were not reading the Bible correctly. He pointed out that the Europeans disregarded the real Sabbath, which was Saturday, not Sunday. As proof, he cited that Jesus was buried on Friday before the Sabbath, and his mother and his disciples did not visit the tomb on the following day because it was the Sabbath, but waited until Sunday.

Under pressure from the British, who wished to limit his holdings, Kakungulu, in 1917, moved his principal residence a short distance farther from Mbale into the western foothills of Mount Elgon to a place called Gangama. It was there that he started a separatist sect initially known as Kibina Kya Bayudaya Absesiga Katonda ("Community of Jews who trust in the Lord"). Recruitment into this community came almost exclusively from what remained of Kakungulu's Baganda following.

The Bible, as a result of the teachings of the missionaries, was held in high regard among the Christians of Uganda. The missionaries had stressed the truth of the Bible by declaring that it came not from the Europeans but from an alien race, the Jews. The purpose of the missionaries was to impress upon the Africans that the Europeans too had found truth from a foreign race. But because of this emphasis, the customs and manners of the Jews became of great interest to Kakungulu's followers. In Michael Twaddle's opinion, Kakungulu's conversion to Malakite Christianity was caused by his disappointment with his treatment by the British authorities, but his subsequent formation of the Abayudaya community was principally the result of his closer reading of the Bible.

In 1922, at Gangama, Kakungulu published a 90-page book of rules and prayers as a guide to his community. The book set forth Jewish laws and practices as Kakungulu found them in the Old Testament, although it contained many verses and sections from the New Testament as well. Despite this interest in Jewish practices, there does not appear to have been any direct contact between Kakungulu and Jews before 1925.

Beginning about 1925, several European Jews who were employed as mechanics and engineers by the British chanced upon the Christian-Jewish community near Mbale. Jews such as these, during what appear to have been chance encounters, told Kakungulu about Orthodox Judaism. As a result, many remaining Christian customs were dropped, including baptism. From these encounters, the community learned to keep the Sabbath, to recite Hebrew prayers and blessings, to slaughter animals for meat in a kosher manner, and some Hebrew.

Kakungulu died on November 24, 1928. Michael Twaddle concluded that at his death, the Abayudaya "remained a mixture of both Christianity and Judaism, with faith in Christ remaining prominent in Kakungulu's beliefs."

Kakungulu is buried a short distance from the main Abayudaya synagogue behind the unpretentious home in which he lived during the last years of his life. The grave, which I visited, has a stone which reads:

SEMEI WAKIRENZI KAKUNGULU
A Victorious General and
Sava Chief in Buganda
Administrator of Eastern Province 1899–1905
President of Busoga 1906–1913
Died 24th 11 1928

In a tantalizing footnote, Twaddle states that after Kakungulu's death, the Abayudaya community divided into those wishing to retain a toehold within Christianity and those wanting to break the ties completely. If so, then during our June 1995 visit, we met only the latter.

Leadership of the Abayudaya community has passed to a group of young married men whose goal is to end its isolation from world Jewry. One of them told me that Twaddle's book, based on interviews held in the 1960s, is outdated. Whenever they learn anything of Jewish prayers and practices, these young men have adopted it into the Abayudaya ritual.

Their knowledge of Hebrew is self-taught and growing. Although the young men know far more about Jewish practice and prayers than their elders, they show great respect and deference to the men who led them after Kakungulu's death. On a visit to the Abayudaya village of Hamanyony, we met Samson Mugombe (the Samusoni Mugombe who was interviewed by Twaddle), now over eighty years old and in ill health. He was introduced to us as "our spiritual leader" and a man who "studied with Kakungulu."

An Unusual Treat For History Buffs

Arye Oded. *Religion and Politics in Uganda: A Study of Islam and Judaism.* Nairobi: East African Educational Publishers, 1995.

Arye Oded has written two remarkable monographs that have been published in a book entitled *Religion and Politics in Uganda.* The first monograph is entitled *Kalema: The Muslim King of Buganda*, and the second, *The Bayudaya: The African Jews of Uganda.* The connecting link between these two studies is Semei Kakungulu, the Protestant general who defeated the armies of the Muslim king, Kalema, thereby stemming Uganda's drift toward Islam, but who later rejected Christianity, adopted Judaism, and established a Jewish community in Uganda.

During the first half of the nineteenth century, before Europeans became interested in the interior of East Africa, Oded writes that Arab traders were regular visitors at the Bugandan court. At that time, the Baganda tribe was a major military and political power in the territory now known as Uganda. The ruling kings (kabakas) of the Baganda tribe were anxious to buy firearms from the Arabs. But the Arabs also brought a religion which the younger chiefs and their sons and daughters found attractive. By the end of the reign of Kabaka Mutesa I (1856–1884), Islam had penetrated among the Bagandan chiefs and the kabaka's pages. Mutesa I declared himself a Muslim in the 1860s, but he was primarily interested in the material benefits he could gain from the Muslim traders. Others among the Bagandan elite were far more devoted to the new faith.

When Kabaka Mutesa I died in 1884, there was a scramble among his sons to replace him as kabaka. By this time, Christian missionaries, both Catholic and Protestant, had penetrated the area. All the religious groups had pretenders to the throne. The Muslim champion was Kalema, a son of Mutesa I. The period from 1884 to 1890 was one of ruthless and brutal struggle between the Muslims, led by Kalema, and the Christians, led by another son of Mutesa I, Kabaka Mwanga. The Christians, under Mwanga, received the active support of the British and completely defeated Kalema and the Muslims in 1890. The struggle, which caused much destruction and death, widened the gap between the followers of the two religions and put an end to Muslim supremacy in politics. From Kalema's defeat until the rise of Idi Amin eighty years later, no Muslim was at the center of power in Uganda.

According to Oded, Semei Lwakilenzi Kakungulu, the founder of the Bayudaya, also known as the Abayudaya, is one of the most important and colorful personalities in Ugandan history. He was born around 1860, and proved himself to be a popular leader and a brilliant military commander. In the late 1880s, Kakungulu became a Protestant and was a major factor in the defeat of the Muslims.

In 1894, Uganda was formally annexed to the British Empire. The British, who respected Kakungulu's military ability, gave him a free hand to subdue tribes to the north and east of Buganda, which then came under British control. Kakungulu cooperated with the British in the hope that they would recognize him as kabaka of the eastern region of Uganda and treat him like the other kings who ruled in Uganda. In this, the British may have actively misled him; at the very least, they disappointed him.

Kakungulu's disappointment with the British brought him closer to a breakaway Christian sect called the Bamalaki. The Bamalaki were native, dissident Protestants whose faith rested on a fundamentalist reading of the Bible. They regarded Saturday as the Sabbath, declined to eat pork, and permitted polygamy. By 1921, there were about a hundred thousand Bamalaki in Uganda. The British exiled their leader to northern Uganda in 1926 where he died after a protracted hunger strike.

Kakungulu's devotion to the Old Testament was noted by a Protestant missionary as early as 1901. In 1919, his devotion to the Old Testament caused him to break with the Bamalaki. Kakungulu demanded that the Bamalaki observe all of Moses' commandments, including the commandment of circumcision. The Bamalaki opposed this, claiming that circumcision was practiced only by Jews, who did not believe in the New Testament or in Jesus Christ. Kakungulu is reported to have replied: "If this is the case, then from this day on, I am a Jew (*Muyudaya*)." In 1919, when over fifty years of age, Kakungulu was circumcised, and he circumcised his firstborn son, whom he named Yuda. He urged his supporters and members of his family to circumcise their sons, and many did so.

In 1922, Kakungulu compiled a 90-page book of rules and prayers in Luganda (the language of the Baganda) for his supporters, who had by this time formed a community in an area just north of Mbale. The book was a guide to Jewish laws and beliefs as he found them from his reading of the Old Testament. Although he declared himself a Jew, he still retained a belief in Jesus, and his book contained several verses from the New Testament.

Until 1926, there is no evidence that Kakungulu had ever met a Jew or had ever read a book written by a Jew—other than the Old Testament. His desire to be a Jew was spontaneous; that is, it developed without external influence. In 1926, Kakungulu met a Jewish trader in Kampala who is remembered only as Yusuf, or Joseph. Joseph was amazed to hear about Kakungulu's "conversion" to Judaism, but he was also astonished at how Kakungulu confused Judaism with Christianity. Kakungulu invited Joseph to his home in Mbale to instruct him and the other Abayudaya in the Jewish religion. As a result of Joseph's instruction, the Abayudaya ceased to believe in the New Testament and Jesus Christ; they stopped the practice of baptizing children, kept the Sabbath strictly, said customary Jewish blessings and prayers, learned to slaughter in the kosher manner, and would only eat meat slaughtered by themselves. Kakungulu began to compile a new prayer book devoid of quotations from the New Testament, but he died before he was able to publish it.

The author, Arye Oded, was born in Jerusalem and studied at the Hebrew University. In 1962, he was a research fellow at Makerere University in Kampala, the capital of Uganda. An Indian Jew living in Uganda told him about African Jews who called themselves Abayudaya. Oded contacted them and arranged for a meeting in Mbale. He was surprised to find waiting for him ten bearded men, dressed in white robes and white turbans. When they learned that he was a Jew from Israel, Oded reports, "their eyes lit up with happiness."

At the time of Kakungulu's death in 1928, there were about three thousand Abuyadaya. By 1962, when Oded first visited them, they were only three hundred. Some of the Abayudaya had returned to the Bamalaki sect, others to Christianity or Islam. Many Abayudaya children became Christian while attending Christian mission schools. Muslims made persistent attempts to convert the Abayudaya, stressing that they were isolated and had no patrons to protect their interests or aid them materially.

The decrease in numbers resulted primarily, however, from the inability of the Abayudaya to maintain the Jewish school that had been established by Kakungulu. The school had come under the control of the Church of Uganda (Anglican) when it could no longer cover its expenses. By the 1960s, the Abayudaya consisted mainly of elderly people, women, and small children. The youth of school age had abandoned the Jewish faith.

Oded spent two days with the Abayudaya in May 1962, and met with them several times over the next five years. The first request of the Abayudaya leaders was to make permanent contact with Jews in Israel and the world. With Oded's help, letters were exchanged with the president of Israel, the president of the World Jewish Congress, and the chairman of the World Union for the Propagation of Judaism. Several editors of Jewish newspapers in Israel, England, and the United States wrote to Samsoni Mugombe, the leader of the Abayudaya. The contacts with world Jewry contributed spiritually and morally to the community and led to an increase in numbers to about eight hundred in 1971.

Just as things were getting better, the Abayudaya were severely hit by Idi Amin's coup in 1971. The community was outlawed by Amin, and all synagogues were closed. The Abayudaya had to conceal their Jewishness or be arrested. Several Abayudaya families, including that of their leader, Samsoni Mugombe, became impoverished and suffered from hunger. Many members of the community left Judaism out of fear.

As long as Amin was in power, all contact between the Abayudaya and the outside world ceased. Oded feared that the community had vanished. It had not, but its numbers had again greatly decreased. The work of reconstruction of synagogues and the school started under the leadership of Samsoni Mugombe immediately after Amin's fall. Youth groups were set up and were given Hebrew names, such as *ne'arim* ("youngsters") and *kokhavim tikvah* ("stars of hope").

Mugombe again wrote letters to many Jewish organizations in Israel and all over the world appealing for urgent help. He asked for books in English on Jewish laws and faith; he asked for a rabbi to be sent to teach them Judaism; he wanted one member of the community to be sent to Israel to study at a yeshiva so that the community would have a leader and a teacher. He also requested financial assistance to maintain the synagogues and school.

In 1994, while serving as Israel's ambassador to Kenya, Oded again visited the Abayudaya. He noted that a new generation of leaders had taken over from Samsoni Mugombe. There were four synagogues, one in Gangama which had been reconstructed with a contribution of $1,000 from an American Jew. Their relations with their Muslim and Christian neighbors had improved. Still, no rabbi had been sent to the Abayudaya; and no Jewish institution in Israel or elsewhere had been found that would admit an Abayudaya and pay for the course of study. Although the Abayudaya consider themselves to be good Jews, none of them has yet been given the opportunity to convert according to the halacha (Jewish religious law).

Oded's monographs are thoroughly footnoted. To a very large degree, his sources are unpublished manuscripts, private correspondence, and interviews, many of which were conducted by Oded himself. Oded is, in fact, the first historian to document the history of the Abayudaya. Most of his research was done in the early 1960s and was published in the 1970s as an article in the scholarly *Journal of Religion in Africa*. The current monograph is an enlarged and more fully documented version of the article. The major additions are three chapters dealing with events after 1970.

Oded's history of Islam and Judaism in Uganda was not written for comparative purposes and does not readily permit a comparison of the experience of the two religions in that country. Nevertheless, having been in Uganda and seen the power and success of the Muslims, I cannot help but ask why the Abayudaya are struggling to survive after seventy-seven years whereas the Muslims fit comfortably into the landscape. The Muslim experience could have been otherwise. Kalema's defeat in 1890 was total. After 1894, when Uganda was a British colony, it is unlikely that the Muslims of Uganda were allowed to receive any significant financial support from their co-religionists in North Africa or the Middle East. Nevertheless, they established numerous mosques and religious schools throughout the country. Did the knowledge that they were part of a world religion with a billion adherents give the Ugandan Muslims the confidence to be fruitful and multiply?

As long as Kakungulu was alive, his high social status and his substantial financial means protected the Abayudaya politically and materially. It may also have sustained their morale so that they could practice their religion in almost total isolation. Once Kakungulu died, that support was gone. They were scorned by their neighbors, by the country's rulers, and by the religious establishment. They had no financial support from the outside; but more importantly, they had no intellectual support from the outside. It would be interesting to know how the Bamalaki have fared since 1921, when they numbered about one hundred thousand, since they, like the Abayudaya, have had to survive without outside recognition.

We Jews differ from other salvationist religions in that we do not proselytize. The theological basis for this attitude is that a non-Jew need only accept the seven commandments of Noah, which are largely moral and ethical laws, to receive a portion in the world-to-come. Thus, there is no theological need for Jews to convert the world. This reasoning does not, however, explain why Jews actively discourage converts. Is there a subliminal fear that converts will undermine the traditional and meticulous observance of Jewish law and customs? Jewish history may well provide support for this fear. But there is also much historical evidence of converts having become faithful Jews. Have opportunities to increase Jewish numbers been lost by a mechanically negative view of converts?

Oded has given us the details of a rare event in Jewish history: a people who spontaneously sought to become Jews and continue to seek to become Jews with no encouragement, active or passive, from their co-religionists. We are entitled to ask ourselves several questions after reading Oded's monograph: Would contact with or support from the world Jewish community have increased the number of the Abayudaya and their chances of survival? What kind of contact with or support of potential converts is permissible under Jewish law ? What kind of contact or support would make us like the missionaries who feel compelled to fish to save souls?

Living with the Abayudaya and Their Non-Jewish Neighbors
Kenneth M. Schultz

This article contains excerpts from the author's anthropology study, completed in the Senior Scholar Program at the University of Rochester. He lived with the Abayudaya for two months in the fall of 1994.

Although the villages of the Abayudaya are near Mbale, Uganda's third-largest city, I recalled the difficult and almost humorous time I had the year before locating the Abayudaya. After several fruitless attempts, I eventually asked a reverend wearing a black T-shirt that read "Believe in Jesus" about the Abayudaya community. He replied adamantly, "Jews in Mbale? If there's a Jewish group living in Mbale, Uganda, I would know about it. I know all the religions practiced, and Judaism, like from the Bible, has never been worshipped here." He paused, shook his head, and then said affably, "You know, you can always stay with us." Maybe ten minutes passed before a teacher at a Christian missionary school appeared and offered, "There's a church by my house where people claim they're Jews. I don't know because I never visited, but a man around here says he's Jewish. I'll take you to him." Surprised, I glanced over to the reverend, who seemed equally shocked. The woman led me to a thin old man who, after being told in his native language of Luganda why I was in Mbale, expressed such exuberance that he immediately put his kippah on and closed his shop.

We then proceeded a few miles to a half-built synagogue. Aaron, Gershom, and Joab, the congregation's leaders, appeared, sweating but nonetheless smiling, once they confirmed that a *mzungu* (white man) was indeed here to see them. Although I was not the first white person to visit, my stay of two weeks last year and the prospect of extending that by two months this year were clearly a sign of respect to the community.

On my first Friday there, Joab said, "Today we will ride to town so you can get your Shabbat food, and then we will immediately return to prepare for the holiday." Since there was no cooking on Shabbat and my body had not adapted to cold food, Joab thought that it was best I buy some American canned food and a thermos to keep it protected. Several times last year, I was asked "What can we do to heat our food on Shabbat? Our kids get sick from the cold food." I suggested that since there is no refrigeration, maybe it is all right to cook early in the morning. A few people nodded, but only out of respect. Nobody took my secular idea seriously.

As we bicycled into town, Joab proudly asked, "Mr. Kenny, do you know how we got these bicycles?" I shook my head. "Rachel. My daughter, Rachel, got them for us. About two months ago, she and some locals went to Kolonyi, which is a nearby health center started by Germans, and sang on behalf of the Farmers' Society for Vice President Kisekka. Kisekka was so impressed with her voice that he donated two bikes to the Society. We still have to pay a small sum to Kolonyi, but we are extremely happy." I asked why he was allowed to keep the bikes, and he responded, "Of course, I am responsible. I am the chairman of the Farmers' Society."

We continued toward town, but before we got very far we heard a rhythmic calling similar to that made from a shofar. It was an announcement that a death had occurred. Joab shook his head and then said softly, "A three-year-old of a nearby family died in the night. Yesterday, he was healthy—today, no. We must go and pay a condolence."

AN ISLAMIC FUNERAL

The home where the burial was taking place was on the way to town. When we arrived, Joab told me that the family was Islamic and that was good because Christian ceremonies last much longer. At first, I was surprised by the seemingly cynical remark, but I remembered Aaron telling me that something like one death occurs every three or four days and mostly to young children, whose developing immune systems are extremely vulnerable to the various diseases, particularly malaria. Naturally, the residents have learned to prefer one ceremony to another. The responsibility of the neighbors to mourn for each death makes attending funerals a weekly occurrence. This is in contrast to the Western custom that one only mourns for members of the immediate family and close friends.

We walked to the table and paid a condolence of 400 shillings (50 cents). We turned and sat down with the men, who were resting comfortably under some trees and chatting quietly. Joab left and walked over to the house and peeked inside, where several women were crying. He raised his hand, whispered something, and walked back across the front yard. An amiable man pushed a cow away from a wooden chair and handed it to Joab. Several people came over, including the father of the deceased, and welcomed us. I offered my condolences, and he acknowledged with a sad smile. A couple of minutes passed before Muslim men, all wearing white robes and a cloth to cover their heads, appeared from the small clay house; they were carrying a wooden coffin that was adorned with a beautiful blue-and-white patterned tapestry. The women, who stood opposite the men, harmoniously began the Islamic mourning prayer as the men placed the casket under blossoming green leaves that draped a pleasant wooden shelter. There, Muslims recited the burial service, which frequently included raising their hands—palms facing upward—to their heads. When the religious leader finished, the coffin was lifted and the rest of us followed the male procession to the grave site, located behind the home. The women kept chanting but remained at the house. I was told that it is not customary for women to join the men. When we reached the site we saw two young men standing in the grave. The tapestry was placed over their heads as they were carefully handled the coffin. The father led the prayers while dirt was poured into the grave. Finally, symbolic drops of water were sprinkled and the ceremony was over.

"Have you ever been to a Jewish funeral?" questioned Joab as we were leaving.

"Yes."

"Is the ceremony similar to this one?"

"Sure, except for the Islamic prayers."

"I'm happy to hear that. The Jewish funeral here is much the same because it does not take too long. We read the right prayers from our siddurim that were sent to us from people in Canada, and then we all help in burying the deceased. Usually the wooden casket is very plain. We can not afford a nice one."

"Hopefully, I will not observe another funeral."

"*Inshallah*," Joab said emphatically, an Arabic term meaning "If God wishes."

"You know," he continued, "you did a righteous thing by escorting the dead. People even said that the boy was blessed because a white man was present at his burial."

Strange, I thought.

In Town

We left the burial area and continued on our ride to town. We were stopped several times by gracious people who wished to greet Joab and me. Although their eyes were fixed on my physical appearance, I did not find the stares intrusive. We arrived at a sparsely-stocked store rented by the Abayudaya. There was no name to the store, but if there were, Joab assured me, it would not be anything in Hebrew. Joab said, "If the owner of the building knew that he was renting to Jews, then of course we would have to leave. Gershom signed the lease 'Mohammed.'"

Seeing a *mzungu*, many children and adults came by to question who I was and why I was staying with Joab. After telling one middle-aged man who had gone to school with Uriah, a member of the congregation, that I was here to study the Abayudaya Community, he shook his head and said, "I never knew there were Jews living in Mbale." He looked at Uriah, who had entered the shop a few minutes before, and asked, "Why didn't you ever tell me that you were Jewish?"

Uriah smiled and replied, "You never asked."

The man looked stunned and said, "But nobody here knows about Judaism. Don't you want to spread the word of Judaism?"

Uriah responded appropriately, "We don't believe in missionaries to attract members." The man was not content; he needed more to satisfy his curiosity.

He glanced over to me and said kindly, "I would like to bring the priest of my church here to talk with the you. I am sure you could enlighten him about your religion. Is it okay if he and I come here sometime next week, like Tuesday?" I gladly accepted without realizing how strange it was that I had been there only a day, while the community has existed since 1919, and just now this man, who was not only a friend of Uriah, but lived close to the synagogue, had for the first time heard of the Jewish congregation. (The man never returned with his priest.)

Uriah was a teacher at one of the prestigious Christian missionary schools that was regarded as the best in Mbale. He took much pride in working there, and rightfully so.

We left the shop and passed a procession of people who were singing and waving thick green leaves wildly around two young boys. The boys were covered with white powder and were waving symbolic fur stripped from the back of a monkey and chanting in Lugisu, the local language. It was the dancing before a traditional circumcision.

"Will the boy be circumcised today?" I asked, amazed by what I was witnessing.

"No, maybe tomorrow, but probably not. Sometimes they will dance for two weeks and some up to a month. Don't worry, you will see one. There will be many around this time," Joab assured me.

Shabbat

On Friday afternoon Gershom and his wife, Seporah, carrying their newborn baby, Moshe, came over and greeted us warmly. I was a bit surprised to see that Gershom had married, considering he had expressed such uncertainty about finding a "Jewish wife" the previous year. I remembered him saying, "This is our greatest problem. The women just leave the community, and what are we supposed to do? They see that Muslim and Christian missionaries provide their people with beautiful buildings and other things, and we just have our little synagogue."

I asked Gershom when he had actually got married and he replied, "Seporah and I were not sure, but we decided to marry early, maybe a few weeks after you left last year. She is a good Jewish woman, and now our son can be a rabbi. I teach him Hebrew everyday," he smiled, "so he will someday be fluent in three languages—English, Luganda, and the language of God, Hebrew." Gershom laughed and walked over to the synagogue carrying a box filled with siddurim, tallitot, and kippot. He was quite anxious to begin the Sabbath.

I followed him over to the synagogue, where Aaron hung a lamp from one of the wooden rafters overhead. Not many members had arrived, but Gershom began the Sabbath with the opening prayer from the siddur. The wind blew slightly through the empty windows and shook the kerosene lamp, causing stints of darkness, but by now Gershom had memorized most of the prayers and the service continued without interruption. A few minutes passed before the religious leader, Mishael, arrived. He was draped in an old, faded white robe that covered his thin, aging body. As he entered the synagogue, he took out a torn white kippah and placed it on his head. He saw me and immediately came over. He bowed his head slightly, smiled, and repeated in a soft, raspy voice, "Shabbat shalom, Shabbat shalom."

Mishael is one of the oldest members of the community. He converted to Judaism with his father while working on one of the fifty acres of land Kakungulu acquired for his military service to the British. Although Kakungulu did not force Judaism on his subordinates and tenants like Mishael, he taught them about Judaism and conferred advantages to them. Like Kakungulu in his old age, Mishael has dedicated his remaining years to the study and understanding of the Old Testament. Aaron once told me that Mishael no longer works on his three acres of land. He has retired to his small hut, where he eats very little and reads the Bible throughout the day. He has already signed over his land to the congregation.

Mishael sat down next to me on the wooden bench. He knew very little English, but this did not prevent him from expressing his happiness. Several times during the prayers he would glance over and just smile. It is difficult to describe the feeling, but the sincerity in his facial gestures alone created the bond we shared in practicing the same religion. Midway through the service, Gershom looked over to Mishael and asked what the Torah portion for the week was. He quickly replied, "Chapter 6, verse 9 of Genesis."

Gershom nodded and thanked him, though he clearly had asked out of respect for the elder. Gershom gave a brief account of what happened in that chapter and followed it with his own moral lesson. He said:

"... The generation of the floods was very arrogant, as it is said in the Bible. Everyone had found his own way, which means the people of that generation were not united. And, what does God do? He brings the floods to destroy that generation. But still there is a lesson that God is merciful. He tells Noah to build the Ark so maybe some people will repent and enter the Ark. But because the generation was arrogant, everyone ignored and despised the words of Noah. The first lesson is that God is merciful. And the other is that the people of that generation were divided because they all went their own way. Now we come to the generation after the flood. They also were arrogant. They resolved to build a tower in order to reach God and talk to Him. They wanted to see how God lived, and this, in my mind, is arrogance. But the difference is that they were united, and instead of God destroying them, He only dispersed them. So there is a lesson—unity toward the right thing is highly blessed by God. So it is a call from me that we unite toward the truth and we shall be rewarded by the almighty God."

The next morning Gershom walked over to a small enclosure and asked me if I knew what it was; at first I wasn't sure. Then I realized that it was a sukkah for the holiday of Sukkot that had been celebrated the month before. Gershom stated, "The purpose is to remember that our fathers lived in such structures when they came from Egypt. The word *sukkah* means 'booth,' and it symbolizes the departure." I asked Gershom whether he lived in the sukkah and he replied that he, Aaron, Seth, and Joab used to sleep in the sukkah when they were little. "But now we don't, because a certain rabbi from Nairobi advised us that if you think the security of the place is okay, then sleep out. Here there are still thieves, so now we stay out there until eight or nine o'clock and eat our meals there. Then we go home. The women do the same."

Members of the congregation began arriving for Shabbat morning services at around 8:30, and the service began at nine o'clock. The men sat opposite the women for the same reason that this is done in Orthodox synagogues everywhere—simply, the fear that physical attraction will interfere with the religious purpose. At first I was surprised to see Aaron leading the service, but after hearing him recite the beginning prayers fluently in Hebrew, I realized that in the past year he had attained a similar fluency to that of Gershom. (Apparently Gershom, Aaron, and Joab have studied very hard from basic Hebrew books sent to them by past visitors.) The congregation participated most energetically when the prayer was recited in Luganda or sung in Hebrew. One prayer, in particular, captured the attention of every member—*Lecha Dodi*. When I heard the soothing voices chanting together, I was entranced by their spiritual expression, which seemed to accentuate the differences between the Abayudaya community and Western Judaism.

The Torah portion of the service was very similar to the one that I am accustomed to at home. It was especially gratifying to witness not only two recently bar-mitzvahed boys who chanted the prayers perfectly in Hebrew, but also two women who read their aliyot in English. Last year, the women primarily sat in the corner and said nothing. I realized, then, that part of the reason the women were fleeing from the Abayudaya community was because they lacked a religious identity. Without inclusion in the service and in the development of the community, Judaism represented no more than a strange word. This year, although there are still moments of exclusion, the women seemed to be more active, and, more importantly, comfortable with their new involvement.

After the Haftarah was read by an elder of the community, there was a break in the service for members of the congregation to say a few words welcoming me back. Joab began and, in essence, thanked God for my safe return to the community. He said, "Mr. Kenny has traveled very far. And he is very brave, because there are many diseases here in Uganda. He has put his faith in God, and we are most pleased. Thank you, Mr. Kenny." Two elderly women stood up at the end and expressed their happiness with a traditional cry that permeated the open room. The service concluded with a unique version of *Adon Olam*.

To each of the congregants, Shabbat is the climax of the week. Aaron told me that even when he is at school, an hour away from home, he never misses a Shabbat. He enters a private classroom and recites all the prayers. Essentially, Shabbat is an expression of their identity. Without this culmination at the end of week, a feeling of emptiness would prevail throughout the community.

SOCCER AND FUNDAMENTALISTS

After the service, we walked home. The rest of the day was spent sitting around and talking. The women sat outside on mats while the men relaxed. Around five o'clock, we were invited to play in a friendly game of football (soccer) at a nearby field; Joab and I accepted. The game was between the elders of the surrounding community, for whom Joab and I proudly played, and the youth. When we arrived, the area was completely filled with people. Everyone wanted to watch the *mzungu* play football. At first people seemed more anxious than excited. But as soon as I chased after the ball and slipped on the wet, muddy field, the game turned into a celebration. People were screaming and dancing after every play. I think that the youth won by two or three goals, but the exuberance felt by everyone overshadowed the importance of the score. I remember Joab looking at me and saying with a smile, "You have made so many people happy." The celebration was carried into the streets, with people singing and dancing the whole way home.

That night, Joab asked me if I had noticed a few of the youth "having long beards and wearing pants rolled up to their knees." I shook my head. He said, "Well, here we call those who dress that way *Tablique*, which means 'fundamentalist,' like the Muslim fundamentalists who terrorize Israelis." I asked when this group had materialized, and he said, "It came about recently, when students from Uganda left here to study in the Middle East, especially in Iraq, where Saddam Hussein is. They return, and maybe there they learn different ways. Right now, we all just laugh at them," he continued, "because it is not very threatening. However, that does not mean we are not wary of them."

At the moment, according to Joab, the *Tablique* do not have any conflict with the Christians or the Jews. The struggle is internal, between the youth and their Islamic elders. In the youths' minds, the elders are not praying according to the Koran, so it is their religious duty to demand changes in prayer and leadership. Joab and many of his Christian peers fear that if this is accomplished, there could be grave danger for both religions. In the past month alone, there have been three incidents in which the Muslim youth have not only disrupted their own Islamic services but have physically fought with the elders. "One time a youth beat up an elder and poured acid into his left eye," Joab said sadly. "Now that elder must wear a covering to hide the empty space."

I thought that since the Jewish community was so small, the Abayudaya did not have much to fear; the real conflict would be between the Muslims and the Christians. Joab's opinion differed greatly. He said, "You know, Sudan is just north of us, and they are governed by shariah [Muslim law]. So the *Tablique* are supported by many people in that country. And when I speak to those who have studied in Iraq, they openly say they are taught that Jews are the most dangerous enemy. So, we are wary, and our joking is a way to keep them out in the open."

FEELING DIFFERENT

A week later, as we prepared for the following Shabbat eve and were about to leave for the synagogue, the rain started. We waited for a few minutes, but the illuminating flashes of lightning only increased. I decided to remain at home. I thought that my night would be spent in solitude, but Mama Debra (the mother of Joab, Aaron, and Gershom), Rachel, and Enos walked in and sat down.

Enos was a fifteen-year-old boy who lived with the family during breaks in the school year. Joab treated Enos as a son, although, strangely, nobody knew who his real parents were. He was an extremely bright and confident boy.

Rachel was a year younger and the daughter of Joab from his first marriage. She was a very quiet girl; Aaron attributed this to her parents' divorce when she was ten. In this society, children are the "property" of the father and usually remain with him, while the woman returns to her family. Rachel had not seen her mother since that day and did not even know where she lived. She seemed to express her despair vividly through her exceptional singing talent.

Mama Debra asked me about my family in America, and then she told me her family history. She said she had five sisters and five brothers. All her sisters have remained Jewish, while her brothers practice either Christianity or Islam. Although there was not a conflict with her brothers, she resented the fact that they had failed to follow their father's wishes and remain Jewish. She concluded, "I do not like what my brothers did, and I do not see them much. But I still speak to my sisters."

I then asked Enos and Rachel about their Jewish identity and whether they faced harassment from their predominantly Christian schoolmates. Enos replied, "In the beginning, it was very difficult and I had few friends. But then I became a school monitor, and the students feared my power to have them caned by a teacher. Soon I had many friends." Enos paused and laughed, and then continued, "And, as they got to know me, they liked me. Only during religious class do I feel unhappy. When we study the New Testament and read that Jews killed Jesus, the students jokingly hit me and point at me like I did it. I feel unhappy, but I also feel happy because I am different—everyone knows that I am a Jew." He smiled as he looked toward Rachel, who was sitting quietly by Mama Debra. I asked her the same question.

She said softly, "I only feel unhappy. I don't like feeling different from my classmates. And I don't know why I have to just because of religion. It makes me sad." She looked over to Mama Debra, apparently for comfort.

"Well, Rachel, do you feel a certain pressure to be different?" I asked.

She shook her head and replied, "No, I like practicing Judaism very much, but I don't like feeling different, especially during religion class."

Mama Debra intervened and added, "Nobody likes feeling different; it makes one unhappy." Rachel nodded. Enos smiled.

I was particularly fascinated by Enos's response when he expressed his ambivalence toward being a Jew. On the one hand, he experienced an uncomfortable isolation from his peers; on the other, he reveled in this difference. I had also found that to be true when I was growing up. I too went to a predominantly Christian school, and when a fight broke out between me and one of my peers, someone would usually cry, "Well, you're not Catholic." At first I would be upset, and then I would feel a tremendous pride in being Jewish. When I saw Enos smile at the end of his statement, he reminded me of myself.

SAMSON MUGOMBE

We celebrated the following Shabbat at the nearby synagogue where Samson Mugombe, revered leader of the community since 1944, leads the services. The building, located atop a small incline along the eroded path that leads to the center of Mbale, was a small clay building sheltered by a roof of rusty sheets of metal. On the outside there were no signs indicating that it was a synagogue. However, the interior was decorated with Jewish symbols meticulously drawn on the old gray walls. We arrived before the other members and sat quietly on one of the wooden benches until I peered through the open window and noticed a tall elderly man draped in a long black garment walking slowly toward the synagogue. He had a wooden cane in his right hand that aided each step. He entered the synagogue and strolled over to where I was sitting. He smiled brightly and said, while shaking my hand, "Shabbat shalom, Shabbat shalom." He turned away and sat at the wooden table that served as the podium. There was something spiritual about this man resting under a painting of a lighted menorah.

Aaron looked over to me and whispered emphatically, "That is Samson Mugombe."

As the rest of the congregation began to arrive, another elderly man, who was the oldest son of Mugombe, stood up at the podium and read the opening prayers in Luganda. Since I was not able to contribute, I sat quietly and observed the surroundings. In one corner, I noticed a beautifully hand-crafted drum. I looked over to Aaron, who said softly, "On Friday a member of the congregation plays the drum to introduce the Shabbat. If you listen around six o'clock on Friday, you will be able to hear."

After half an hour or so, Mugombe rose from his chair and began his lengthy sermon. In the beginning, Aaron tried to translate, but the attempt was fruitless as Mugombe spoke without pausing. He talked for nearly ninety minutes, and by the end, everyone seemed to be exhausted. Although I did not understand the service, after observing a Shabbat conducted by Samson Mgombe and witnessing the pride he had in Judaism, I refused to believe that the service was any less Jewish than the one at the larger, brick synagogue.

As we walked out of the service, I asked Mugombe's son, also an elderly man, if he ever had thought of converting during the time of Amin's regime. (In the 1970s Idi Amin had outlawed Judaism and some Abayudaya synagogues were destroyed; faithful adherents went underground.) He replied in Luganda, which Aaron translated, "Ah, Amin was a very bad man and he did very evil things to us, but it is our religion that kept me strong. This is all that I had. And if I let go of it for something I did not believe, then I would no longer have been a person."

"What about the people of the congregation who did convert to Christianity or Islam?"

"That is okay for them, but it is not me. This is what I was taught by my father, and this is what I am."

Later Joab said to me, "You see, I don't like so much the service here. I get very tired. But I must respect it. Mugombe has done very much for our community and I am grateful. And do you know what he also said in his sermon? He said that we must always remain together, and I agree."

THE CIRCUMCISION

We returned home and ate a small lunch. I had some bread and porridge that was kept warm in a thermos. After getting dysentery the first week, I decided that I would rather eat a big, warm dinner than satisfy my appetite with cold food that was possibly infested with parasites.

At around three o'clock, Joab and I set out for the circumcision. We walked away from town and through *shambas* (yards or gardens) that were divided by man-made plateaus on the beautiful green hills of Uganda. We approached the Christian home where two brothers were going to be circumcised, and according to Joab, this was common. He clarified, "There could be one, two, three, or four boys being circumcised at once. You see, when a boy of the Bugisu tribe, which is most people in this area, reaches eighteen, he must be circumcised. And if he has brothers who are younger, maybe as young as fourteen, they might also do it with him. We Jews are the only ones who do not participate in this tradition."

"Have you ever seen any of these boys cry?" I asked, wondering if a fourteen-year-old could be as brave as his older brother.

"Yes, a few do. And it is very interesting to see. Here it is the custom that if you cry or do such things as show fear, like shaking, then you are called a coward and unfit for the community. And you are abused all the time. Another thing is that the friends who have given gifts might ask for them back, and the circumciser, who has to perform under great pressure, fines the father of the boys three goats and some money."

"Does the father protect his son from the abuse?"

"The father is usually the first one to hit him. One father even wanted to kill his son with a *panga* [machete]," Joab replied excitedly.

"What does the son do? Does he remain at home?"

"Yes, where is he to go? He has no money. But the son usually does not get married. The women no longer respect him."

We heard the procession approaching. The rhythmic chanting with the beat of drums permeated quickly throughout the small neighborhood. People at once left their homes, and owners closed their restaurants.

We walked over to the place of the circumcision, which I suppose was the home of the family. In the middle of the courtyard, there was a big white circle. As the two brothers walked confidently down the road, their male friends screamed at the top of their lungs, "Be brave! Don't move! Don't cry! Don't shake!" The boisterous crowd filled with young, sanguine women surrounding the circle, while young boys feverishly climbed the trees to witness their eventual fate. The two stoic boys were taken behind the house for one more moment of encouragement. The father, who was strangely draped in a beautiful, flowery dress holding a rusty *panga*, walked over to the anxious crowd and playfully threatened anyone who entered the circle. His face looked strained with anticipation. I glanced over to the circumciser, who was holding the sharp knife in preparation and standing quietly by himself. I asked Joab about him and he joked, "Don't worry. He is trained in a proper manner. In the past, ah, it was very dangerous, but now the circumciser must go through a course. And the first thing he learns is to sterilize the knife."

Suddenly the younger brother emerged from the group of his friends and entered the circle. He was wearing only gray shorts, and his body was covered with a white powder. His eyes looked bloodshot, but his face was expressionless. His father whispered one last thing to him, and he nodded. The circumciser then unzipped the boy's pants and pulled out his penis, which was also covered with the powder. The circumciser quickly pulled the foreskin forward and sliced it as his friends increased their pitch and cried, "Don't move! Don't shake! Never fear!" The boy remained still, although his eyes seemed to redden. Fortunately, he did not glance down as the blood began to drip. The circumciser paused for a second, covered the penis in brick ashes to protect from slippage, and then quickly made the second and final cut that caused the blood to freely flow into a small puddle. The shouting increased until the father walked over to his youngest son, smiled, and told him to sit down on a wooden chair to get treated with a bandage and antibiotics.

The older son was now ready. He walked confidently down to the circle with his hands raised in the air. Joab looked over to me and said, "This boy chooses to do it the brave way." The circumciser, who now had a different sterilized knife, quickly made the first cut. The boy smiled boldly, raised his pumped fists, and went dancing into the streets with his male friends, who sprinkled symbolic water all over his thin body. Blood dripped from his open shorts leaving a dark path on the red soil. During this time of waiting, I noticed the severed skin of the boy lying on soil that covered a plastic bag. I asked Joab what they did with the dead skin, and he replied, "The parents of the boy will bury the skin in a secret place. There is a tradition that if someone takes the skin, it might disorganize the boy. He might not marry, or other things bad could happen. The boy does not even know where it is buried."

After twenty minutes, the boy returned, and the circumciser made a second cut. The crowd went into a frenzy as the boy again left the circle and went dancing throughout the neighborhood. Joab smiled and cried, "I have never seen a boy do it twice. He is most brave. People are very, very happy." The boy returned about fifteen minutes later, and before he received his final cut, he danced in front of everyone. The crowd joined in as the ceremony became a fantastic celebration. Finally, he went bravely back into the circle and was officially circumcised.

On the way home, I inquired about the future of the two boys. I was interested to know how the rite of passage affected their lives. Joab responded, "It will take them about one month to recover. Then, with all the gifts they have received, the boys will begin their new lives. You see, now the boy no longer plays sex with various women and seeks one woman to marry. That is why you saw many women there, because they first want to see if he is brave. So, you will see, he will be married very soon, maybe just after he recovers."

When I returned home and explained to Aaron what I had just witnessed, I realized that this tradition united the entire community and transformed it into a communal society. In a way, this rite of passage transcended all the barriers that divided the people according to their respective religions and became an all-encompassing spiritual experience. Throughout the ceremony there was not one mention of tenets of Christianity or the beliefs associated with Islam that might alienate a certain person or group of people; everyone was free to participate in the mystical event.

However, according to Aaron, the ceremony was ever-changing. Besides the beneficial introduction of safety precautions, the government was attempting to alter and possibly abolish the practice. Aaron said, "The government of Uganda is already discouraging it in some areas. Sometimes, they [the people of the ceremony] dance almost a whole part of the year and do nothing but celebrate. This is causing economic problems because people do not work. Dancing has even been restricted this year until nine o'clock."

The Bris

I finally had an opportunity to see an Abayudaya bris when Judah's new son reached the age of eight days. Gershom and Uriah, the only two in the whole community who performed circumcisions, were preparing for the bris. I asked Gershom who had taught them, and he said, "It was a training. My father and Uriah's father did it, so we followed them."

"Well, then, how did you learn to do a bris ceremony according to Jewish law?"

"From the siddur, of course," Gershom replied as he pointed to the black book in his hand.

The short service started with prayers read in English. Then Gershom removed a tiny sterilized blade from his pocket, read a few prayers in Hebrew, and began the circumcision. Uriah held the screaming baby as Gershom carefully made the first incision. He was very precise and patient as he struggled to control the cheap blade. At one moment, he even stopped to wipe the sweat from his forehead. Before the final cut, I turned away and noticed the mother of the child standing, alone, outside the circle, and every time her son released a horrifying shriek, her face cringed with fear. Only after Gershom was finished, and she realized that the baby was fine, did she and her friends rejoice by chanting the traditional cry. Gershom read the concluding prayers in English, and everyone drank a cup of wine to celebrate.

We then returned inside the home while the women tended to the boy. I asked Gershom if he had been nervous, and he replied, "Ah, I was very nervous. I was shaking, man. I must take very long to separate those skins from the real body because the blade is not good. It is very dangerous to use. Also, you know, what makes us shake is the environment. The people become very frightened and scream, especially when they see blood. They yell, 'Please stop there. You are hurting him. You might kill him.' And if you take a long time people say, 'Why don't you do this quickly? This is very bad, what you are doing. This is mutilation.' That is why we get nervous."

Aaron looked at Gershom and said, while shaking his head, "These men are most brave. What they do is much more difficult than the circumcisers for the older boys. They must be precise, man. We are very thankful for having them. I don't think I could do it."

On the way home, Joab and I discussed what the surrounding people think of the Jewish custom to circumcise the son after eight days, compared to the African tradition of circumcising the son as a rite of passage into manhood. He said that when he was young and would try to watch the traditional circumcisions, the kids would treat him badly. He stated, "I would be called a coward because they did not like that I was circumcised as a child. They thought I was avoiding their custom. So, immediately, I was alienated from the rest of the kids."

"Did you ever want to be part of the African tradition?"

"Yes, when I was a kid. I like to dance very much, and when the kids yelled at me to stop and threw things at me, I was very upset because I wanted to join them."

"What made your feelings change?"

Joab paused and then replied, "I do not know exactly, but I began to realize that at times I would always be different than them, and it made me feel strong and happy."

"Do the kids still harass Jewish boys?"

"Not in the same way, because now they recognize our existence and we are all friends. But there are still comments made against Jews in school."

CHANUKAH

My final week was spent in preparation for my farewell Chanukah party, which would take place at home. At first, Aaron refuted the location, but Joab replied convincingly, "Mr. Aaron, how can we not have it here? This is where Mr. Kenny stayed with us and got to know the neighbors. The guests will not just be the Abayudaya people but everyone in the area." He looked at me and said, "That is how we have a party in Africa. You cannot leave anyone out. Ah, that is very bad." Joab and I were in charge of the party. We bought two huge turkeys, three kilos of cow and goat meat, fish, a barrel of African beer, and all the trimmings, like spices, tea, and sugar. The additional food [bananas, sweet potatoes, and beans] were taken from the *shamba*.

When we purchased the meat, I asked Joab if anyone in the family ate it. He answered, "Miriam and the children enjoy the meat very much, and sometimes I will buy it for them. Miriam is free to make her own decisions, and so are our kids. Would it be fair if I said, "No, you can not eat that?"

"Me, I do not eat it because Muslims slaughter all the meat and do not properly cover the blood. And this restricts me because I am kosher. However, I do not know if I would buy it even if I were not kosher. The Muslims are very arrogant when it comes to their business. They feel they are superior to us and the Christians and are the only ones with the right to slaughter animals. I was even arrested for slaughtering an animal. During Amin's regime, I owned a calf who accidentally swallowed a plastic bag that got caught in the digestive system. The calf was suffering terribly so I slaughtered it. The Muslims became outraged and brought me to court. Thankfully, the court let me go after hearing that the calf was mine."

The party was extremely entertaining. The elders sat in one corner drinking the entire barrel of African beer and two bottles of whiskey, while the young people danced to the musical tapes played on Aaron's radio. In the middle of this festive occasion, Joab signaled to everyone that the food was ready. Everyone took a short break from their respective activities and ate the deliciously prepared food. When we finished eating, there were a few kind speeches thanking me for coming and inviting me to return the following year. The party finally ended when the last sip of alcohol was drunk.

After the party, Miriam went inside her home and brought her beautiful newborn baby over to me. The baby girl had been born during my stay. Joab smiled and said, "Mr. Kenny, have we told you her name?" I shook my head. He paused for a second and then answered, "We decided to call her Stacey after your sister in America. We think she will be our bridge to your family."

23

Peru

Converting Inca Indians
Rabbi Myron Zuber

It all began in 1966, in the Peruvian city of Trujillo, with a man called Villanueva, a good Catholic who frequently attended church. It was customary for the people to sing a psalm en route to church. On that particular Sunday they were singing Psalm 121, "I will lift my eyes to the hills . . ." When he came to the fourth verse, "Behold, the Keeper of Israel neither slumbers nor sleeps," he began to ponder: why shouldn't he join the people who have twenty-four-hour Divine supervision? Discussions with his priest could not reconcile his difficulties. After a period of time Villanueva came to the conclusion that the Catholic Church could not satisfy his spiritual search; he decided to embrace Judaism.

However, in a staunchly Catholic country like Peru one cannot offhandedly dismiss the religion of the country and become Jewish without encountering severe obstacles. Villanueva was excommunicated from the Church, which posted a sign proclaiming that no one could socialize with him or marry into his family. He remained undaunted. The following week, more extreme measures were employed, and Villanueva discovered that he had no electricity or plumbing. Still he refused to capitulate.

Villanueva's children were afraid that the tension would erupt into physical blows, so they encouraged their parents to go to Spain. While there, Villanueva studied Rambam and Abrabanel in Spanish and visited the small Jewish community in Madrid to acquire as much knowledge as possible. After six months, when the furor dissipated, he and his wife returned to Peru.

In the interim, the priest had been defrocked by the bishop for having failed to adequately guide his flock. Villanueva wasted no time and immediately set about educating his friends and associates with his newfound knowledge. It did not take long for him to amass five hundred people who also wished to convert to Judaism. Now he faced the problem of what to do with all these people who wished to become Jewish. The small Jewish community in Lima, composed of post-World War II refugees of Polish and Hungarian descent, callously looked down on the Inca Indians as social inferiors. If the Indians attended shul, the Lima Jews would intentionally exclude them; they gave no encouragement, no aliyah, no honors. Nobody was receptive to them, nobody invited them home or helped them in any way. The Indians returned to their homes totally disheartened.

Villanueva tried to obtain Spanish siddurim and, not being cognizant of the correct *dinim,* constructed his own tefillin out of wood. (Incidentally, this unusual pair of tefillin, a labor of love and self-sacrifice, is presently housed in the Museum of Jews of the Diaspora in Israel.) For twenty years Villanueva struggled single-handedly to find a solution to his dilemma.

In 1985 he contacted the Lubavitcher Rebbe, and Lubavitch Rabbi Chadakov immediately got in touch with me, since he felt that I was "proficient in the laws of ritual slaughter and adept at mingling with people." I agreed to travel to Peru to aid these Inca Indians in their quest to become Jewish and immediately enrolled in intensive Spanish studies.

I arrived in Peru in 1988 and discovered that the people were genuinely committed. They davened every day, but, due to the scarcity of tefillin, Villanueva wore the tefillin first, and after his turn a big line formed and people took five-minute turns using the tefillin.

On Shabbos the entire community got together at long tables for a meal of fish and vegetables. There was an obvious absence of meat or poultry in their diet because nobody there knew how to properly slaughter an animal according to Jewish law. Trujillo is eleven hours from Lima, so transporting kosher meat in this hot climate would not be feasible. The women baked their own challah, and participants were generally optimistic and jovial.

The Jews in Lima displayed unwarranted prejudice in their refusal to allow these people to use the mikveh. Therefore the people in Trujillo use the ocean as a mikveh, and the Jews of Cajamarca, further inland, use a nearby waterfall.

Although I was most interested in instructing the congregation about practical matters such as kashrut or Shabbat, they were especially interested in more esoteric concepts, such as *gilgul* (reincarnation) and *Mashiach* (Messiah). These people were extremely self-sacrificing. They constantly thought about being Jewish and were prepared to offer all their possessions in order to practice Judaism properly. For example, one woman sold all her jewelry at the market in order to obtain money to pay for tefillin for her son on his bar mitzvah. The woman's husband, who usually finds work only two days a week, traveled to Ecuador to work in the mines so that he could earn enough money to purchase a new suit for the child and a new dress for his wife.

Villanueva traveled to Lima in order to have a bris. The mohel (ritual circumciser) was more lenient than other Jews there; he felt that if these people sincerely wanted to become Jewish he would not stand in their way.

The people would gather around a table each Sunday to discuss the *sidra* (weekly portion), and Villanueva would lead the discussion. One time during the *sidra* discussion a person interrupted to comment that he was having car trouble. Villanueva immediately stopped the trivial side-talk, insisting that a table was comparable to an altar, and only holy ideas could be expounded in its presence. On another occasion it was discovered that a man had profaned Shabbos. Villanueva immediately excommunicated him despite the man's tears and protests.

The situation came to a head. What would become of these people? It was not possible for them to achieve their potential as Jews if they continued to live in such isolated conditions. The community decided that it would have to relocate either to the United States or Israel. Villanueva opted for Israel, and everyone agreed to abide by his proposal. He was very respected in the community, and his advice was always taken.

A beth din from Israel came to Peru and converted many members of the community. Then two groups of approximately three hundred emigrated to Israel in 1989 and settled in Elon Moreh, on the West Bank. Most were young people, the oldest being only forty-three years of age. They rapidly integrated into Israeli society, far more successfully than the Russian or Ethiopian Jews. Some Inca Indians joined the Israeli army, while others found jobs and became productive members of society. Some got married and relocated to Jerusalem. The children of these marriages are real Sabras. They speak Hebrew, have forgotten their Spanish, and have become one with their new homeland. They have merged into Israeli mainstream society and have settled down to a relatively comfortable lifestyle.

* * *

After this mass exodus took place, I was under the false impression that there was nothing left of Inca Jewry in Peru. A small number of individuals had chosen to remain because of their jobs. Others voluntarily chose to stay because they felt incapable of starting over and relocating to a foreign country. In no time at all, more people became interested in the Jewish phenomenon, and before long 250 new members had joined the group of committed Jews.

A neighborhood of about thirty Jewish Inca Indians also grew in Lima, and they experienced difficulty with the city's other Jews.

One problem was that the excellent school established by the Jewish community refused to register a seven-year-old child of a Jewish Incan mother, saying the tuition was too expensive for her (the mother thought the real reason was that they were prejudiced against Indians). The school had accepted two Catholic girls, children of the vice president of the country, and hired a Catholic teacher to provide them with religious instruction. I was quite upset that the Jewish school was more prepared to provide for Catholic dignitaries than for their own Jewish brethren who happened to be Indians. I approached the staff of the school and was adamant until they finally relented and admitted the Incan child.

The Lima Jews do not permit the Inca Jews to enter their synagogue, even though the Incans were converted by a beth din from Israel.

One day I was approached by a group of women in Trujillo who wished to speak with me privately about *nidah* (family purity). I was embarrassed by the subject matter and relatively unfamiliar with the intricate details. I decided to suggest that in the future a husband-and-wife team should visit the Inca Indian Jews, so the woman would be available to discuss matters pertaining to women.

On Shabbos the children sang beautifully, songs they already knew, and other *zemiros* I taught them. Each week somebody would come to the community as a curious observer. One week a man by the name of Serna, a professor of French at the University of Trujillo, came. Much impressed by the melodious singing, he suggested that the youngsters sing on public television. The children were very excited at the possibility and I began to prepare them for the occasion. However Valderama, Villanueva's successor, refused to allow this. He did not think it a good idea for the Jewish community to be in the limelight, fearing that it would promote antagonism and foster ill feeling.

Before my departure, I helped the group organize *shiurim* (lessons) on the weekly Torah portion. I was happy to note that these people are thinking individuals able to figure out resolutions to questions. I invited them to call me collect if they ever encountered questions they were unable to resolve.

I encouraged them to sing and dance, and advised them to incorporate their Indian melodies to Hebrew songs. I taped a beautiful Indian melody used to sing Psalm 121, "I lift up my eyes to the mountains." I did not want them to abandon their culture, but to merge it and make it a part of their newfound Judaism. I encouraged them to dance Indian dances for Yiddishkeit enhancement. Trujillo had a community of 180 when I left.

I traveled to the small community in Cajamarca to make my farewells and planned to stay only a few days. The people were disappointed and asked what it would take for me to stay. I replied that they only numbered eight, not enough for a minyan. However, if two additional men would agree to have themselves circumcised, I would remain. Two men immediately agreed to this proposal and traveled to Lima to have the operation performed. I extended my stay. The community of Cajamarca eventually plans to go to Israel, but the Israeli government wishes to verify their commitment to Judaism. If they are still Jewish after a two-year waiting period, Israel will accept them.

The Incan Jews have all taken new Jewish names to augment their Jewish identity. However, many still retain their Spanish names. One man, ironically, is called Jesus, and it is amusing to comment that Jesus read the Torah portion nicely today. It takes a while to make a total switch from the old Spanish names to the new, unfamiliar Jewish names.

Valderama, Villanueva's successor, longed for a Torah scroll for his shul. He approached the shul in Lima with his request, but the congregants refused to give him anything, even though there are a large number of Sifrei Torah decomposing in the basement of the Lima shul. I opened one at random and was shocked to witness the escape of numerous cockroaches. The Sefer Torah is permitted to house repulsive insects but is forbidden to the Inca Indian Jews.

Undaunted, Valderama set about making his own Sefer Torah. Unfamiliar with the *dinim* entailed in writing a Torah scroll, he proceeded to painstakingly photocopy each page of the Chumash (the first five books of the Bible) onto parchment. He then sewed the pieces of parchment together to form a scroll. An Israeli museum asked to display the Sefer Torah he made because they were impressed with the effort he put in.

I always tried to be accommodating and flexible in trying to merge the two cultures. When a congregant asked if he should sit *shiva* (the seven-day mourning period) for his Catholic mother, I compromised by telling him that he could sit for one day. Another asked if he should continue placing fresh flowers on his mother's grave. I responded that since flowers were expensive, it would be more productive to convert this expenditure into tzedakah and give charity in her honor. I sympathize with these people and tried to satisfy their old ties so long as doing so did not interfere with their Jewish affiliation.

I have been back in the States for a few years now. I remain in telephone contact with my friends in Peru, and my wife visits twice a year to help the women. I spend much of my time giving lectures about these courageous Jewish Incans, trying to raise donations for their many needs. In early 1996, I traveled to Washington, D.C., to speak at the quarterly Kulanu meeting and to alert officials at the Israeli embassy about the spiritual needs of the Incans remaining in Peru and practicing Judaism under such adverse circumstances. I was accompanied to the embassy by Kulanu president Jack Zeller; we met with the director of public and interreligious affairs, requesting consideration regarding the conversion and immigration of the Peruvians. We are hopeful that a beth din will be sent from Israel to convert the remaining 250 Incans practicing Judaism in Peru.

What will ensue after the arrival of the beth din in Peru (assuming it does come) is difficult to foretell.

* * *

Meanwhile, back in Israel, when the government began discussing the possibility of returning land on the West Bank to the Arabs, the Incans asked the government what the future had in store for them. The government comforted them by claiming that they would be placed elsewhere. The Jewish factory owners in Elon Moreh sold to the Arabs while the selling was good, and all the Jews there were pushed out fairly rapidly. Many Incans lost their jobs, were being moved around, and claimed they were discriminated against. Whether they will stick it out in Israel or return to Peru remains to be seen. Either way, they will remain Jews.

* * *

I hope that the Incan Jews in Peru will soon have an autonomous Jewish community with all the amenities—a rabbi, mikveh, shul—and that none of them will lack for the necessities that will enrich their practice of Judaism.

Toward that end, I am always soliciting tefillin, taleisim, mezuzahs, and money for Spanish-Hebrew prayer books (these can be bought in Mexico or Argentina). I also collect cash donations for the people to buy appropriate clothing (I do not ship clothing donations). Poverty permeates the community to such an extent that women quite frequently have to wear the same dress for an entire week. In order to have a change of garments for Shabbos, they turn the dress inside out so that it will look different from what is worn on weekdays! (A man's typical wage for day work is $1.50 per day.) The women would also love to have silver Jewish charms, like Stars of David or mezuzahs, for their necklaces. Money for food is also desperately needed.

Despite the problems, I am happy about my work. Isn't it marvelous to hear a fantastic tale of mass conversion when there is 82 percent intermarriage among the mainstream Jews of Lima and 52 percent intermarriage in the United States?

24

India

"*Discovering" the Telugu Jews of India*
Jason L. Francisco

Among the most successful Christian missionary efforts in India has been the conversion of approximately 40 percent of the populace in the coastal districts of Andhra Pradesh. The majority of the converts are Harijans, the so-called untouchables, who generally own no land and form the bulk of the agricultural laboring class. The Christianization of the working poor in the Indian countryside has produced one result almost certainly unforeseen by the missionaries: a small number of families have embraced Judaism.

Although the Bible is well known and widely taught, it was not until several months into the year I spent in the Andhra countryside that I discovered the Telugu word for Jews, *yudulu*, an uncommon word. The Christians I came to know, and indeed most people I asked, had never heard of Jews or Judaism, and seemed to think it a Christian sect (I did meet one person who described Jews as high-caste Americans). When a friend told me of a Jewish family living nearby, I was incredulous. I was shocked when I saw the mezuzah on the door of the family's home and was greeted with a hearty "Shalom, brother!" I was introduced to the world of a tiny Jewish community which makes up in effort and desire what it lacks in certainty about its destiny.

Shmuel Yakobi, currently living in the city of Vijayawada, is the oldest of six children of an untouchable family originally from the village of Kesara, some 25 miles north of the Krishna River, in Krishna District. His father enlisted in the Indian Army during the Second World War, and so acquired an education and knowledge of English, a language used by elites in India. After the war he found work as a schoolteacher in the town of Chebrolu, in nearby Guntur District. Shmuel's father's achievement was extraordinary. For generations his family, like virtually all untouchables, had worked as farm laborers, sometimes as bonded laborers. According to Yakobi, his father instructed the first three children—Shmuel, Vijayalaxmi, and Sadok—in English and a range of subjects, determined in his intent to pass to them as much of his learning as possible. Yakobi remembers his father as an intense and far-sighted man. He died in the mid-1960s, not yet fifty years old, having educated only half of his children.

The family had converted to Christianity, according to Yakobi, sometime around the turn of the century. However, both Shmuel and Sadok Yakobi remember their grandmother and their father telling them that though they were called Madigas, a Telugu untouchable caste, and practiced Christianity, in fact they were Jewish. Neither of the Yakobi brothers knew precisely what this meant, except that their heritage was somehow concealed from them. The information remained dormant until the mid-1980s.

Capitalizing on the education his father had given him, Shmuel Yakobi decided to become a Christian preacher, which afforded advanced training in English, a good salary, and upward mobility. Often Protestant clergy develop ties with foreign churches, preside over the disbursement of foreign-donated funds, and receive invitations and money to travel abroad. Yakobi built a successful career. He developed relationships with evangelical Christians in the United States, where he has traveled several times; he married the daughter of a successful Madiga Christian and received a healthy dowry.

As his career progressed, however, he felt a growing disaffection socially and spiritually with the Christian world. Somehow his disquiet attached itself in his mind to the lost Jewishness passed to him in stories from his father and grandmother. He began to study the Old Testament of the Christian Bible with increased seriousness. In the early 1980s, while still a preacher, he arranged a trip to Jerusalem, where he encountered living Judaism for the first time. He experienced a powerful, intuitive identification with the Jewish people and the Jewish religion. He returned to India intent on leaving Christianity and living as a Jew.

Sadok and Aaron, a younger brother, decided to join Shmuel. The three Yakobi brothers in time convinced approximately thirty families in their home village of Kottareddipalem, near Chebrolu, to join them in living as Jews. There are, I think, four principal reasons for their success.

First, the Jewish emphasis on a direct, rather than a mediated, relationship with God, combined with the Jewish emphasis on God as the redeemer of the poor and the vulnerable, resulted in a strong sense of what might be called Jewish liberation theology. The Telugu Jews, as much as any group of afflicted Jews, have come to identify strongly with the Torah's promise of deliverance by the God of universal justice. Understanding the importance of this promise demands a closer look at what I would call the community's socioeconomic vulnerability.

Like other rural Indian untouchables who depend on farm and menial labor for a living—the lowest-paid, lowest-status work in the Indian countryside—most of the families survive on less than $300 per year. As the poorest of the poor, they generally lack access to the most rudimentary health care, housing adequate to the seasons, and balanced nutrition. As a result of the seasonal unemployment built into agriculture (only planting and harvesting require labor), combined with the fact that the area generally supports only one crop per year and there is a tremendous surplus of unskilled labor, borrowing money even for food is necessary, at interest rates as high as 36 percent. Emergency loans for medical and other expenses are usually given, when they are given, at interest rates as high as 120 percent. Many families are driven into debt from which they never emerge. They become subject to the harassment of thugs and collectors. In general untouchables lack an autonomous political organization to assert their interests, and must seek the protection of contending groups of political or social elites—whose protection is, as often as not, fickle and shrewd.

The Torah's promise of the redemption of the vulnerable is closely tied to the second reason for the decision to become Jewish. It is an audacious, and in some ways a defiant, act of self-determination. The choice to become more zealously Christian, a choice they could conceivably have made, would not have been so bold. Christian liberation theology is not practiced in India. Christianity is practiced as a faith of conciliation, of reconciliation, whose trappings of deliverance more closely reflect the sheen of Western investment than the imminence of the Second Coming. Gratitude for grace given, for gifts given, rather than the moral passion of the prophets and the extraordinary power of the Exodus narrative, characterize church teachings. The choice to remain Christian, another option, might have earned them some of the benefits that befall many Telugu Christians: foreign-subsidized cement and tin houses (rather than the standard mud-and-dung thatched-roofed houses, which many people admit are actually cooler and better suited to the climate), opportunities to attend missionary-run English-language schools, perhaps better chances to qualify for university seats reserved for untouchables, perhaps access to missionary hospitals. For all the undeniable benefits Christian relief has brought, it comes at the cost of an authoritarian church structure and deference to a sometimes unscrupulous clergy who wield substantial power. The choice to remain Christian, for all its benefits, in many senses amounts to a forfeiture of self-determination. More than that, it is compatible with and does not challenge the rudiments of socioeconomic suffering.

The forms of self-determination attendant on becoming Jewish were not merely nominal—and this is the third reason for the Telugu

Jews' choice to become Jewish. As Jews they are required by God to act on their own behalf, concretely, in the world. They are required, importantly, to observe the Sabbath, a day of rest denied to most agricultural laborers. As Jews they become entitled both to work and to rest—an option denied most unskilled laborers, routinely exploited by landlords and factory owners who demand a seven-day work week. Indeed, the choice to become Jewish initially guaranteed aggravation of their material suffering. Employers simply replaced many Jewish workers because of their religious views. Still, the right both to work and to rest proved so humane and so civil that its holiness could hardly be doubted. The community's increased suffering in the years following its emergence seems, in fact, to have bolstered the members' convictions, and enhanced the value of being Jewish. Further, as Jews they are required to observe Jewish holidays and lifecycle events commemorating covenant, freedom, survival, and atonement. In becoming Jewish they did not merely call themselves by a new name, but found a sanction to act for themselves materially and spiritually, under the wings of a compassionate universal justice.

The fourth reason to become Jewish concerned reclamation of the past. Shmuel Yakobi began to navigate what he calls the lost history of Jews in south India. Now more than ten years into his research, he believes that Jews, possibly descendants of the Lost Tribe of Ephraim, migrated from northern India, perhaps Afghanistan or the North-East Frontier region (Manipur, Mizoram), sometime during the ninth or tenth century C.E., and settled around the area of Nandial in what were at that time nascent Telugu-speaking areas. He claims currently to be writing a comparative philological study of Hebrew and Telugu, which argues that Hebrew is the unrecognized source of many words in proto-Telugu, the still-unreconstructed Dravidian language that anteceded Sanskrit influences. Yakobi also claims that Telugu Jews for centuries formed a distinct *kulam* (birth-marriage-occupation group, or, as it is often poorly termed, caste). They maintained, he says, distinct customs, eating habits, occupations, and literacy in Hebrew. In my discussions with him, I must say that he was not forthcoming with artifactual evidence for these claims—a Hebrew Torah, genealogies, ancient Telugu Jewish ritual objects. I am under the impression that these have not survived. He was equally not forthcoming with details of historical evidence in the form of folklore and linguistic analysis. He is currently appealing, so far unsuccessfully, to the Archeological Survey of India to fund his investigations.

To the rest of Hindu society, the Telugu Jews, if they did exist historically, were grouped with outcastes, and associated particularly with the Madiga community of untouchables. Thus the community might have assimilated into Christianity when colonial missionaries reached the Telugu areas during the British period. Precisely why the community might have been assimilated then, after so many centuries, remains an important question. One provisional answer might be as follows. Scholars of South Asia have drawn a reasonably clear picture of the intensification of economic pressure on the peasantry during the colonial period, which was often extremely severe and widely produced a feudalization of agrarian relations. Such pressure has in many respects not subsided, and it is clear today that poor rural Indians need material and financial relief wherever they can get it. Well-funded and eager Christian missionary groups service economic desperation, building homes and schools in exchange for a pledge of loyalty. It seems possible that sheer economic need broke apart the nineteenth-century Telugu Jewish community, driving many of its members to embrace Christianity, along with millions of other poor Indians. However, this remains to be determined.

For economic reasons Shmuel Yakobi's formal break with Christianity was long in coming. His financial connections were critical to the building of the community's synagogue in Kottareddipalem, The House of the Children of Yakob, which opened in 1992. In the late 1980s, Shmuel moved his residence to the nearby city of Vijayawada, where he founded, also with the assistance of foreign

Christian donors, an independent open university offering correspondence courses in Torah and Hebraic Studies to Christian seminary students across India. Sadok and Aaron Yakobi became the resident leaders of the community, studying and teaching Torah and Hebrew with materials Shmuel Yakobi brought from Israel. Aaron Yakobi died of tuberculosis in 1992.

While the details of the community's ancestry remain cloudy, its members are firm in their choice to be Jewish, and become Jewish. My own opinion is that the importance of the community for world Jewry lies not in its history, but in its having developed independently and by its own initiative a Jewish response to the realities it faces. It has developed a spiritual and ethical practice which is solidly within Jewish tradition. The members of the community have assumed and not merely inherited their Jewish commitments, and in this they honor and extend the best efforts made by any Jew.

The Judaism they have developed is, at this point, virtually devoid of talmudic and rabbinic influences. Rather, it focuses on God's sheer power and commitment to His people, on the ethical imperatives of the prophets, and on the strength of their covenantal relation. The community cherishes the biblical account of the Exodus, and identifies deeply, I would say ardently, with its promise of liberation in exchange for the practice of justice and kindness, and religious observance. These promises form the backbone of the community's spiritual life; in group and individual prayer these Jews plead to God for it, demand their right to it, thank God for it, and struggle to be patient waiting for it. For them the living God delivers signs and responses to their prayers daily, in small ways. Sadok Yakobi, the leader of the community, whom the members support with weekly donations, spends his days moving from hut to hut leading prayer and giving support. Though neither a preacher nor a healer, he tells many stories of having witnessed miraculous healings, as well as small, inexplicable changes of fortune, which he and the community attribute to God's direct intervention. Sadok is convinced that the power of the community's prayer and the faithfulness of the God committed to them are responsible for their survival under otherwise insufferable conditions.

The community distinguishes itself from its Christian, Hindu, and Muslim neighbors—a distinction that is as important to them as it has been to Jews throughout the centuries—by keeping the Sabbath and major Jewish holidays, and following Jewish dietary laws. The more learned members of the community are engaged in ongoing, intensive discussions with one another and with their neighbors, particularly about the difference between Jewish teaching and the Christian doctrine they have comparatively recently rejected. The subjects include why Jesus is not the Messiah, the meaning of the redemption at Sinai, how to be a people of priests and a holy people, how Jews communicate with God, what the prophecies of the ingathering of the Jewish people mean for them. The discussions arising from these and related questions are vital to the community's development. They continue as live spiritual investigations. I spent three Sabbaths with the community, during which I studied the Torah with Sadok Yakobi, Abraham and Reuben Koshi, and a group of other men in sessions lasting all day. Our sessions were provocative and beneficial to all.

Telugu Sabbath services are original and moving, much of them dedicated to song. The congregation—men and women together—poignantly and powerfully sings the Hebrew of the psalms to Telugu folk melodies. The synagogue itself is a spare structure of bricks, a large room with a high ceiling and a single table on which stands a perpetually burning flame. It is the only brick building belonging to the community (all the member families live in mud-and-thatch huts), and everyone is exceedingly proud. Next door to the synagogue lives a Hindu family which donates its electrical connection to the synagogue on the Sabbath, providing everyone with the pleasure of electricity once a week (an irony much appreciated when I explained that many Jews will not turn on an electric switch on the Sabbath).

In my visits with the Telugu Jews I tried repeatedly to verify the authenticity of the community's Jewish commitment. I asked myself: Is it possible that their Jewishness is merely a vehicle to escape their economic suffering? Is their Jewish ancestry a fabrication? Perhaps it is a far-flung fantasy, born of intense suffering, to emigrate to Israel, a comparatively affluent country, much in the way other Indians dream of relocating to the United States or to Europe? Is their Judaism practiced for the sake of being Jewish regardless of where they live and die? I asked these questions of them in a variety of ways. I drew two conclusions. First, the clarity and calmness of their comments, and the passion of their worship, convinced me of the truth of their Jewish commitment. I believe they have made an irrevocable choice to be Jewish; they treat the choice as a destiny. Their commitment, I believe, is so strong that they will strive to live their Jewishness in spite of the resistance of the people around them, and regardless of their reception by other Jews. I believe they will die as Jews, whether in India or elsewhere. Second, because material poverty pervades their lives, I believe it is unreasonable to expect them to make any choices, including being Jewish, independent of their day-to-day struggles. Such struggles have been an active force in their decision to become Jewish.

Still, other Jews' acceptance of their choice to be Jewish matters greatly. Rabbi Avichail's visit to the community in 1994 and Kulanu's efforts have reassured them that their existence does matter to other Jews. Naturally they hope that fellow Jews will help them in their religious observance and also in their struggle to ameliorate their economic condition. Many of the Telugu Jews express a desire someday to make aliyah to Israel. Shmuel Yakobi's son has emigrated and obtained Israeli citizenship. These positive developments have been accompanied by a damaging series of articles from Israeli sources appearing in Indian newspapers, claiming that the Council of Eastern Jewry, the steering committee for the Telugu community, considers all Indian untouchables to be lost Jews, and proposes a mass exodus of millions of untouchables to Israel. Sadok Yakobi denies these claims, but such rumors have been strong enough in Israel to block even tourist visas to these Indians.

The sheer existence of the Telugu Jewish community is something of a miracle. For the community to have reached Judaism by striving to be true and just to itself in its uniquely Indian circumstances is, to me, extraordinary. Will their Jewish commitment challenge other Jews to honor their own Jewish commitments? Will other Jews admit the lives of the Telugu Jews into the story of the Jewish people? Will Jews around the world witness Judaism as a liberation theology in the experience of the Telugu Jews? Whether or not they are the Lost Tribe of Ephraim, they are a young community of devoted Jews, suffering and surviving with their God. Perhaps enough Jews around the world still know the isolation and the drawn-out urgency of having to live partly by wits and partly by faith that the wonder of a Jew in Andhra Pradesh is not so unbelievable.

(Further information about the Telugu community can be obtained from The Synagogue of the Children of Yakob, Kottareddipalem, Chebrolu Mandal, Guntur District, Andhra Pradesh, 522 212 India.)

25

Ghana

This letter appeared in the Autumn 1995 Kulanu newsletter.

Judaism in Ghana
David G. Ahenkorah

The name of our group is House of Israel (Zion). It was founded in 1976 by the late brother Aaron Ahomtre Toakyirafa. This brother Aaron, one day in 1976, had a vision about the lost tribes of Israel. Aaron was able to tell us about our ancestors who were scattered to so many lands from the Bible in the Old Testament. He opened our minds to know that all he taught from the Old Testament was the customs and the traditions that our forefathers were doing during thirty years past, when Christianity was not much in our area here. We then knew that through this Christianity we lost our customs, so we started practicing Judaism.

Aaron Ahomtre obtained an address from some American Jews and he wrote to them, and they delayed for about two years before he had a reply from them. Yet all those days we were still practicing Judaism. Their reply made us very happy, since they also cling to the Old Testament. When brother Aaron Ahomtre died, I stood at his position to maintain the group. I am brother David G. Ahenkorah, a teacher. Kofi Dwateng is secretary, Joseph Armah is chairman, Joseph K. Nippah is adviser, Isaac Aidoo is treasurer.

None of us speaks Hebrew; some of us can read and write. Others can't do so. We meet every Sabbath and the holidays. We cling only to the Old Testament. Therefore, we only believe in one God who created the Heaven and the Earth. None of our members practice any other religion or believe in any created image. We have few prayer books, not in sufficient numbers for us. We all wish to convert to Judaism. We are ready to cooperate with you in every way and request help from you.

Our meeting place for every Sabbath service is done in a classroom. With its problems we are making our own meeting place for the Sabbath and the holidays.

The Ghanaian Village That Wants to Be Jewish
Daniel Baiden with Robert H. Lande

For the last several years there have been scattered reports—such as the one above—that a group of about 150 people in the village of Sefwi Wiawso, Ghana, has embraced Judaism. As anyone with even a little knowledge of Jewish history knows, group conversions to Judaism are rare. For anyone proud to be Jewish, this Ghanaian event is therefore intriguing. For me, however, news of this group had singular importance. This is because I am a Jew who was born in Ghana.

I was born in 1950, to Jewish parents. My family's oral history says that our ancestors were from Ethiopia, and that our family originally came from Israel. As a child I heard many times that we were part of one of the Ten "Lost" Tribes of Israel. Like many Ethiopians, we moved a lot. Hundreds of years ago, to flee conquerors of Ethiopia, my ancestors migrated west, eventually settling in Ghana. My extended family in Ghana (including cousins) is quite large—at least seventy-five people. Until recently, I thought we were the only ones in Ghana with a tie to Judaism. When I heard through Kulanu about the village of Sefwi Wiawso, I was sure that my family must somehow be responsible for the village's turn toward our faith.

I grew up always aware of my Jewish heritage. My father, Emmanuel, had learned much about modern Judaism from a friend, Rabbi Weiss, a Polish refugee who lived in Ghana in the late 1940s and early 1950s. My father learned some Hebrew from Rabbi Weiss and taught his children about Judaism as best as he could under the circumstances. We observed the Jewish holidays, and, while we did not have weekly services, we did avoid cooking or other work on Shabbat. My family possesses various Jewish ritual objects that are quite old, including tallitot, Stars of David, and prayers written in Amharic, the Ethiopian language. Sadly, many members of my family who are still in Ghana no longer practice Judaism.

I moved to the United States in 1979. I joined Congregation Oseh Shalom, in Laurel, Maryland, where Rabbi Gary Fink has served as my spiritual teacher, and my friend Harry Rosenbluh has patiently taught me Hebrew. I regularly attend Shabbat services, keep a kosher home, and am active in Jewish causes.

When I heard that in the remote village of Sefwi Wiawso there was a group that practiced Judaism, I had to see for myself. I borrowed the plane fare from Harry Rosenbluh and was given a number of siddurim and other books by Rabbi Fink. In addition, Kulanu gave me a student Torah to present to them. (It looks like a real Torah and is complete in every way, but it is printed, not handwritten, and is made with ordinary paper.) Kulanu also provided me with additional prayer books, Israeli flags, etc., that the Jewish Book Store in Wheaton, Maryland, was kind enough to sell at a reduced price. I contacted my relatives to tell them that I was coming and then left for Ghana.

On May 8, 1996, I arrived in Accra, the capital of Ghana. I had a joyous reunion with my family in the nearby town of Cape Coast, and even more joy that Shabbat when I led services for them. I led a Shabbat morning service for many members of my extended family and a few onlookers as well—seventy-five people in all. They especially liked the Shabbat songs that I taught them, *Ma Tovu* in particular.

I then started to plan the best way to reach Sefwi Wiawso—no easy task, since it is in a remote portion of the country, far from Accra. I prayed for guidance as to which route to take, and decided on the coastal route. I wanted to time my arrival for Shabbat, so I set out at 3:00 a.m. on Friday morning, together with Samuel, my brother.

The journey by "bush taxi" (actually a small crowded bus) took until 8:00 p.m. The driver left us off at a village called Takoradi with instructions to start climbing a small mountain if we wanted to reach the village. After an hour of climbing we arrived at a police station and asked for the village of Sefwi Wiawso. When pressed, we said that we wanted to meet the Jews who lived there. They first professed to have never heard of the place, and then said that the village contained "thieves and bad people." When we protested that the village must exist if "thieves and bad people" lived there, they threatened to put us in jail. The impasse was broken when a small boy, who had overheard everything, offered to take us there for a fee.

By 10:00 p.m. the boy brought us to the house of Joseph K. Nippah, one of the group's leaders. We were delighted to see that their Shabbat candles were still burning. We were warmly greeted even before we could announce who we were. When they discovered that we were Jewish, they were even more delighted to see us. Despite the late hour they took us to a second house, the home of Joseph Armah, the group's chairman, where twenty-five people quickly gathered. Despite my fatigue I could not resist such a wonderful crowd, and led them in Friday night services. As my adrenaline pumped I taught them Lecha Dodi and other appropriate Shabbat songs and prayers.

My brother and I stayed overnight with the Armah family and awoke the next morning to find that we were in the middle of a compound of approximately fourteen Jewish households that contained, I was told, about a hundred people. The Jewish community also had perhaps an additional eight households that were not in the compound. All told, approximately 150 people are members.

The community is affluent by Ghanaian standards. The houses are relatively large and well built, with electricity and running water. The Armah family had a television, but I could not watch because it was Shabbat. The villagers are mostly farmers (they grow cacao and palm trees, and I saw many cows, goats, and other animals) and also earn money by baking bread, operating a grocery store and taxi service, photography studio, etc.

They led me to their synagogue, which is an old, cramped building with three rooms. One of the rooms was used for prayer. In addition, many members of the community stayed at the synagogue all day to make it easier for them to avoid such Sabbath prohibitions as watching television. The other two rooms were for resting during Shabbat, one for the men and one for the women.

I delighted them by putting on my tallit and taking out the student Torah that Kulanu had given to the community. They had never seen a Torah before, so it was an object of great interest to them. The children especially wanted to touch it. I assumed the role of rabbi, leading the enthusiastic congregation of fifty-five in a service. I thought about the prayers and melodies that Rabbi Fink, at Oseh Shalom, had taught me as I did my best to teach this eager group a small bit of modern Judaism. I conducted most of the service in English because they did not know Hebrew. But I also attempted to teach them a few Hebrew prayers, including the Shema, Kaddish, and Yigdal. I conducted the Torah service in Hebrew, explaining that every synagogue in the world was reading the same Torah portion that same day. I read it in Hebrew because I wanted them to experience an authentic Torah service emotionally, even if they could not understand it.

The service I led for them was totally unlike their normal service, where they mostly read the Old Testament together. They did this because they lacked modern Jewish prayer books. My gifts of prayer books were received with the utmost gratitude.

After the service we had a late, leisurely lunch. The meal was cold because they do not cook on Shabbat. We talked for hours about a wide variety of matters.

During this conversation I solved the mystery of the origin of their Jewishness. The solution was one that I had in part suspected. In 1976 a man named Aaron Ahomtre Toakyirafi had a vision that he and the other members of the village were descended from one of the Ten Lost Tribes. He convinced some of his neighbors that they should return to the customs of their ancestors and follow only the Old Testament. Although he has since died, the community is his legacy.

There is more to the story, though. My older brother, Isaac, had attended and taught at a nearby teacher-training college in the late 1950s. Clearly, Isaac (who is no longer living) was an excellent teacher. As they told me about my brother, the memories came back to me. I remembered that, as a small child only about six years old, I had once accompanied him to this very village! How amazing that the seeds that Isaac had planted in the 1950s had grown a generation later. How incredible that they had maintained their Jewishness for another generation with almost no contact with the outside Jewish world. How appropriate that I, more than a generation later, would be the one to continue my brother's holy work. I believe that it is my destiny to lead them to a higher level of Jewish belief, knowledge, and observance.

We talked about many other subjects. They told me that they have named their community the House of Israel. Several members told me they embraced Judaism because, to them, the Old Testament contained more truth than the New Testament. They reject Jesus Christ in all forms and consider themselves to be Jewish, although they would like to convert formally. They also told me that although Ghana does not have an ambassador from Israel, in February 1996 the community's leader, David G. Ahenkorah, had journeyed to a nearby country, the Ivory Coast, to meet that nation's Israeli ambassador. Unfortunately he offered no assistance to the community. They expressed to me a great interest in visiting Israel but asked almost no questions about the United States.

Late that afternoon we concluded our conversation and went back to the synagogue, where I gave the House of Israel a Havdalah candle I had brought with me, and led the congregation in making Havdalah. They insisted on calling me "rabbi"; this embarrassed me, of course, but it was perhaps understandable, since I was the closest thing to a rabbi they had ever encountered. In fact, I was the first outside Jew to enter the village since my brother's visits many years before!

It is my prayer that my visit will be the start of world Jewry's contact with this village. They sincerely want to join the Jewish people and have a great thirst for Jewish knowledge. They practice no other religion. Although none of them knows Hebrew, many of the men and the children can read and write English. This makes the task of giving them Jewish knowledge very difficult, but not impossible.

One can only speculate as to how much longer they can maintain their desire to become Jewish, and their feeling that they are Jewish, without help from the outside world. We must immediately start taking steps to dramatically increase their level of Jewish knowledge, to help them become the Jews they want to be. We must send them Jewish educational materials, including books for children, prayer books, beginning Hebrew books, and audio tapes with songs and prayers in Hebrew. We must also correspond with them—perhaps a pen-pal program for the children would be appropriate. They also need a much larger synagogue; they have a half-built one that they would be delighted to dedicate to anyone generous enough to send them the funds necessary to complete it. In addition, my family, in Cape Coast, would like to build a synagogue and dedicate it to Rabbi Fink in appreciation for all that he has done to teach me and enable me to bring Judaism to Ghana.

We should also organize a visit by a fact-finding and teaching delegation. I hereby offer to be the expedition's guide, and beseech every rabbi reading this to consider becoming our expedition's spiritual leader. We must let them know that if they sincerely want to be Jewish, we will provide them with a warm and friendly welcome to the Jewish community.

Part VI
Reflections

26

Genealogy on a Grand Scale
Jonina Duker

I teach Jewish genealogy. No matter what flavor my talk is in—whether I'm entertaining elderly Jews for an afternoon or teaching serious students for six weeks—the title is always the same: "Jewish Genealogy: Reconnecting the *K'lal*." I am trying to inspire as many people as I can to trace their family histories. If enough of us do it, then we will be able to put back together what the world keeps splitting asunder, generation after generation. We Jews are connected to each other by many bonds; I believe that being able to describe the links more concretely strengthens the bonds.

To me, it seems obvious that the work of an outreach organization like Kulanu is merely Jewish genealogy from another perspective—Jewish genealogy on a larger scale. Look at large groupings of family units of similar ethnicity and figure out how and when a group "split off." More importantly, help the descendants reconnect with *K'lal Yisrael* (the entire Jewish people) in whatever way they want to reconnect.

I believe that issues of Jewish genealogy and continuity are fundamental to Judaism. As Jews we attach a great deal of importance to how people and things are named. We refer to God as HaShem—"the Name." We are Semites, descendants of Noah's son Shem. We believe that "a good name is rather to be chosen than great riches" (Proverbs 22:1). Genealogy is about connecting names. A basic tenet of our faith has to do with the respect we owe our ancestors: "Honor thy father and thy mother, that you may long endure" (Exodus 20:12 and Deuteronomy 5:16). If you honor your ancestors by passing on what they cared about, you will teach your descendants by example to honor you by doing the same. That is the only way an individual human being can endure—by passing on what matters to him or her.

I am more fascinated by the historical linkage than by the contemporary decision to return by converting. An acute sense of loss compels me to spend my time on genealogy. As a human being, I do not deal well with loss. I think about those who struggled and suffered to pass on Judaic traditions and values, and how the sacrifices they made were not always enough to ensure the continuation. I feel as if something has been stolen personally from me. That is why I feel a personal sense of deprivation when I hear about a group of Jews that has been lost or dispersed. Correspondingly, that is why I feel a personal sense of victory when I hear about someone returning—yes, we've gotten one back!—one who had been tragically lost to us as a people. We are reclaiming our own.

With one caveat, I do not feel that same sense of victory when I hear about someone converting. (I do feel a sense of welcome, but not victory.) When speaking about Jewish genealogy, I am always careful to tell my audiences that Jews by choice should not feel left out in a discussion of Jewish genealogy. Without singling anyone out, I tell the audience that those who are Jews by choice need to remember three things.

First of all, they have chosen an alliance with the Jewish people, so the odds are good that a loved one will be descended directly from Jews. What a wonderful present for people you love—tracing their Jewish roots.

Secondly, with the influx of resettled Russians into the United States there is a wonderful opportunity to do Jewish genealogy as a mitzvah. Many resettled Russians arrive clutching fifty-year-old letters from North American family members with whom contact has been lost. Reconnecting people with real, living, flesh-and-blood relatives can be an even headier experience than making a historical linkage.

The third reason is not a matter of fact; it is a mystical belief of mine. I firmly believe that many Jews by choice are descendants of Jews where the knowledge of the historical linkage has been lost. What draws them back in is some kind of subconscious historical memory. I defy anyone who doesn't believe this to read Julius Lester's autobiography. When he wrote about his long-term attraction to Judaism and his eventual discovery that one of his ancestors was an immigrant Russian-Jewish peddler, my reaction was profound and visceral.

When people ask me when I first became interested in genealogy, I always answer "I was born that way." At family gatherings I always listened to groups of older relatives telling family stories and talking about who did what and why. As a child I always had the comforting feeling that certain deceased ancestors of a scholarly persuasion were with me. They were looking over my shoulder, and it was my obligation to make sure that my behavior fitted what they would want for their descendants, given the new frame of reference for the Judaism of the time.

There is a famous story about a rabbi who used to go into the woods to say a prayer on certain occasions. After his passing, his followers only remembered where to go but not what to say. After their passing, only the memory that someone would go somewhere remained. I feel as if we, through organizations like Kulanu, have been given an opportunity to help others find the place in the woods and remember what to say again. We can make the words of Joel (1:3) live again for those who were lost for generations:

Tell your children of it,
And let your children tell their children,
And their children another generation.

27

Conversion and the Purpose of Jewish Existence
Lawrence J. Epstein

One of the characteristics of a really successful and important Jewish organization is that it be able to define its own unique contributions to Jewish life and be able to draw a variety of people to do its important work. Kulanu's mission—to revive Judaism among those thought lost to the Jewish people—is such a unique effort. As I interpret that mission, Kulanu seeks to help people of Jewish ancestry to return to Judaism and helps those who sincerely wish to join the Jewish people. Those with such ancestors include the descendants of people forcibly converted during the Inquisition, people with Jewish ancestors who were forcibly assimilated, people whose Jewish ancestors assimilated through lack of knowledge about Judaism, people who believe themselves to be part of the ancient Jewish people, and others. Sincere converts are those who do not have any known Jewish ancestors but who find Judaism an attractive religion and wish to join the Jewish people on its historic spiritual journey. Kulanu's uniqueness is its international perspective and its willingness to deal with people often neglected by other Jewish organizations.

This vital effort brings together people with very different motivations. Some join Kulanu for demographic reasons. They see increasing the numbers of Jews, especially in Israel, as valuable because the more Jews there are, the more safe and secure is the

Jewish future. Others join for religious reasons. Some of them see the return of people who may have been Jews at one time as the dawn of redemption. Still others participate because Kulanu is engaged in a vast humanitarian rescue mission. Some find the stories of the rescued inspiring and hope they will influence other Jews to have a deeper attachment to their heritage.

I think all of these are excellent reasons, and I find some value in all of them. I know that the plurality of reasons for joining strengthens an organization, and I find the various reasons why people become interested both fascinating and revealing. I would like to discuss the principal reason why I became involved with Kulanu.

I have a long-standing interest in the subject of conversion to Judaism. I have written two books on the subject and edited a third. I've also written a curriculum on conversion for Jewish schools, a bibliographical and encyclopedia article, and many other articles on the subject. I've worked with various national and local organizations to promote conversions to Judaism.

While I have no personal, emotional stake in the subject of conversion, the subject nevertheless became more and more important to me as I studied it. At first, my interest was simply practical. I saw increasing the numbers of conversions to Judaism as a way to increase the number of Jews and decrease the number of intermarriages. As I studied, I realized that I had a connection with those who convert to Judaism. I had been raised in a very secular Jewish home with only a little Jewish upbringing. My knowledge of Judaism was weak, and my attachment to Judaism was tenuous. When, in my early twenties, I rediscovered my Jewish heritage, I felt very much like what a convert must feel like. Thereafter, I felt a spiritual kinship with those who voluntarily choose to become Jewish.

Despite my minimal Jewish background, I had somewhere learned that converts weren't really Jewish and that conversion was antithetical to Jewish beliefs. However, as I began reading the sacred Jewish texts and books of Jewish history, I discovered that quite the opposite was true. Judaism, traditionally, was very open and welcoming to converts. Large numbers of people had converted to Judaism. It suddenly struck me that the Bible showed that every Jew alive today has at least two ancestors who were converts, even if their genealogy goes all the way back to Abraham and Sarah, who weren't born Jewish. I read the midrashic literature. I read why persecutions had forced Jews to stop encouraging conversion.

Somewhere along the way, it became clear to me that the Jewish mission to be a light unto the nations had not been taken seriously enough for too long. I saw welcoming converts as part of the covenantal obligation that Jews had accepted at Mount Sinai, an obligation that was not being met. I determined to do my part to fulfill this mitzvah, this religious commandment.

When I read of the work that Kulanu was doing, helping people who thought they had Jewish ancestors re-embrace Judaism through a formal conversion, I knew that this was an organization for me. While I maintained a healthy skepticism about the claims of some people that they were members of the Ten Lost Tribes, I nevertheless found the claims intriguing. I thought Rabbi Eliyahu Avichail to be an inspiring figure, willing to travel great distances, often into dangerous areas, to help people he didn't know learn about traditional Judaism and become Jewish. Whatever the accuracy of the claims, I felt that people who wished to join the Jewish people for any reason should be encouraged, helped, and welcomed.

Kulanu's international efforts also were important to me. Conversions are often seen only in the context of combating intermarriage and assimilation in the United States. I think that encouraging conversion to Judaism needs to be seen from an international view. After all, if such encouraging is a divine obligation, part of the very purpose of Jewish existence—as many believe from the teachings of the Talmud—a theory of encouraging conversion that encompasses the entire world is necessary. Kulanu's efforts exemplify that theory to me.

My guess is that not many people who have become active in Kulanu have done so for a reason similar to my own. Perhaps not many even would agree with the conclusions I have drawn. But I think such differences are enriching. The ability to draw people for so many varied reasons is Kulanu's great strength. It is an organization that is needed. It is an organization that will make an historical contribution to Jewish life.

28

A Philanthropist Speaks: Zionism for the 1990s
Irving Moskowitz

Dr. Irving Moskowitz financed the air transportation of scores of Shinlung descendants of the tribe of Manasseh from northeastern India to Israel.

Yes, I helped the Shinlung. I helped them with my time, my energy, my enthusiasm, and my money. People always ask why. Of all of the causes in the world, why have I picked this one to become my number-one priority?

I believe that the Shinlung are one of the Ten Lost Tribes of Israel. I believe, in other words, that they are my brothers and sisters. Their faith faltered over the years, but now they want to return to Judaism and to Israel. How can I not help them?

The instinct of every Jew should be to help his or her fellow Jews when they are in trouble. Right now I am secure and comfortable in the United States. But who knows what will happen tomorrow? Who can say for sure that my grandchildren will not one day be isolated and persecuted, with only their fellow Jews willing to go to great lengths to help them? History has shown that we frequently are isolated and weak. If we do not help each other when times are good, who will do so when times are bad? Jews who have everything of a material nature that they could ever want often get complacent. They forget that we as a people have to be strong.

I am also struck by the beauty—dare I say, miracle?—of a people who have been separated from mainstream Jewry for two thousand years but have clung to a remnant of their faith, and now want to return to the Jewish people. I feel that long-lost brothers and sisters want to return home, but that they cannot do it by themselves. How can I not help them? How can I not embrace them?

If an Israeli pilot were captured by enemies, we would spare no expense, do everything possible, to rescue him. All we have to do for the Shinlung is to give them airplane tickets to Israel and some money to get them started in a new life. It is so simple. How can we not do it?

Yes, the idea of bringing dozens—and one day thousands—of Shinlung back to Judaism and to Israel is crazy. About as crazy as the dream of founding a Jewish state after two thousand years.

I firmly believe that helping the Shinlung is the essence of Zionism. It is Zionism for the 1990s. When the history of this era is written I don't want anyone to say that I didn't do enough to help my brothers and sisters and, by helping them, to help the Jewish state and the Jewish people.

This also is a way to renew the Jewish people and the spirit of Zionism. Think what a message this sends to Jews all over the world! We must have something really special for this to occur. Perhaps Jews will be less likely to abandon Judaism when they find out about these remote people who wish to rejoin us.

Why do I help the Shinlung? The truth is that they are the ones who are helping me. They are allowing me to perform a great mitzvah. For doing something that to me is only instinctive, I feel very good. It is I who must say thank you to the Shinlung.

29

Nathan's Prayer
Nathan Bliss

This prayer was included in the author's Bar Mitzvah in February 1966 at Beth El Hebrew Congregation, Alexandria, Virginia.

Dear God,

I know you're very busy, but I'd like to take a little of your time this morning to reflect on this special day that you have allowed me to reach. My Bar Mitzvah means a lot to me. It is a high point in my Jewish life and a time to prove that I am a responsible person.

The Torah and Haftarah portions I read today described your instructions for holy buildings. In a sense, you instructed us to build a house for you, God. Whether it be the traveling Tabernacle or the first Temple in Israel, they both house you. In my portion, we were instructed how to make this house a holy place that is suitable for our worship to you.

Today, you present us with other opportunities to build holy places to worship you. Many who seek to worship as Jews around the world do not have the resources to create houses of worship in their communities. Many Jews are isolated, unknown to most in the outside world, and lack even the basic necessities of life, such as food and clothing. It is the job of those who are more fortunate to help these people with their life needs and their spiritual needs. As my *tikkun olam* project for my Bar Mitzvah, I have become involved in an organization that helps Jews in remote communities.

This organization is called Kulanu. I was introduced to it by our own Rabbi Jacques Cukierkorn, who is one of the organization's founders. *Kulanu* means "all of us." It was created to find lost and dispersed Jewish people and help them to become a part of the larger Jewish community. They offer financial assistance, contacts with Jews in other countries, instruction in Judaism and Hebrew language, and help in setting up places of worship. In some cases, they also help people to relocate to Israel. Kulanu has helped the Telugu Jews of India, the Abayudaya Jews of Uganda, as well as Jews from Peru, Ethiopia, and China.

The work of the Kulanu organization is very interesting to me. It is hard to believe that these isolated Jewish communities even exist. I contacted Rabbi Mendel Zuber, a rabbi in New York. He works primarily with the Incan Jews of Peru. These people live in three small communities in the Andes Mountains. They are very poor and in need of many things. They have no synagogue in which to pray to you. They have to travel to Lima, the capital, if they want to visit a place of worship. They are not able to keep the commandment of building a house for you, God.

There were close to five hundred Jews in these communities when they first came to the attention of the Lubavitch movement. Rabbi Zuber was sent to teach Hebrew, Jewish religious beliefs and practices, and helped three hundred of them relocate to Israel. However, there are now still 250 remaining Incan Jews in Peru. These people are still very poor and are still trying to follow your commandments. Rabbi Zuber put me in touch with the Salagar family in the town of Trujillo, Peru. Through this family, which includes eight children, I have donated prayer books in Spanish and Hebrew so that these Jews can conduct a worship service and all follow from the same text. Our family has also sent Star of

David necklaces, which the young Incan Jews especially want to wear in order to proudly show their identity. I am looking forward to continuing my personal contact with this community, and I hope someday that I will be able to visit them, either in Peru or in Israel.

As I look to the future, God, I hope for a world in which people from all different places and cultures can understand each other and live together peacefully. Help the fortunate to realize what they can do for the less fortunate, as you commanded us to do in the Torah and Haftarah portions I read today. Help them see what a small contribution can do to improve the lives of others. Help them see that our world is in need of a lot of healing, and we are the only ones who can heal it.

I thank you for all of my family and friends who are with me today. May you guide us as we help make this world a better place for all people in all communities to live and grow in peace. Amen

30

Celebrating Jewish Diversity
Myra D'Gabriel

I feel a great deal of sympathy for the Marranos, perhaps because my own background is so varied. My mother fled from the pogroms in Russia as a child and came from a very Orthodox Jewish family. My father was born in India, a member of the Sikh religion and a leader of the Sikh community in England for many years. I was born in Scotland and brought up as a Jew, knowing no other religion.

I married a Cuban Jew after emigrating to Canada, where our oldest son was born; our two other sons were born in the United States, where we lived for years, and I now live in Brazil. Perhaps my mother's nickname, Tsigayner ("Gypsy"), has something to do with it. I was born at the beginning of World War II and thank God that I was born on the right side of the English Channel. Had I been born 26 miles away, I would have been another statistic of the Holocaust.

I grew up with youngsters who had survived the concentration camps. I learned to run very fast from postwar supporters of [Sir Oswald] Mosley [the British fascist leader], to whom Jews were anathema. I was bullied and heckled by children who called me "half-caste" and learned to defend myself at an early age. Yet these things were comprehensible, even understandable to one who has lived through a war.

What I do not understand, and do not think I ever shall, is how a Jew can possibly be racist! Is it because he must find a victim—any victim—to transfer his humiliation to? How can there be enmity between two Jews because one is Sephardi and the other is Ashkenazi? How can a person who was born a Jew and brought up in the Jewish faith not sympathize with and accept the Marrano who wants to return to the faith of his ancestors and must work very hard to become a Jew?

I enjoy my mixed ancestry and consider myself a better person because of it. But my father was a wise man, and he insisted that I be brought up only in the Jewish faith, because he admired that faith and claimed that it was safer to be a Jew than to be called a "half-caste." To some people that may be considered a derogatory term; to me it means that I am more than the sum of one person!

31

Irony
Karen Primack

I've been donating some time to a Jewish outreach organization since its inception, but two recent events in my life have helped me focus on why I should support the organization financially as well.

First, I read the August 1993 issue of *Moment* magazine, which had as its cover story and theme "Jews in Cults." While I had read much about cults before, some of the information was new to me. I learned from Arnold Markowitz's article that three-quarters of those who join cults are relatively balanced, successful people from upper-middle-income, intact, and educated families. The author suggested three reasons for the disproportionate number of Jews in cults or cultlike groups: they are open to alternative political and theological ideas, they attend college or university (where cults recruit most energetically), and Jewish families are sometimes too close and don't allow for appropriate separation. Committed Jews are not immune. The article by David and Livia Bardin gives a moving account of their son's involvement in a destructive cult—even though he had graduated from Jewish day schools and young adult programs, spoke Hebrew, had lived in Israel as a boy, and returned twice as a youth. The magazine noted that the average cost to deprogram a former cult member ranges from $18,000 to $30,000.

The very next day I encountered a long-time acquaintance at the supermarket. We had not seen each other in several years and quickly got caught up. Our sons had gone to high school together, and I knew that their family was fundamentalist Christian and that their son had been pulled out of biology class when the topic of evolution was discussed. I now learned that their daughter teaches second-graders in "a messianic school for Jews."

That night my husband and I wrote out a check for $600 to cover the cost of transporting a Shinlung immigrant from India to Israel. I began to feel much better!

Yes, we all know we are losing Jews to intermarriage, to cults, to other religions, to indifference. I agree with many that education is a vital tool in turning the situation around. Unlike some, however, I do not place my focus on replacing lost numbers; quality is more important than quantity to me.

What I have come to appreciate, though, is the irony that allows many Jews to wring their hands in despair over the intermarriage rate and yet to ignore the plight of our cousins, shown by impressive scholarship to be from the Ten Lost Tribes, who have maintained their identity through twenty-seven centuries of hardship. Many are practicing Jews eager to study further in Israel, and some to relocate there. They deserve at least as much attention—and financial support—as those who are *leaving* Judaism.

Don't you agree?

32

Facilitating Returnees
Brian P. Haran

Kulanu is doing something of immense importance. I don't have stronger words at my command to tell readers just how vital it is.

Kulanu, Amishav, and other outreach organizations are very important. Had I known of them years ago, I have no doubt that they would have made a big difference in the process of my own "return." It has taken me many years on my own. One feels alone, isolated. Neither fish nor fowl, and certainly not realizing that one is part of a large and significant piece of Judaism.

The more publicity and practical help that is made available, the better for the whole of the community. The old Jewish connection is a key that can unlock a door enabling our brothers and sisters to come back into the light, having lived in the shadows for so many years.

33

Should We Provide a Warm Welcome to Anyone Who Sincerely Wants to (Re)join the Jewish People?

Robert H. Lande

The issues discussed in this book raise many questions in my mind. For example, how much do we have to know before we can conclude that a person might be a lost Jew or a part of a lost Jewish community? What kinds of help should we provide? How far should "helping" or even "welcoming" be taken? How do we know whether people who say they want to become Jewish are sincere? What if someone with no proven Jewish roots sincerely wants to join the Jewish community? Are we missionaries?

SUPPOSE WE ARE UNSURE OF THEIR JEWISH ROOTS?

Most of us have encountered people whose Jewish roots are uncertain, and have heard about communities and individuals without Jewish origins who want to practice Judaism. So long as someone sincerely wants to become Jewish, shouldn't we attempt to assist him or her in this quest?

Two examples illustrate that it often is extremely difficult to determine whether someone actually has Jewish roots.

The Jewishness of the Beta Israel of Ethiopia was doubted by many for decades. They were officially declared to be Jewish by the Israeli Chief Rabbinate only in the 1970s. Even today their origin is disputed. The Chief Rabbinate believes that they are descendants of the Tribe of Dan, whereas the Beta Israel believe that they descend from King Solomon and the Queen of Sheba. And while many academic historians believe that they are descended from the Jews of Yemen, a few scholars believe that their ancestors were medieval converts. If the activists in the American Association for Ethiopian Jews had waited until the Jewish community came to a consensus about the true origin of the Ethiopian Jews, all the Beta Israel would still be waiting and suffering in Ethiopia.

Similar problems arise concerning people who believe they are descended from Spanish and Portuguese Jews who were forced to convert to Christianity five hundred years ago. Few of them can trace their maternal line conclusively back to unquestioned Jews in the 1490s. How many of us could do that? If we cannot meet this test, perhaps we should not be so strict with people who have an oral tradition that says they are of Jewish descent.

One creative solution toward these issues was devised by a Liberal rabbi in Brazil when a descendant of Marranos presented himself and asked to be considered a Jew. The rabbi devised and required a "reunification" ceremony rather than insisting upon a normal conversion. This enabled the individual to keep his pride and respect his family traditions, and also satisfied the rabbi's desire for a ceremony acceptable under halacha.

We should learn from these examples. We should be welcoming, not overly suspicious or formalistic. Above all, we should search for creative solutions. We must not simply reject individuals or groups of uncertain origins.

Still, there is a certain romance to assisting people who wish to return to their Jewish roots. If a Marrano's ancestors for five hundred years stubbornly clung to some remnants of Judaism, perhaps out of a desire that their children's children might one day be able to worship freely as Jews, it surely is wonderful—in fact a privilege—to play some small role in this miracle.

Picture a secret Jew lighting Sabbath candles in a special, nonpublic room with her daughter in the hope that her daughter's daughter would one day be able to light the candles openly. Now, twenty generations later, their descendants want to worship openly as Jews. How can we not help them to do so? We can never erase the effects of the Inquisition from Jewish history. But we can at least help a few of its victims' descendants validate their ancestors' stubbornness.

Are We Missionaries?

Are we missionaries? The short answer is no. The longer answer must depend upon how the term "missionary" is defined, but under any reasonable definition, the answer is still no.

Judaism has generally refrained from missionizing for many reasons, including the trouble we often would have caused for ourselves if we had engaged in missionizing. Since we oppose others who missionize among Jews, it seems unfair or inappropriate for us to be doing this. Moreover, many of us have an image of a missionary as someone with a Christian Bible in one hand and a whip in the other. We know that historically many Jews and non-Jews were forced to adopt Christianity, Islam, and other religions, or were forced to convert if they wanted to be educated, to obtain various economic benefits, or just to fit better into the dominant culture. Naturally, we want nothing to do with conversions that are forced, induced, or, in effect, purchased.

Still other missionaries proselytize to everyone. Although they don't use coercion or economic inducements, they knock on doors and stop people on the street in an attempt to persuade them to join their religion.

Jews have never done anything even remotely approaching missionizing behavior of this kind. Every situation in which rabbis have been involved has started with a group or an individual who has evidenced a strong interest in Judaism well before they had any contact with the rabbi. First they decided they wanted to become Jewish.

Thus, our highest priority is and should remain lost Jews. The more sure we are that someone is a lost Jew, the more we should extend ourselves to welcome him or her to the Jewish people. The more evidence we have that someone is in fact Jewish, the more we should do to help in the journey back. But we should not turn any sincere person away—once he or she has first expressed an interest in Judaism.

How Do We Know Whether Someone's Interest Is Sincere?

Like many outreach activists, I often give talks about current projects. I describe how groups of Jews became lost but now some of their descendants would like to rejoin the Jewish community. I also discuss how groups around the world with no proven connection to Judaism have decided they want to become Jewish. Inevitably, some members of the audience react with suspicion and hostility.

In part they are asking why anyone would want to become Jewish, with an implication that people rarely would do so sincerely. There is sometimes even a suggestion that the would-be converts must be expressing an interest in Judaism to achieve economic benefits.

These questions make me sad, because they imply that Judaism has so little to offer as a religion that anyone wishing to join must be suspect. It makes me wonder about the Jewish knowledge, awareness, and spiritual beliefs of those who view potential converts with hostility. Do they view Judaism as a joy or a burden?

It appears that Judaism is for some people similar to an exclusive country club that you can join only if you are rich, white, and have parents who also were members. If this is Judaism, then conversions are not permitted. But what if Judaism is instead a religion, albeit one mostly comprised of rich and middle-class white people?

There is no denying that some might believe that converting to Judaism could benefit them financially. But the economic motivation simply is not a generally plausible one, for three reasons.

First, consider two of the groups highlighted in this book. The Abayudaya embraced Judaism in 1919. Yet, before Kulanu's historic visit in 1995, they had only scattered contacts with world Jewry. It is hard to believe that they even knew that Jews on the average are wealthier than Christians. If they had wanted to please their British rulers, they would have become Christians, not Jews. If they had wanted to please Idi Amin when he ruled Uganda, they would have become Muslims. It is inconceivable that they adopted Judaism in 1919 so that their descendants might, in 1996, obtain some economic benefit.

The Shinlung/Menashe also began to embrace, or reembrace, Judaism in the 1950s and 1960s. As of that time they had no hope of emigrating to Israel or of achieving any form of assistance from world Jewry. Again, it seems inconceivable that their decades-ago decision could have been so cynical. Charlatans out for economic gain won't change their lives, risk their neighbors' hostility, and endure the problems and burdens of being Jewish for decades just for some tiny probability of assistance from a community they have barely heard of.

Many more examples could be given. How long must someone live as a Jew before we believe that he or she honestly wants to be Jewish?

Second, the vast majority of the people written about here wish to formally convert to Judaism. This means convincing a beth din of three rabbis that they are sincere in their desire to join us, as opposed to wanting to convert to obtain some advantage. Rabbis are not perfect, of course, and they can be fooled on occasion. But it is part of their training and their business to assess whether a convert is sincere, and we should have faith that they are good at their profession.

The third reason is based upon the observations of Jews who have visited the groups we have been working with. These visitors are for the most part worldly, mature people with a cynical streak who have "heard it all" many times before. Yet all who return from a visit to the Shinlung, the Abayudaya, or the other groups, uniformly report how impressed they were with the honesty of the group's devotion to Judaism. Their accounts are filled with stories of the group's spirituality, devotion, and sincere interest in Judaism. They testify that the interest is long-term and persistent.

WHAT TYPES OF ASSISTANCE SHOULD WORLD JEWRY PROVIDE?

Tough decisions sometimes arise because of the extreme poverty of some of the people that we get to know. A visitor to the Abayudaya or the Telugu community, for example, inevitably feels compassion for these extremely poor people. Should world Jewry give aid that goes beyond religious material and instruction?

It is tempting to draw a firm line and say no, agreeing to pay only for religious material, such as books and ritual items. But what if a poor person cannot read Hebrew and wishes to learn? Surely we should pay for books, tapes, or lessons? Moreover, what if they cannot read at all? How can we expect illiterate Abayudaya or Telugu Jews, who cannot read English or any other language, to be fully Jewish?

As a practical matter it is extremely difficult for people to be Jewish if they are illiterate. For this reason we should consider including education as one of the types of assistance that we will provide.

Should we go further? This depends on the availability of monetary resources and whether we have the expertise in economic development to be successful. (There is another consideration: Economic assistance could open us to the canard that we were obtaining insincere converts who profess an interest in Judaism only for financial gain. However, this argument would be blunted if we limited our aid to recipients who have sincerely been practicing as Jews for a very long time.)

Conclusion

I vividly remember a friend's quandary. His young daughter asked, "Daddy, you and I are Jewish, right? That's because Judaism is the best religion in the world, right? Isn't Mommy the best mommy in the world? Then why isn't Mommy Jewish?"

Why shouldn't Jews have that child's attitude toward our religion? And if we do, why should we be so surprised, indifferent, and even suspicious when someone wants to join or rejoin us?

We certainly should point out to potential converts the disadvantages of becoming Jewish, including potential anti-Semitism. And we should be grateful that our rabbis will only convert people they believe to be sincere, with a persistent, long-term interest in Judaism.

One occasionally hears that modern Jewry is adrift and rudderless. The possibility that people all over the world are interested in embracing or reaffirming their Jewishness, however, should be thought of as a historic opportunity for the Jewish people. We should view it as a challenge rather than a burden. The fact that so many people want to become Jewish should be trumpeted to those in our community who might assimilate away, for it would show them that Judaism is indeed something to keep and to cherish.

It is my hope that mainstream Western Jews will ask why all of these people, from all over the world, want to join our religion, and will realize how wonderful our religion is. I pray that Western Jews will look with amazement at these people who have stubbornly clung to their scraps of Judaism for centuries secretly, under great hardships. Perhaps they will be less likely to abandon such a wondrous religion. It is my fervent hope that when we warmly welcome those who would (re)join us as our brothers and sisters, we will be helping and renewing ourselves in many ways.

Appendix
What You Can Do!

The suggestions that follow are suitable for individuals as well as for schools, congregations, and community groups.

1. Become informed about lost and developing Jewish communities.
2. Correspond with and *visit* one or more of these communities to reduce their feelings of isolation.
3. Invite a speaker to address your group about one or more of these communities (contact active organizations, scholars, or a member of the community).
4. Give information about and recognition of one of the communities at your bar or bat mitzvah (see Nathan's Prayer, above, chap. 29).
5. Incorporate readings about lost and developing communities at holiday observances (see the suggested Passover reading about the Bnei Menashe, above, chap. 7).
6. Match up your synagogue, havurah, service organization, Hadassah chapter, school, or social group with one of these communities for continuous interaction. Enrich yourselves and others!

7. Become active in one or more of the following organizations, all of which assist lost or developing communities:

Kulanu
11603 Gilsan Street
Silver Spring, MD 20902-3122
(TEL 301-681-5679; FAX 301-681-1587)
kulanu@ubmail.ubalt.edu
http://www.ubalt.edu/www/kulanu

Amishav
Epstein 3-B
Jerusalem 96555, Israel

Sino-Judaic Institute
2316 Blueridge Avenue
Menlo Park, CA 94025
(TEL 415-323-1769)

China Judaic Studies Association
c/o Dr. Beverly Friend
Oakton Community College
1600 Golf Road
Des Plaines, IL 60016

Society for Crypto-Judaic Studies
2000 Avenida Cesar Chavez
Monterrey Park, CA 91754

Washington Association for Ethiopian Jews
11603 Gilsan Street
Silver Spring, MD 20902

North American Conference on Ethiopian Jewry
165 East 65th Street
New York, NY 10022
(TEL 212-752-6340)
http://www.cais.com/nacoej

Casa Shalom Institute for Marrano (Anusim) Studies
PO Box 66 Gan Yavneh
Israel 70800
(TEL/FAX 972-(0)8-573-150)

Friends of Righteous Converts in Israel
PO Box 7589
Jerusalem 92428, Israel

Glossary

Abayudaya. Members of the Baganda tribe of Uganda who practice Judaism.
Adon Olam (lit. "Lord of the world"). Hymn that often ends the Sabbath service.
Aliyah (lit. "to ascend"). (1) The honor of being called to read a Torah portion or to recite a blessing before the reading of the portion. (2) Immigration to Israel.
Amishav (lit. "my people return"). Organization founded by Rabbi Eliyahu Avichail in Jerusalem, helping descendants of the Ten Lost Tribes of Israel and other communities with Jewish roots.
Ashkenazic. Of Central and Eastern European Jewish descent; Yiddish-speaking.
Balemba. Southern African tribe, possibly of Jewish descent.
Beth Din. Rabbinic tribunal.
Bnei Menashe. Descendants of the tribe of Menashe, one of the Ten Lost Tribes of Israel, many of whom have been traced to northeastern India.
Bris (brit). (lit. "covenant"). Male circumcision ritual performed at the age of eight days.
Chag Ha-azmaut. Israel Independence Day.

Chanukah. Eight-day midwinter festival commemorating liberation and rededication of Temple by Judah Maccabee.
Chanukiah. Nine branched candelabrum used for Chanukah ritual.
Chazan (pl chazanim). Cantor.
Cheder. Religious school.
Cholent. Slow-cooking stew set in the oven before sundown on Friday to cook slowly overnight, so as to provide a hot meal for the Sabbath without kindling a fire.
Chumash. The Five Books of Moses (Pentateuch).
Converso. A convert.
Crypto-Jew. One who practices Judaism in secret.
Daven. Pray.
Dayan (pl. dayanim). Judge in rabbinic court.
Dinim. Religious laws.
Drash. Sermon.
Etrog. Citron; used in ritual of Sukkot.
Ger. A convert.
Haftarah. Reading from the prophets at the Sabbath service after the Torah reading.
Haggadah. Liturgical text read at Pesach Seder.
Halacha. Jewish law.
HaShem (lit. "the name"). Symbolic designation for God.
Havdalah (lit. "distinction"). Ritual separating the end of a Sabbath or festival from the beginning of the following weekday.
Havurah (pl. havurot). Group of Jews who pray, study, and/or socialize together.
High Holy Days. Rosh Hashanah and Yom Kippur.
Kaifeng. City in China where Jews settled beginning around 1000 C.E. and which had a thriving Jewish community until approximately 1700.
Kibbutz. Israeli collective settlement.
Kippah (pl. kippot). Skullcap worn by Jews.
K'lal Yisrael (lit. "whole of Israel"). The entire Jewish people.
Kashrut. The Jewish dietary laws.

Kol Nidre. Solemn prayer that opens the service on the eve of Yom Kippur.

Kosher. Ritually clean and prepared according to Jewish dietary laws.

Kulanu (lit. "all of us"). Organization, based in the United States, helping lost and dispersed Jewish groups.

Lecha Dodi (lit. "come, my beloved"). Prayer welcoming the Sabbath.

Levirate marriage. Marriage in which a brother marries the wife of his childless deceased brother (Deuteronomy 25:5–6).

Lulav. Bunched palm, myrtle, and willow branches used in ritual of Sukkot.

Menorah. Seven-branched candelabrum.

Marranos. Spanish and Portuguese Jews forced to convert to Christianity in the fifteenth or sixteenth century who continued to practice Judaism in secret.

Matzah (pl. matzot). Unleavened bread, used during celebration of Pesach.

Mezuzah. Case enclosing a parchment with biblical texts (Deuteronomy 6:4–9, 11:13–21) placed on the doorpost of a Jewish home, business, or school.

Mikveh. Ritual bath.

Minyan. Quorum of ten adult Jews necessary for public services (only males qualify in Orthodox Judaism).

Mitzvah (pl. mitzvot) (lit. "commandment"). The performance of an act required by halacha; more generally, a good deed.

Moshav (lit. "settlement"). Cooperative village in Israel combining features of collective and private farming.

Pesach (Passover). Spring festival commemorating Exodus from Egypt.

Pirkei Avot (lit. "Ethics of the Fathers"). Talmudic tractate widely studied for its moral and ethical content.

Rosh Hashanah. Jewish New Year festival.

Seder. Family home ritual dinner on first and second nights of Pesach.

Sefer Torah (pl. Sifrei Torah). Torah scroll.

Sephardic. Of Spanish-Portuguese descent; Ladino-speaking. (Sometimes used loosely, and incorrectly, as a designation for all non-Ashkenazic Jews.)

Shabbat. Sabbath.

Shabbat Shalom (lit. "Sabbath of Peace"). Sabbath greeting.

Shabbos. Sabbath.

Shaliach. Emissary.

Shavuot. Festival commemorating giving of Torah at Mount Sinai.

Shema. The central prayer of Judaism, beginning with "Hear, O Israel, the Lord is Our God, the Lord is One," and comprising three biblical passages (Deuteronomy 6:4–9, 11:13–21; Numbers 15:37–41).

Shinlung. People residing mainly in northeastern India and Burma, considered to be descendants of Manasseh (Menashe), one of the Ten Lost Tribes of Israel.

Shochet (pl. shochtim). Ritual slaughterer, according to laws of kashrut.

Shofar. Ram's horn, used in synagogue services on Rosh Hashanah and Yom Kippur.

Shul. Synagogue.

Shulchan Arukh. Code of Jewish law followed by Orthodox Judaism.

Siddur (pl. siddurim). Prayer book.

Sukkah. (lit. "booth"). Temporary structure in which Jews eat during the eight-day agricultural thanksgiving festival of Sukkot in the fall.

Tallit. (pl. tallitot). Prayer shawl.

Talmud. Massive compilation of rabbinic discussions on Jewish religious and civil law dating between 200 and 500 C.E.

Tefillin. Small leather boxes containing scriptural texts (Exodus 13:1–10, 11–16; Deuteronomy 6:4–9, 11:13–21) which are bound with leather thongs to the forehead and left hand, usually worn by Orthodox men during morning prayers (except on Shabbat).

Tikkun Olam (lit. "repair of the world"). Activities, including charity, undertaken to help improve some aspect of the world.

Tisha B'Av (lit. "ninth of Av"). Late-summer fast day commemorating the destruction of the First Temple in 586 B.C.E. and the Second Temple in 70 C.E.

Torah. The Five Books of Moses (Pentateuch). See also Sefer Torah.

Tu Beshevat. (lit. "fifteenth of Shevat"). "New Year for Trees," sometimes called the Jewish Arbor Day.

Tzedakah (lit. "righteousness"). Charity.

Tzitzit. Fringes on the four corners of the tallit.

Yeshiva. School for rabbinic studies.

Yom Kippur. The Day of Atonement.

Zemiros. Table songs sung on the Sabbath.

Printed in the United States
65664LVS00002B/277-285